CYBERINSURANCE POLICY

INFORMATION POLICY SERIES

Edited by Sandra Braman

The Information Policy Series publishes research on and analysis of significant problems in the field of information policy, including decisions and practices that enable or constrain information, communication, and culture irrespective of the legal siloes in which they have traditionally been located as well as state-law-society interactions. Defining information policy as all laws, regulations, and decision-making principles that affect any form of information creation, processing, flows, and use, the series includes attention to the formal decisions, decision-making processes, and entities of government; the formal and informal decisions, decision-making processes, and entities of private and public sector agents capable of constitutive effects on the nature of society; and the cultural habits and predispositions of governmentality that support and sustain government and governance. The parametric functions of information policy at the boundaries of social, informational, and technological systems are of global importance because they provide the context for all communications, interactions, and social processes.

CYBERINSURANCE POLICY

RETHINKING RISK IN AN AGE OF RANSOMWARE, COMPUTER FRAUD, DATA BREACHES, AND CYBERATTACKS

JOSEPHINE WOLFF

The MIT Press
Cambridge, Massachusetts
London, England

The MIT Press would like to thank the anonymous peer reviewers who provided comments on drafts of this book. The generous work of academic experts is essential for establishing the authority and quality of our publications. We acknowledge with gratitude the contributions of these otherwise uncredited readers.

This book was set in Bembo by Westchester Publishing Services. Printed and bound in the United States of America.

Library of Congress Cataloging-in-Publication Data

Names: Wolff, Josephine, author.
Title: Cyberinsurance policy : rethinking risk in an age of ransomware, computer fraud, data breaches, and cyberattacks / Josephine Wolff.
Description: Cambridge, Massachusetts : The MIT Press, [2022] | Series: Information policy series | Includes bibliographical references and index.
Identifiers: LCCN 2021045988 | ISBN 9780262544184 (paperback)
Subjects: LCSH: Computer insurance. | Computer security—Management. | Cyberspace—Security measures—Management. | Computer crimes—Prevention. | Risk management.
Classification: LCC HG9963.5 .W65 2022 | DDC 658.4/78—dc23/eng/20220114
LC record available at https://lccn.loc.gov/2021045988

10 9 8 7 6 5 4 3 2 1

For Perri Klass and Larry Wolff, who took care of the Chompo Bar until I was ready to give it to Gloria (who is not yet old enough to eat a whole Chompo Bar).

It was the day before Frances's little sister Gloria's birthday. Mother and Gloria were sitting at the kitchen table, making place cards for the party.

Frances was in the broom closet, singing:

> *Happy Thursday to you,*
> *Happy Thursday to you,*
> *Happy Thursday, dear Alice,*
> *Happy Thursday to you.*

"Who is Alice?" asked Mother.

"Alice is somebody that nobody can see," said Frances. "And that is why she does not have a birthday. So I am singing Happy Thursday to her."

"Today is Friday," said Mother.

"It is Thursday for Alice," said Frances. "Alice will not have h-r-n-d, and she will not have g-k-l-s. But we are singing together."

"What are h-r-n-d and g-k-l-s?" asked Mother.

"Cake and candy. I thought you could spell," said Frances.

"I am sure that Alice will have cake and candy on her birthday," said Mother.

"But Alice does not have a birthday," said Frances.

"Yes, she does," said Mother. "Even if nobody can see her, Alice has one birthday every year, and so do you. Your birthday is two months from now. Then you will be the birthday girl. But tomorrow is Gloria's birthday, and she will be the birthday girl."

"That is how it is, Alice," said Frances. "Your birthday is always the one that is not now."

—*A Birthday for Frances*, Russell and Lillian Hoban, 1968

CONTENTS

SERIES EDITOR'S INTRODUCTION

SANDRA BRAMAN

"Freedom," "rights," and "democracy" are words that often come up when we talk about information policy, but as Josephine Wolff makes clear in *Cyberinsurance Policy*, "risk" should also be there as well. The word was coined mid-fifteenth century by the Italian shipping insurance industry, concerned as it was about *risco*—"that which cuts"—the reefs that threaten cargo on high seas. Historian of statistics Alain Desrosieres points to the launch of the first secular democracy in France in the late eighteenth century as the moment when that field became formalized. Historians of insurance such as François Ewald and Daniel Defert document its first stages of development by actuaries who had to distinguish among not only types of risk, but also population segments, behaviors, causal thresholds, and other matters we now think of as the subjects of "social science."

Actuaries did so in order to develop insurance products that combine these diverse types of data according to a particular set of rules. This makes insurance a form of political imaginary itself—one that, according to anthropologist Mary Douglas and political scientist Aaron Wildavsky, in turn depends upon the extent to which any given combination of individuals recognizes itself as a group and on the extent and nature of rules considered appropriate for governance. Thomas Hobbes was big on risk, seeing its assessment as the basis of all political arrangements. From that regard, the dominance of the Chinese cybersecurity insurance market in 2019 by the four firms *Cyberinsurance Policy* tells us about—two American, one German, and one Swiss—is particularly interesting.

It has already been over four decades since Ulrich Beck explained that our capacity for coping with risk has gone down as technological and societal complexity have risen. Causal relations aren't always discernible, and thus accountability can be impossible to assign. Damaging processes may not become visible until long after irreversible harm can be prevented. The range of types of cybersecurity risk, as Josephine Wolff so superbly walks us through, is vast and multiplying. It is deeply intertwined with every other category of risk so far contemplated, and will become ever more so. Identifying perpetrators can be difficult or impossible, as can all of the types of harm caused or the actual cost of any of it.

The author carefully works through each of the policy options available to governments, offering shrewd critical insight regarding just why each has been discussed for so long without much in the way of effective action. It has been up to national governments and the European Union to develop cybersecurity-related policies on behalf of all parties, but the major cybersecurity insurance firms are transnational. Insurers look to states for forms of support—data, funding pools, technical standard setting, and guidance—provided for other of their products. Governments do not yet make these things available, but at the same time insurers also shy from the increase in regulation that is a necessary concomitant of the use of such policy tools.

There is a dance in policy-making discussions about the sociotechnical system of the Internet. Technologists often point to the law as responsible for preventing or solving problems; lawmakers and analysts in turn assign responsibility to those who design and produce technologies to ensure that the goods and services they produce aren't themselves the cause of policy problems. The most promising approach to achieving effective cyberinsurance policies may be that introduced in a 2020 experiment by a firm that offers cybersecurity support with a warranty that comes into play should its protections fail. Going this route, too, though, requires what the other side of the sociotechnical problem has to offer, including technical standard setting in addition to data and perhaps a funding backup as is done with, for example, flooding, given the shared nature of the infrastructure—and, thus, of any cybersecurity risk.

This book can be read in many ways. It provides a comprehensive and systematic history of cybersecurity insurance in the internationally dominant country in the industry, the United States, as well as elsewhere around the world. The author's detailed analyses of court cases offer nuanced insight into the legal concepts, and the issues, at stake, doing so in a manner that lets the drama behind accounting figures show through. And it offers insight into the multifaceted negotiations underway among diverse types of entities, some geopolitically and/or commercially recognized, some not, for the most value that can be extracted at the conjunction of social, informational, and technological systems that is the subject of cybersecurity policy.

Josephine Wolff's first book, *You'll See This Message When It Is Too Late*, provided a detailed history and analysis of nine cybersecurity attacks motivated by financial gain, espionage, and public humiliation of victims. She concluded that because there is always another way into a network on the technical side, it is on the way out—when perpetrators of cybersecurity incidents try to do something with their access or with the information they get out of it—that prevention, intervention, and/or mitigation are most likely to be successful. In *Cyberinsurance Policy: Rethinking Risk for the Internet Age*, she takes up her own challenge by looking at one of the most fundamental of ways in which those behind cybersecurity incidents engage with all three classes of their victims—their targets, those whose intelligent networked infrastructure is used to achieve cybercrime or cybersecurity goals, and those in society at large who experience the consequences of damage to cybersecurity targets and who therefore, as is classically the case with terrorism, are the actual targets.

ACKNOWLEDGMENTS

I purchased insurance for the first time in 2015, not long after I had started thinking about cyberinsurance as a possible area of research. Risk averse to my core, I selected the most expensive option for every type of coverage my new employer offered, except pet insurance. I had not even known before then that a person could buy insurance coverage for accidental death and dismemberment or long-term disabilities, but now that I knew such policies existed, I never wanted to be without them again. To be clear: I loved insurance and I knew absolutely nothing about it.

Over the course of writing this book, many people who know much more about insurance than I ever will very patiently explained to me some of the industry's inner workings and history. I am especially indebted to Daniel Schwarcz, who invited me to speak at the 2021 symposium on The Role of Law and Government in Cyber Insurance Markets and provided invaluable feedback on several chapters, and Daniel Woods, who offered thoughtful notes on this manuscript as well as many crucial reading suggestions. I'm also grateful to Lori Bailey, Tom Baker, Adam Bobrow, Kevin Coughlin, Arnold D'Angelo Jr., Tom Finan, Steve Haase, and Trey Herr for taking the time to talk with me and offer their perspectives on cyberinsurance. Bill Lehr worked with me on some of my earliest forays into cyberinsurance and provided many important economic insights. David Clark gave me the confidence to extend my interest in cybersecurity incidents and liability to topics outside my expertise and a sense of unshakeable optimism about the potential for new ideas and approaches to improve cybersecurity.

Torie Bosch at *Slate* let me write my first ever piece about cyberinsurance back in 2014 and has been a source of ideas, friendship, and above all, incredibly clear-eyed, crisp editing ever since graduate school. It was a joy to get to work with Susan Rigetti at the *New York Times* and have the opportunity to appreciate her skills not just as a brilliant writer but also as an extraordinary editor.

I feel very fortunate to have had another chance to work with Sandra Braman and Gita Manaktala at the MIT Press, who provided crucial guidance and encouragement for this project from start to finish. I am also grateful to the New America Cybersecurity Initiative, the Atlantic Council Cyber Statecraft Initiative, Cisco Systems, and the Charles Koch Foundation for supporting this project.

I began working on this book at the Rochester Institute of Technology, a school that provided me with many benefits beyond insurance, including incredible friends and collaborators in Sarah Burns, Stephanie Godleski, Andrea Hickerson, Eric Hittinger, Priti Kalsi, Mehdi Mirakhorli, Sumita Mishra, Yin Pan, Sandra Rothenberg, Jamie Winebrake, Matthew Wright, and Bo Yuan. In 2019, I moved to the Fletcher School of Law and Diplomacy at Tufts University and was fortunate to join another group of remarkable scholars and generous colleagues. I am especially grateful to Steve Block, Bhaskar Chakravorti, Tom Dannenbaum, Dan Drezner, Alnoor Ebrahim, Leila Fawaz, Kathleen Fisher, Jeff Foster, Kelly Sims Gallagher, Carolyn Gideon, Francesca Giovannini, Ian Johnstone, Sulmaan Khan, Michael Klein, Rachel Kyte, Susan Landau, Abi Linnington, Melissa McCracken, Chris Miller, Cyndi Rubino, Julie Schaffner, Elaine Schaertl Short, Jeff Taliaferro, Joel Trachtman, Dan Votipka, and Matthew Woodward.

Returning to Cambridge allowed me to reunite not just with Fenway Park and Formaggio Kitchen, but also with several friends in the Boston area and along the Northeast Corridor, including Kendra Albert, Eileen Costello, Sharon Gillett, John Hess, Alex and Claire Jacquillat, Patrick Gage Kelley, Alexis Levinson, Lily Hay Newman, Emily Prud'hommeaux, Adrienne Raphel, and Alicia Solow-Niederman, who provided much needed distractions and even occasionally pretended to be interested when I talked about insurance.

Bob and Renee Wolff entrusted me with the maintenance of their email account and gamely agreed to move their Great Books group of more than fifty years online when COVID-19 prevented them from holding their monthly meetings at the local library. Whenever a particularly grim cybersecurity incident left me feeling dismayed, nothing restored my faith in the Internet faster than watching them and a dozen of their octogenarian and nonagenarian friends discuss *The Turn of the Screw* from little Zoom boxes (some with virtual backgrounds!). Sheila and Mort Klass did not live to see this book, but I can vividly imagine the conversations I would have had with each of them about it—Mort would have believed it was going to change the world, and Sheila would have told me that it sounded very impressive but she really couldn't understand a word I was saying. She is, as ever, the person whose work ethic I most aspire to channel when I sit down to write.

Most of this manuscript was written during 2020 and early 2021, when the world very suddenly went into lockdown in the face of the global COVID-19 pandemic. I was lucky during that period not just to have hundreds of pages of research on cyberinsurance to throw myself into but also to have the company of Lisa Ho, Anatol Klass, Tommy Leung, and Nathan Perkins. We ate dinner together every night for some 400 nights—performing carefully controlled, triple-blind science experiments to determine the best type of vanilla bean, the tastiest Greek yogurt, and the perfect olive oil, playing bridge and *Mario Kart*, celebrating half-Christmas on half-Thanksgiving, eating Lynne Rosetto Kasper's Friday-night spaghetti with tuna and black olives, and assembling a cheese journal worthy of entry into the *Congressional Record*. Lisa introduced me to the joys of homemade ice cream and let me introduce her to a Midori ten-year diary. Tommy carefully tracked everyone's dessert consumption, designed a highly demanded DuckDuckGo weather widget with hourly precipitation predictions, and took three days off from work to cook a Chinese feast for my birthday. Far and away the most competent member of the pod, Nathan endured endless abuse about Siri's gaffes as well as his mispronunciation of German composers and Cantonese phrases, but he still fixed all of our Apple devices, assembled the enormous nineteenth-century post office desk where I wrote this book, and gave me the computer I wrote it on. As for Anatol, he mostly sang songs about Pete Buttigieg (and occasionally mee goreng), taking breaks every now and then to have a meltdown about whatever he was cooking, or to comment on this manuscript, or to read hundreds of books on modern Chinese history in preparation for his oral exams—in short, he was indispensable. It has been a true pleasure and privilege to get to watch him beat Excitebike Arena and grow into a formidable scholar and remarkable researcher. I will be forever grateful to the four of them for their company during that strange, scary, and sad year of quarantine and for filling those days with tremendous, unexpected joy.

While the rest of us were blithely blindfolding vanilla beans, Orlando Klass spent the pandemic working long shifts in the hospital, but he somehow still managed to find time to take incredible care of our grandparents and to ship a Cheez-It cake to Cambridge.

Perri Klass and Larry Wolff are my very favorite people in the whole world, and I strongly suspect that would still be true even if they weren't my parents (though in that case I might have to cede the hotly contested title of their favorite daughter). Growing up, I learned how to write books from watching them: stay up too late, don't clean the house, and don't let anything get in the way. Over the years, they bought me so many books that I am still using the discounts they accumulated at Harvard Book Store; they read me so many books that I still hear their voices when I read Louisa May Alcott, Jane Austen, E. F. Benson, and Maud Hart Lovelace; and they wrote so many books that I just assumed someday I would, too.

INTRODUCTION: A MARKET-DRIVEN APPROACH
TO CYBERSECURITY

On June 17, 2017, the most destructive piece of malware ever detected started spreading through computer systems across the globe. It took out 10 percent of all computers in Ukraine within twenty-four hours and paralyzed the operations of major companies across multiple industry sectors and countries, irreversibly encrypting their data and flashing error messages on hundreds of thousands of screens.[1] The Danish firm Maersk, the largest container shipping company in the world, was hit. So, too, as was the British consumer goods manufacturer Reckitt Benckiser, which makes Durex condoms, Lysol, Clearasil, and Mead Johnson baby formula. The snack company Mondelez International, headquartered in Deerfield, Illinois—maker of Oreos, Trident gum, and Ritz crackers—suffered the same fate, unable to operate many of its computers and other devices because of strange and threatening messages in red and black text that refused to go away, some warning victims not to turn off their computers, others offering the alarming alert "oops, your important files are encrypted."[2]

At first, the malware looked like a piece of ransomware because some of the infected computers displayed messages demanding that the victims make a payment in anonymous cryptocurrency to unlock their machines in order to retrieve their data. In fact, at first glance, the malicious program closely resembled a ransomware program dubbed Petya that had surfaced the previous year. But it soon became clear that whatever this was, it was not Petya—it spread much faster than any malware that had come before it, and even if the victims paid the ransom that was demanded, there was no way to decrypt the affected data.

NotPetya, as the malware came to be known, was designed purely for destruction and it was very good at its job. The White House later estimated that the damages caused by NotPetya totaled $10 billion—far more than had been attributed to any earlier cyberattack in history.[3] Fortunately for Mondelez, which had suffered an estimated loss of $188 million just from trying to get its systems back up and running after 1,700 of its servers and 24,000 of its laptops were infected, the company had insurance to cover these kinds of costs—or so it thought.[4] The property insurance policy Mondelez had purchased from Zurich American Insurance covered "physical loss or damage to electronic data, programs, or software, including physical loss or damage caused by the malicious introduction of a machine code or instruction."[5] This addition to Mondelez's standard property policy was part of a growing trend in the insurance industry to sell add-on coverage products that specifically included certain types of online, computer-based risks, including data breaches, denial-of-service attacks, computer viruses, and ransomware—the types of risks that only two decades earlier would have seemed too infrequent, inexpensive, or sector-specific to bother insuring. In the late 1990s and early 2000s, many companies conceived of cyber risks fairly narrowly as being primarily tied to accidental programming or IT errors—for instance, fears about a widespread Y2K computer malfunction—or to data breaches that targeted retailers and other organizations that stored large databases of credit card numbers. Nothing, in other words, that would be likely to target an Oreo manufacturer.

By 2017, those risks had become so pervasive and costly that a growing number of companies, like Mondelez, were desperate to protect themselves against not just the looming technical threats but also the economic consequences of those threats. And so, insurers like Zurich developed new policies and provisions to meet that demand and a small, but rapidly growing, market emerged for cyberinsurance. Cyberinsurance options on offer took many different forms: there were add-on products that introduced additional clauses to existing policies, like the one in Mondelez's property insurance, specifying that those policies extended to online threats, as well as stand-alone policies devoted exclusively to insuring firms against specific online threats like data breaches. Cyberinsurance coverage included policies that covered the costs of lost business if a company's computer infrastructure went down, policies that would provide customers with funds to pay online extortion and ransom requests, and even policies for high-networth individuals concerned that their data or online bank accounts might be compromised.

Because cyberinsurance can take so many different forms, it can be tricky to measure the size of the market, but it's clearly growing. In 2015, total cyber premiums written for both stand-alone and add-on package coverage in the United States came to just over $1.4 billion. Just two years later, in 2017, the year of NotPetya, premiums for cyberinsurance policies in the United States had doubled, totaling more than $3 billion, and 471 US insurers reported that they offered cyberinsurance products, according to data collected by the National Association of Insurance Commissioners.[6] Meanwhile, non-US firms were beginning to join the market, predicting that the implementation of the European Union's General Data Protection Regulation (GDPR) in May 2018 would send several European firms in search of coverage.[7] Even so, cyberinsurance remains a relatively small portion of the overall insurance market. By comparison, auto insurance premiums in the United States total more than $200 billion annually. But by 2017, after two years of consecutive 30 percent increases in premium sales, no other type of insurance was experiencing as much growth and interest from new customers as cyberinsurance. That growth slowed slightly in 2018, when premiums increased only about 20 percent, to $3.6 billion, but by then hundreds of carriers were already beginning to ramp up their cyberinsurance offerings. It was not yet a major source of income for insurers—but they expected, and hoped, it soon would be.[8]

"Cyberinsurance is the hot hot hot area of the insurance world," Nick Economidis, then a cyber liability underwriter at Beazley, explained in early 2018.[9] Companies were eager to buy cyberinsurance, but it wasn't simple to figure out what kind of coverage they needed or even what the different options on offer actually covered. And correspondingly, carriers were eager to sell these policies, but writing and pricing them wasn't simple. The market for cyberinsurance was—and is—characterized by profound uncertainties on both sides for buyers and sellers alike. By the time they began to craft policies for online risks in the mid-1990s, insurers had accumulated decades of actuarial techniques, policy-writing experience, and tactics for screening the risk profiles of potential customers gleaned from developing insurance products for everything from risk of illness and injury to risk of being sued, risk of natural disasters, risk of being robbed, and risk of car accidents. In some ways, cyber risks were similar to other kinds of risk that insurers were used to dealing with, like car crashes, earthquakes, burglary, and cancer, except that cyber risks were newer and continuing to evolve rapidly. The earliest computer viruses date back to the 1980s, but already by the 2000s those early incidents bore little resemblance to the types of intrusions and malware that companies were facing. That meant insurance firms lacked the decades of claims data that informed the actuarial models for their other insurance offerings and were therefore less able to predict how frequently cybersecurity incidents would occur or how much they were likely to cost. But this was not a novel challenge for insurers. After all, when the car was first invented it took a while to figure out how to sell insurance for the new kinds of risks that personal automobiles presented—it made sense that the personal computer and all its attendant and difficult-to-anticipate risks would take time for insurers to figure out, as well.

But cybersecurity risks weren't just new, they were also different from other types of risk in certain profound ways that made them a unique challenge for insurers. For instance, insurers had no obvious way to protect themselves against having to pay out claims to all of their cyberinsurance customers at once. It would be unheard of for an insurer's entire customer base to simultaneously experience car accidents or health crises or natural disasters or robberies and file claims all at once. For risks like natural disasters that do affect large numbers of policyholders at once, insurers deliberately diversify their customers to be certain they are not all concentrated in any one place or demographic that might be hit especially hard specifically in order to avoid correlated losses. But cyberattacks like NotPetya were not restricted to any single location or industry sector. For insurers, that meant potentially facing a massive number of claims simultaneously with no obvious path to diversifying their customer base in a way that would reliably prevent correlated losses.

Customers filing those claims also faced risks, as Mondelez discovered after it had dutifully documented its losses from NotPetya and filed a claim with Zurich for the damage that had been done to its computer systems. On June 1, 2018, nearly a year after it was hit by NotPetya, Mondelez received a response to its claim. Zurich was denying Mondelez's claim on the grounds that NotPetya was a "hostile or warlike action." The property insurance policy Mondelez had purchased from Zurich included an exception for losses or damage caused by:

> hostile or warlike action in time of peace or war, including action in hindering, combating or defending against an actual, impending or expected attack by any:
>
> (i) government or sovereign power (de jure or de facto);
> (ii) military, naval, or air force; or
> (iii) agent or authority of any party specified in i or ii above.[10]

It was a standard exception for insurance policies, dating back many decades, and intended to absolve insurers of having to rebuild entire cities or nations that had been decimated during wars. This type of exclusion in insurance policies serves as a sort of insurance policy itself that the insurers would not be bankrupted or held liable for destruction on a scale beyond anything their customers might expect in the course of daily life, catastrophic disasters that would be far beyond any the insurers themselves could predict or afford to pay for. It's a perfectly reasonable provision in many ways. Zurich can model the likelihood of a robbery or a fire at Mondelez's Deerfield headquarters, but they can hardly be expected to anticipate—much less cover the costs of—a direct attack by a foreign government. If the Russian military were to bomb Deerfield, Zurich would be off the hook, so why shouldn't they be similarly protected from the effects of a computer virus developed and distributed by the Russian military?

But computer code—even computer code that causes disastrous damage—isn't obviously analogous to a bomb, and in the case of NotPetya the Zurich exemption was not quite so clear-cut. On the one hand, NotPetya did appear to have been the work of a government or sovereign power, specifically the Russian military, aimed at compromising critical infrastructure in Ukraine in the midst of ongoing hostilities between the two nations.[11] But was it really a "warlike action" just because it was state-sponsored? And, if so, was it really reasonable for Zurich to be excluding all such attacks from the coverage they were selling given how commonplace they were becoming? After all, it was the second large-scale cyberattack to be launched by a national government in the span of two months, following the WannaCry ransomware released by North Korea earlier that year, in May 2017. Increasingly, states were coming to view cyber capabilities as a standard complement to their other modes of espionage, sabotage, and conflict—a more mundane and ongoing form of engagement than kinetic warfare, one that governments and businesses alike were realizing that they would have to come to terms with in the future. A "warlike action" suggests something extreme and anomalous and infrequent; but by 2018 large-scale state-sponsored ransomware was on the verge of becoming exactly the kind of routine business threat that insurance policies were designed to cover.

In October 2018, Mondelez filed a lawsuit against Zurich for breach of contract. The filing followed a protracted back-and-forth with Zurich, during which the insurer initially adjusted the claim and offered Mondelez a $10 million partial payment but then reversed course and refused to make any payment or to continue processing the claim. The case, which has not yet been decided, speaks to many of the different tensions surrounding the growing cyberinsurance market. For insurers, this tension centers on balancing their anxiety about losing insurance customers and premium payments to competitors with their concerns about having to cover the costs of unpredictable large-scale attacks like NotPetya. On the one hand, insurance firms like Zurich want to persuade customers that cyber risks are manageable just like any other kind of risk—through insurance. On the other hand, those same insurers do not want to be on the hook for the kinds of risks they do not yet know enough about to be able to model and anticipate. Meanwhile, governments around the world have begun to take an interest in cyberinsurance, looking to insurers to provide privatized, market-driven solutions to the cybersecurity challenges their countries face as an alternative—or in some cases, a complement—to what they fear might be onerous and heavy-handed regulations. Rather than imposing strict cybersecurity requirements on businesses, regulators often look to insurers to define what criteria and controls their customers must meet to qualify for policies. Rather than defining clear liability regimes about which types of stakeholders are responsible for different cybersecurity practices and outcomes or what constitutes negligence when it comes to protecting data and networks, regulators have largely left it up to insurers to fight these battles in court when they choose to deny policyholder claims.

This book is about the creation and regulation of the cyberinsurance industry from its origins in the late 1990s up through the present day. It presents a history of the development of this market as well as an in-depth analysis of the legal disputes that have surrounded cyberinsurance claims and policies since the early 2000s and how those disputes have, in turn, shaped insurance coverage and purchasing decisions. It looks at how insurance firms have approached—and continue to approach—computer-based risks and cyber-related coverage, both internally, in crafting and pricing policies, and externally, in responding to claims filed by policyholders and engaging with policymakers around the globe. This analysis also examines how policyholders have interpreted their cyber risk coverage and how they have often found themselves confused and disappointed, sometimes leading to costly and extended litigation with their insurers. It reviews the role that policymakers in the United States, the European Union, China, Brazil,

India, and Singapore have played in shaping the market for cyberinsurance as customers, data aggregators, and regulators. It also looks to regulatory interventions in other types of insurance, including auto insurance, terrorism insurance, and flood insurance, to examine what insights or ideas those may offer for potential policymaking related to cyberinsurance.

Beyond offering some practical policy recommendations, this book builds on theoretical frameworks introduced by risk and insurance scholars about the nature of systemic risks, the role of insurance as governance, and the complicated interplay between law and insurance. In understanding the scale and potential scope of cyber risks, it is helpful to consider some of the literature on other risks with the potential to cause widespread damage across multiple sectors, including the risks posed by climate change, nuclear weapons, and financial crises. Ulrich Beck theorized that the emergence of large-scale ecological and high-tech risks have challenged our existing methods for measuring and managing risks. He wrote of these risks: "In the afflictions they produce they are no longer tied to their place of origins—the industrial plant. By their nature they endanger *all* forms of life on this planet. The normative bases of their calculation—the concept of accident and insurance, medical precautions, and so on—do not fit the basic dimensions of these modern threats. Atomic plants, for example, are not privately insured or insurable. Atomic accidents are accidents no more. . . . They outlast generations."[12] In the face of these new types of risks, Beck argued, "the calculation of risk as it has been established so far by science and legal institutions *collapses*. Dealing with these consequences of modern productive and destructive forces in the normal terms of risk is a false but nevertheless very effective way of legitimizing them."[13] The same cannot be said of cyber risks, but Beck's analysis offers some relevant insights into the challenges insurers have faced in trying to develop cyberinsurance coverage. While cyber risks do not share all of the features Beck points to in atomic accidents—they do not endanger all forms of life on the planet, nor do their impacts necessarily outlast generations—they do exhibit some of the invisibility, geographic reach, and complexity of the threats Beck describes. Cyber risks challenge some established risk calculation techniques but the effort to silo those risks in stand-alone policies has not legitimized them so much as isolated and minimized them from their complex interactions with other types of risk. Scholars have previously pointed to the disciplinary barriers in academic fields as an obstacle to cyber risk research, but the same is equally—if not more—true of the organizational barriers within insurance carriers separating those who work on cyber risk from their peers who model other types of risks.[14]

Just as Beck's conception of a risk society dominated by invisible catastrophic threats does not exactly apply to cyber risks, neither does the existing literature on systemic risk illuminate all of the important elements of what makes these risks significant and different. The notion of systemic risks, or large-scale risks that affect an entire system rather than individual components, emerged from international financial crises though it has also been applied to environmental risks, societal inequality, and cybersecurity.[15] According to Ortwin Renn, Klaus Lucas, Armin Haas, and Carlo Jaeger, the key properties of systemic risks are that these risks are global, highly interconnected, that they often involve unknown tipping points, allow for more than one future, and are caused by the interplay of "individual micro- and global macro-processes within the system under consideration, combined with exogenous processes that modify the internal dynamics of the system."[16] Here, again, some elements of these characteristics are relevant to cyber risks—which are certainly global in nature and highly interconnected and intertwined—but others appear to be entirely irrelevant to considerations of cyber risks, including the notion of nonlinear cause-effect relationships and stochastic effect structures. Some cyber risks may seem analogous to systemic risks in their scale but many—indeed, most—are not. Even NotPetya, devastating and expensive as it was for many companies, does not clearly meet the criteria of a systemic risk, unless the system it affected is defined as Microsoft Windows. If anything, cyberattacks like NotPetya are too diverse in their targets, too widespread in their victims, to be considered systemic risks because they do not affect a particular sector or system, instead snarling a particular piece of many different, interconnected systems. In their analysis of the systemic risks created by globalization, Ian Goldin and Mike Mariathasan suggest that "risk in our hyperconnected environment can no longer be treated as something that is confined to particular sectors or domains."[17] This is perhaps the most important insight about cyber risk to be gleaned from the literature on systemic risk—that it requires breaking down some of the barriers that separate different types of risk from each other and taking a closer look at how cyber vulnerabilities and interdependencies serve to connect many of these existing risks in new ways.

Prior work on the governance role of insurance companies and insurance regulation also informs this analysis, particularly in its consideration of the potential for insurers to supplant regulators in strengthening private sector cybersecurity and the potential role of regulators to stabilize and encourage the development of a robust cyberinsurance market. In their work on the insurance industry, Richard Ericson, Aaron Doyle, and Dean Barry argue that "Insurance is *the* institution of governance beyond the state. The insurance industry uses methodologies of law, surveillance, expertise, and policing in collaboration with the state."[18] When it comes to cyberinsurance, however, many of the governance mechanisms that they identify insurers as carrying out are largely absent or ineffective. Insurance contracts do provide a "legal bond" but the auditing and surveillance systems intended to help carriers decide who to insure offer little guidance about how secure a policyholders' networks truly are and the "private policing apparatus" intended to allocate blame and responsibility has proven similarly ineffective. This work helps shed some light on the limitations of insurers to promote cybersecurity and also on why policymakers have continued to champion cyberinsurance initiatives in spite of these limitations. Ericson, Doyle, and Barry contend that "as part of its efforts to downsize itself, the state actively promotes individual responsibility for risk. . . . Reconfiguring itself as but one player in the interinstitutional field of insurance, the state limits its role to turning people into responsible risk takers and managers who purchase private insurance, offering at best a temporary safety net when things go wrong."[19] This framing of government stakeholders as providing "at best a temporary safety net" and pushing individuals toward insurance as a risk management strategy resonates with the enthusiasm regulators have exhibited for cyberinsurance as well as their reluctance to directly implement more aggressive cybersecurity measures.

In its analysis of the role of government actors in the cyberinsurance market, this book looks to the work of Virginia Haufler on the critical role of the insurance industry in shaping global trade.[20] Haufler traces the evolution of insurance covering international commerce from purely private insurance to increasing involvement from governments and argues that this public-private model of insurance enabled the growth of international trade from the late nineteenth century through the late twentieth century. "The development and evolution of an international risks insurance regime over the course of the twentieth century depended on the initiative and authority of the private sector participants," Haufler writes. "By the end of the century, a marked shift had occurred in the relationship between the public and private sectors in providing insurance and managing the risks of international commerce. Changes in demand, industry norms, and the financial resources available to the insurers transferred greater influence over the regime to public sectors."[21] This book extends Haufler's theory of how increasing public-sector involvement is required for the development of insurance products intended to govern global risks and examines how it applies to cyber risk as well as its limitations in the face of different nations' sometimes conflicting interests in cybersecurity and data protection.

Kenneth Abraham has analyzed the ways that the insurance industry has developed in parallel with tort liability law during the twentieth century. Drawing examples from worker's compensation funds, medical malpractice insurance, auto insurance, and environmental liability coverage, he elucidates the constant interplay between the two systems during that time as each fundamentally shaped the other, particularly with regard to how each addresses the importance of loss spreading, or distributing losses among different parties, versus giving those parties incentives to prevent those losses in the first place.[22] He argues:

> Tort law continually seeks an available source of recovery, creating or expanding the liability of individuals and businesses that are likely to be covered by or have access to liability insurance. And liability insurance has usually responded, by creating new forms of insurance to meet the new liabilities when such insurance was not already available. . . . Tort liability increasingly has performed a loss-spreading function that is also the core purpose of insurance. Correspondingly, though to a lesser degree, insurance has come increasingly to duplicate the deterrence function of tort, by attempting to create incentives on the part of policyholders to prevent their losses from occurring. From both directions, the two systems have moved toward each other and have tended to overlap.[23]

By examining a series of cyberinsurance lawsuits between carriers, their customers, and occasionally other third parties, this book builds on Abraham's theory to explore the deterrence function of cyberinsurance and its effectiveness at creating incentives for policyholders to prevent losses in addition to spreading losses. It argues that, unlike other types of insurance, cyberinsurance has been largely unsuccessful at contributing to deterring losses and has instead served an almost entirely loss-spreading function, despite regulators repeatedly looking to insurance as a way to improve cybersecurity standards and safeguards. Additionally, this book makes the case that the legal disputes between insurers and their policyholders have, in large part, supported carriers' efforts to carve coverage for many cyber-related risks out of their existing non-cyber-specific policies because the precise wording of those policies was often not developed with modern online threats in mind. These rulings have also motivated carriers to make those carve-outs clearer and more explicit, and, in doing so, have helped drive the shift toward insurers covering more cyber risks under stand-alone policies rather than trying to fit that coverage into the larger landscape of other, interconnected types of risks and the insurance policies that govern them. This growth in stand-alone cyber policies has resulted in cyber risks being treated as increasingly isolated or siloed from other types of risks within insurers' organizational and analytical frameworks at precisely the moment when cybersecurity is becoming more central than ever before to the protection of physical property, business operations, automobile safety, and many other areas covered by other insurance lines.

In its analysis of regulators' and policymakers' involvement in the cyber-insurance industry, this work also builds on Kenneth Meier's analysis of the political economy of insurance regulation. Meier posits that "the political economy of insurance regulation results from a complex interaction of industry groups, consumer interests, regulatory bureaucrats, and political elites," and the final section of this book aims to trace the influences of these different parties in the ongoing debates about how regulators should approach cyberinsurance.[24] Meier also argues that insurers do not dominate insurance regulation decisions, despite the industry being ripe for regulatory capture, given its complexity and relatively low profile. "Capture does not occur because the industry is too divided to agree on policy goals," he explains, and these differences in insurers' opinions and priorities are an important part of understanding why many discussions of cyberinsurance regulation have been so circular and have yielded so few legislative results.[25] Despite the lack of legislation around cyberinsurance, policymakers' interest in the industry has played a significant role in raising awareness about cyberinsurance. Furthermore, the resources created by government working groups to promote more extensive, standardized data collection about cybersecurity incidents have at times been useful to individual carriers even when regulators have decided against using them to implement larger-scale data repositories. Finally, the data protection regulations implemented by several countries, many of which include reporting requirements, financial penalties for compliance failures, and in some cases even baseline security standards and certifications, have influenced cyberinsurance coverage. These laws have created new sources of data for insurers, thanks to mandatory incident reporting, as well as new regulatory risks—including fines and liability—for firms to insure themselves against and, in some cases, also offered greater clarity about how those firms' exposure to cyber risks and regulatory penalties should be assessed and mitigated.

Just as courts and policymakers have helped shape the cyberinsurance industry, so too has cyberinsurance shaped the cybersecurity threat landscape. With the emergence of ransomware as a major threat, for instance, insurance policies that help victims cover the costs of online ransom payments have changed the calculus for victims about whether or not to make the payments demanded by their attackers. For instance, on May 29, 2019, a police department employee in Riviera Beach, Florida, opened an email attachment that turned out to contain a ransomware virus and quickly spread to infect the entire city government's computer systems. Within a month, the city of 35,000 people could not process utility payments online; city employees could not access their email, or even phones, in some cases. Less than three weeks later, the Riviera Beach City Council unanimously voted to have its insurance carrier pay the attackers 65 Bitcoin, the equivalent of nearly $600,000 at the time.[26] Just two weeks later, Lake City, another Florida city, was facing the same crippling computer system outages due to ransomware, and authorized a 42 Bitcoin ransom payment, or $460,000, of which the town paid only $10,000. The rest was covered by the city's insurer.[27] "With your heart, you really don't want to pay these guys," Lake City Mayor Stephen Witt told the *New York Times*, "but, dollars and cents, representing the citizens, that was the right thing to do."[28] That cost-benefit equation—the tallying of Lake City's dollars and cents— was weighted in large part by their cyberinsurance policy and the extent to which the city officials were insulated from not just the size of the payment but also the decision to fund the criminals attacking them.

In cases like Riviera Beach and Lake City, cyberinsurance policies can normalize—even legitimize—the payment of online ransoms. By paying for insurance to cover the bulk of the ransom payments, victims are able to view themselves as making reasonable risk management investments rather than acknowledging that in fact they are direct contributors to criminal enterprise. In this manner, the ransom payments that fuel the profitability of these criminal organizations become a regularized and accepted part of firms' costs, rather than a highly discouraged act of last resort that only serves to encourage more criminals. By the time Riviera Beach and Lake City were dealing with their ransomware crises, both cities had already been paying premiums for their cyberinsurance coverage for some time—they had little incentive to talk themselves out of using a service they had already paid for, and every reason to cave to the attackers' demands.

Transforming the costs of cybersecurity incidents into regularized and accepted elements of industry budgets is, in some sense, the whole point of cyberinsurance. As with other types of insurance, it is intended as a means of risk transfer to eliminate large, unexpected costs and replace them with smaller planned payments charged at regular intervals. But there is a significant difference between transferring the costs of replacing infected software and devices or business interruptions or even legal fees associated with class action lawsuits and transferring the costs of directly funding criminal organizations. In the case of online extortion payments, there is value in not accepting these losses as a routinized cost of doing business because those payments go directly to criminals, further supporting their continued efforts and encouraging others to enter this profitable criminal industry. Insurance coverage for ransom payments can enable or even encourage victims to accede to these ransom demands when the overall cybersecurity goal should be exactly the opposite: disincentivizing such payments in order to try to make ransomware less profitable and discourage cybercriminals from distributing it.

The history of cyberinsurance reveals the changing and sometimes overlapping goals of the industry that led to coverage for costs like ransom payments. The earliest policies were designed primarily to cover third-party costs—that is, the costs associated with vendors or individuals outside the targeted firm who were affected by an incident. While the earliest policies date back to the late 1990s, the motivations for purchasing cyberinsurance became clearer in the early 2000s when many states began passing data breach notification laws. In 2003, California passed the first such law mandating that companies report data breaches of personal information to the affected individuals. By the end of 2007, thirty-three other states had followed suit, implementing their own versions of breach notification regulation. These laws imposed various obligations on breached companies to announce publicly when their customers' data had been stolen and those announcements, in turn, made it possible for customers and states to sue companies they believed had provided insufficient protections for the stolen data.

The breach notification laws spurred the development and sale of a very particular type of cyberinsurance: data breach insurance. Aimed primarily at retailers, who collected the payment card information that was the chief target of many early data breaches, data breach insurance provided coverage for the costs of notifying customers about a breach, providing credit monitoring to affected customers, and hiring lawyers to help deal with any resulting lawsuits.[29] Even with the wide adoption of breach notification laws, data breach insurance was slow to win customers outside the retail sector and by 2008, premiums for cyberinsurance were still hovering below $500 million.[30] The back-to-back years of 30 percent premium growth would not arrive until 2012—around the time when policies first began covering a wider range of first-party losses and many other threats besides just breaches of personal information.[31]

Trey Herr links this 2012 spike in the sales of cyberinsurance to the 2011 decision by the US Securities and Exchange Commission (SEC) to issue guidance to companies advising them to disclose their cyber risk profile, including any relevant insurance coverage, to investors as part of their financial filings.[32] The SEC guidance, like the state data breach notification laws before it, is an example of policymakers indirectly influencing the market for cyberinsurance. These mechanisms drove the cyberinsurance market forward not by encouraging companies to purchase cyber-specific policies but rather by signaling to them that they would not be permitted to stay silent about the online risks they faced and might well find themselves liable to their customers or shareholders in the event of a serious incident.

By 2012, the US government was sufficiently invested in promoting cyberinsurance directly that the Department of Homeland Security's National Protection and Programs Directorate (NPPD) convened a series of public roundtables and workshops on the topic. The convenings, which spanned October 2012 through April 2016, brought together representatives from industry and government to examine "the ability of insurance carriers to offer relevant cyber risk coverage at reasonable prices in return for an insured's adoption of cyber risk management controls and procedures that improve its cyber risk posture."[33] From their outset, the purpose of these meetings was to encourage cyberinsurance as a means of preventing cyber-related incidents and losses through requiring policyholders to adopt security controls. This framing suggests a disconnect between the ways that insurers and their policy-holders typically viewed the goal of cyberinsurance policies and the ways that policymakers perceived those same goals. While insurance carriers and their customers were primarily focused on cyberinsurance as a mechanism for risk spreading and loss compensation, policymakers were looking to those same insurance policies as a tool for risk reduction and loss mitigation. Insurers, to a great extent, encouraged that view, repeatedly reassuring regulators that they could help promote cybersecurity best practices among their policyholders and prevent incidents from escalating, even in the absence of any clear evidence that they were succeeding at these goals. But that framing of cyberinsurance as a means of strengthening cybersecurity was crucial to government support for the industry as a key component of creating the right incentives for the private sector to better protect itself. Predicated on the idea that insurance could serve a deterrent function by helping firms prevent cybersecurity incidents, in addition to its typical loss-spreading role, the NPPD-organized meetings centered on government officials asking representatives from the cyberinsurance industry what assistance, if any, they could provide to hasten the development and growth of the sector.

By that point, harnessing private market forces to take the lead on managing cybersecurity risks of noncritical infrastructure had already long been a priority of the US government. The National Strategy to Secure Cyberspace, released by George W. Bush's administration in February 2003, emphasized that "the private sector is best equipped and structured to respond to an evolving cyber threat." It noted, "Some businesses whose products or services directly or indirectly impact the economy or the health, welfare or safety of the public have begun to use cyber risk insurance programs as a means of transferring risk and providing for business continuity."[34] This idea that civilian cybersecurity was—and should be—primarily the business of private companies was a recurring theme for the US government during the early 2000s. Even as the government was taking an increasingly active role in cybersecurity, for instance by publishing that first national cybersecurity strategy in 2003, or by establishing the military Cyber Command in 2009, regulators returned, repeatedly, to the idea that the security of civilian data and networks was, primarily, an area for companies to tackle with their superior technical expertise and greater resources.

This push was often couched in calls for "public-private partnerships" between industry and government. In the introductory letter to the 2003

National Strategy, George W. Bush writes: "The cornerstone of America's cyberspace security strategy is and will remain a public-private partnership." But while the terms of those public-private partnerships were made somewhat more explicit through National Infrastructure Protection Plans for designated critical infrastructure sectors, such as transportation, finance, communications, and power, many private companies received no clear guidance from the government about how they should be protecting their computer systems or managing cyber risks. Subscribing to the view that the private sector knows best how to handle these risks, the federal government remained relatively hands-off when it came to mandating security best practices or clarifying the expectations for what companies must do to avoid liability for cybersecurity incidents. The National Institute for Standards and Technology (NIST), within the Department of Commerce, has provided the most guidance to these firms, through publications cataloging different security and privacy controls as well as a high-level Cybersecurity Framework, published in 2014, that organizations can use to organize their cyber risk management efforts. But these high-level initiatives and voluntary standards have still left many organizations in need of more guidance, particularly smaller firms without the resources to devote to a dedicated cybersecurity team.[35]

The cyberinsurance market that has emerged to fill those gaps is an example of "private governance," Herr argues.[36] This private governance emerges not as the result of state retreat or governments neglecting their governance duties, he finds, but rather because of private advance, or regulators finding "some financial benefit in setting and enforcing standards" in a manner that satisfies "the demands of those seeking regulation."[37] Undoubtedly, insurers have derived significant financial benefits from the cyberinsurance market. As insurers have faced the limitations of their own technical expertise and partnered with a growing number of security firms, those partners have also benefited. Whether the demands of cyberinsurance customers like Mondelez have been met, however, is a more complicated question. Meier suggests that "the purpose of insurance regulation is to protect the consumers' interests," whether by improving the financial stability of insurance companies so that claims can be paid out, regulating rates for insurance, or increasing access to insurance, as well as improving the choices and information available to customers.[38] The frustrations of cyberinsurance consumers suggest that there may be a need for some greater government involvement in working toward some of these aims and trying to help resolve the challenges that insurance customers and their carriers face in buying and selling cyberinsurance.

In addition to Haufler's work on government's evolving roles in insurance markets, Meier's work on insurance regulation, and Abraham's analysis of the interplay between tort law and liability insurance, this book also owes much to the existing body of scholarship focused specifically on cyberinsurance. Prior work on cyberinsurance includes significant theoretical modeling of the cyberinsurance industry and the challenges it presents, such as correlated losses.[39] Related research has used modeling techniques to look at how insurers might try to mitigate the risk of correlated losses by seeking out customers who do not use the most popular computing platforms.[40] A theoretical framework for classifying different cyberinsurance market models has identified five key components of these markets: networked environment, demand side, supply side, information structure, and organizational environment.[41] Yet another theoretical model has tackled the question of how insurers can improve the software security of their customers.[42] While this book deals with many of the same challenges identified in these theoretical studies, it does not model the cyberinsurance market or its effects. Rather, it examines the historical origins of this market and its evolution through analysis of lawsuits, cyberinsurance policies, interviews, government records, and media coverage, aiming to describe the cyberinsurance market as it is—and has been—rather than modeling it quantitatively. Accordingly, this work is heavily influenced by previous empirical analyses of cyberinsurance policies that addressed the questions of what types of costs and incidents they cover, how they are priced, and what exclusions they carry. Daniel Woods, Ioannis Agrafiotis, Jason Nurse, and Sadie Creese analyzed twenty-four cyberinsurance self-assessment questionnaires in the UK and the US to understand whether the security controls they mentioned corresponded with accepted industry best practices.[43] Sasha Romanosky, Lillian Ablon, Andreas Kuehn, and Therese Jones performed a content analysis of boilerplate cyber policies to assess the different types of costs and incidents covered by cyberinsurance products, as well as the pricing structure for those products and the questionnaires used by insurers to assess potential policyholders.[44] This book draws heavily on their conclusions, especially in its discussion of how insurers audit customers' cyber risk exposure. Robert Morgus conducted a similar analysis on a set of policies to categorize different coverage types.[45] Shauhin Talesh conducted interviews and observations of insurers and analyzed industry manuals, concluding that cyberinsurers act as security compliance managers for their customers, helping them comply with privacy laws and better understand their legal obligations.[46]

This book aims to build on the work done by these and other scholars to characterize the market for cyberinsurance both theoretically and empirically by adding a layer of historical perspective on how cyberinsurance markets have changed over time and the role of legal disputes and policies in influencing those changes. This analysis examines the emergence of the cyberinsurance market through the lens of regulatory developments, legal battles, and shifts in public policy, not just in the United States, where the vast majority of early cyberinsurance policies were sold, but also in the markets where insurers are currently looking to ramp up their cyber coverage, including the European Union, China, Brazil, and India, expanding the geographic scope of previous cyberinsurance scholarship. Using legal records, government reports, interviews with regulators and insurers, and cyberinsurance policies collected from insurers and regulators, this book maps the global growth of the cyberinsurance market and considers how that growth has challenged earlier notions about the quantification, management, and assessment of risk.

At the heart of this analysis are three related arguments about the roles of insurance carriers, courts, and policymakers in shaping the cyberinsurance market and the impacts of that market on both cybersecurity threats and risk management, more generally. The first argument is that courts in the United States have supported insurers' efforts to exclude cyber risks from non-cyber-specific policies related to liability and crime, even in the face of sometimes ambiguous language in those policies governing their applicability to cybercrimes and cyberattacks, thereby enabling insurers to shift their cyber risk coverage into stand-alone policies. Those stand-alone cyber risk policies cover many first- and third-party costs related to different kinds of cybersecurity incidents, ranging from network outages and data breaches to social engineering attacks and regulatory penalties, but they often do not account for the many complicated ways cyber risks are intertwined with other types of risk covered in separate policies. These connections with so many other types of risk are what differentiate cyber risks from other types of risk previously tackled by the insurance industry and contribute to the limitations of insurers' existing tools and approaches for modeling risk. Second, this analysis indicates that this effort to silo cyber risks, in their own isolated policies and departments within insurance companies, has contributed to the challenges insurers face in modeling and pricing these risks by preventing them from keeping up with the ways computer networks and data have become increasingly embedded into other systems and coverage areas. The final overarching theme in this book relates to the role of policymakers, who have encouraged the further development of cyberinsurance in many countries, based on the idea that a robust insurance market will reduce organizations' overall cyber risk exposure. But, in fact, due to a combination of a lack of data, a lack of expertise, and an inability to scale rigorous security audits, cyberinsurance has not appeared to play a significant deterrent role in reducing cybersecurity incidents or exposure to cyber risks. Instead, the pressure to grow their cyberinsurance portfolios and compete for customers has actually forced many carriers to limit the rigor and depth of their assessments of potential customers' security postures. Taken together, these arguments explore the disconnect between how policyholders understand their coverage for cyber risks and how their carriers interpret that coverage, as well as the disconnect between how regulators have viewed cyberinsurance and how it has actually functioned in practice, looking to the industry's origins and legal history to understand why and how these discrepancies emerged. So much of the history of insurance is the story of how an industry managed to quantify and measure and predict different types of risk, using quantitative methods to transform primitive risk-sharing mechanisms—for instance, shipowners agreeing to share the costs of sunk vessels when there was no way of knowing whose ships would sink or preventing them from doing so—into a vast, profitable industry. But in many ways cyber risks have challenged those actuarial methods and returned insurance to its earlier form, serving as a basic means of risk sharing and loss compensation for victims, without any ability to predict who will be targeted or how they should protect themselves, rather than a carefully modeled, statistically sophisticated mechanism for understanding when risks will occur, how big they will be, or whom they will affect.

The first section of this book looks at the development of cyberinsurance and lays out the history of the industry alongside that of other, more developed insurance sectors, including car and flood insurance. The following chapter examines the different roles of regulators and government agencies in helping each of these insurance products develop and the applicability of these approaches to cyberinsurance. Early efforts in cybersecurity regulation are discussed alongside analysis of how those policies influenced both the content of cyberinsurance policies and their adoption by different customers. This analysis includes a discussion of how the types of threats and costs that cyberinsurance policies cover have changed over time to include coverage of incidents related to online extortion, network outages, and social engineering.

Following this historical analysis, the second section of the book is focused primarily on legal disputes between insurers and policyholders about whether cyber-related losses were covered under policies designed for liability, crime, or property and casualty losses. The third chapter draws on legal disputes about cyber risk-related claims under commercial general liability (CGL) insurance policies to provide an analysis of how cyber risks were effectively excised from the coverage provided under CGL policies, spurring demand for data breach insurance crafted specifically to cover this type of liability. The fourth chapter looks at a corresponding set of legal disputes for denied cyber-related claims under commercial crime insurance policies. Not all of these incidents fit clearly or exclusively into definitions of computer fraud or cybercrime as financially motivated crimes carried out through computers or the Internet, so this chapter explores the issues that arise when computer risks and the associated insurance coverage overlap with other types of crime and coverage. Court rulings on the cases discussed in these two chapters left insurance customers increasingly uncertain about whether their policies included coverage for damage caused by viruses or phishing attacks even if those online threats targeted insured assets. This uncertainty contributed to the demand for stand-alone cyber-specific insurance products. Even as insurers sought to develop a new market for cyberinsurance products, they often grappled with the question of whether and how to incorporate cyber risks into other, existing policies that covered more general risks. These chapters look at early efforts by insurers and courts to figure out how cyberinsurance fit into the larger picture of insurance coverage and what could be done to disambiguate the overlapping threats and concerns that fell under the umbrella of cyber risk. The fifth chapter follows legal disputes over denied property and casualty insurance claims for cyber-related damages, examining how even after buying add-on insurance products intended explicitly to cover computer-related risks, customers sometimes found that exceptions ported over from other insurance policies left their coverage incomplete or inadequate. In particular, this chapter reviews a series of cases that rely on "act of war" exceptions, mentioned earlier, to deny coverage for cyberattacks perpetrated by states and actors and considers how the unique nature of cyber risks and uncertainty surrounding what constitutes cyberwar has left cyberinsurance customers unable to exercise their coverage when they most need it.

The final section of the book looks at the trend toward stand-alone cyberinsurance policies that cover a growing number of first-party risks, the challenges these policies present to insurers, and the approaches different governments have taken to helping carriers address those challenges and bolstering the cyberinsurance industry. The sixth chapter tackles the particular challenges that cyberinsurance underwriters face in trying to design and price stand-alone cyber risk policies, as well as the challenges of auditing and assessing potential cyberinsurance customers and the extent of their exposure to computer-based risks. It looks at the ways that insurers have tried to deal with incomplete or unreliable data, the interconnectedness or correlation of cyber risk (or the possibility that all of an insurer's customers might be simultaneously affected by the same cyberattack), and the challenges of trying to assess customers' level of security and risk when determining whether or not to sell them a policy. These challenges have forced insurers to resort to industry partnerships and more primitive pricing schemes, among other approaches, in the face of the unique characteristics of cyber risks.

The seventh chapter explores the role of policymakers in helping insurers address these challenges, and also traces global growth of cyberinsurance in the late 2010s. Governments have influenced the development of the cyberinsurance industry in the United States, the European Union, China, Brazil, India, and Singapore, through the passage of data protection regulations as well as, in some cases, focused initiatives aimed at growing the cyberinsurance industry. This analysis also considers the role of governments as customers for cyberinsurance and the broader agenda of policymakers in stabilizing and encouraging the growth of the cyberinsurance industry. Drawing on other regulated types of insurance, including auto insurance, flood insurance, terrorism insurance, and health insurance, this chapter identifies different models of how policymakers can intervene in insurance markets and ultimately recommends a set of policy proposals to address the most pressing challenges and concerns in the cyberinsurance sector.

Finally, the conclusion (chapter 8) summarizes some of the recurring themes related to the balance between stand-alone and add-on cyberinsurance products, liability for cybersecurity incidents, whether cyberinsurance can strengthen cybersecurity overall, and the role of policymakers in this ecosystem. It also considers future directions for the cyberinsurance industry and emerging threats and challenges that carriers and policyholders will face in the coming years,

Insuring cyber risks is a fundamentally risky proposition at a time when there is still so much we do not know about the threat landscape. The insurance industry, by contrast, is fundamentally risk-averse—insurers like to be certain they have a clear handle on exactly what future years will hold for their customers. Indeed, their business model depends on knowing roughly how much they will have pay out in claims and pricing their premiums accordingly. At the same time, at a moment when cyberinsurance is the fastest-growing sector of the insurance industry, many firms are eager to cash in on the growing demand even in the absence of robust models and reliable data about how often cybersecurity incidents occur, how much they cost, and how they can be most effectively prevented or mitigated. This book traces the efforts of insurers to grapple with the challenges of insuring cyber risk and speaks to the larger themes of how an industry built on being able to model risk reliably deals with new technologies before the risks those technologies present can be fully characterized or understood. It looks at the legal disputes that have surrounded this industry and the interplay between courts and insurers in defining coverage for cybersecurity incidents as well as the origins of the insurance ambiguities that gave rise to this litigation.

By setting out this history of cyberinsurance alongside the development of other types of insurance, it is possible to better understand which challenges faced by the cyberinsurance market today are due to cyber risks being relatively new and which are due to cyber risks being substantively different than other types of risk because of how interconnected and integrated into other risks they are. These comparisons reveal that while every new insurance market faces growing pains, there are also some ways in which the cyberinsurance market is tackling a qualitatively different kind of risk than insurers have modeled in the past. Only some of the challenges facing the cyberinsurance industry today will be resolved by time and better data alone—some will require further litigation, regulatory interventions, and even new ways altogether of thinking about and dealing with risk.

I

HISTORY OF CYBERINSURANCE

BREACH ON THE BEACH: ORIGINS OF CYBERINSURANCE

Only twenty people showed up for the Breach on the Beach party at the International Risk Insurance Management Society's annual convention in Honolulu in April 1997. It was a small gathering but it marked a huge achievement for Steve Haase, who was then an insurance broker and senior vice president at Hamilton Dorsey Alston Co. For more than two years, Haase had been trying to persuade colleagues in the insurance industry to back a new product that would protect companies whose data had been stolen from their computer servers, but no one had been willing to bite—until now. The Breach on the Beach luau marked the official launch of Haase's brainchild, called Internet Security Liability (ISL), an insurance policy tailored to the risks of e-commerce underwritten by insurance firm American International Group (AIG).[1] "[AIG] was willing to take the risk to get the market share," Haase told *Inc. Magazine* in an article published later that year. Insurance is an industry that trades in risk and depends on being able to estimate and assess different types of risk—but the risk that Haase was referring to was that there might not be any way to effectively measure the types of online risks he was aiming to insure companies against. The challenge, as Haase described it then, was that "there aren't really any actuarial studies of Internet commerce. . . . Banks and other merchants aren't too forthcoming with that sort of information."[2]

At the time, Haase had been selling insurance policies to technology companies for a decade and he was fascinated by how the Internet was becoming a platform for business. Online commerce was still very much in its infancy in 1997 but it was already showing signs of rapid growth. In 1995, Microsoft started offering a web browser, Internet Explorer, with its popular Windows operating system, giving millions of computer users worldwide an easy way to access the Internet. From 1996 to 1997, the number of Internet users worldwide grew from 40 million to 100 million people, the number of registered domain names grew from 627,000 to 1.5 million.

Amazon, which started in 1996, sold $148 million worth of books in 1997, up from $16 million the previous year.[3] The ISL coverage that Haase had persuaded AIG to back was aimed at protecting retailers like Amazon who were collecting customer credit card numbers and storing them on servers. In 1997, the standard ISL plan would provide coverage up to $250,000 in legal costs and settlement fees if customer credit card numbers were stolen off those companies' servers and a credit card company subsequently sued the firm for failing to protect them. The premium for the plan was priced starting at $2,500 annually, but websites that had their security audited and certified by the National Computer Security Association qualified for a 25 percent discount, bringing the cost down to $1,875 per year.[4]

Two decades later, all of those numbers would seem absurd—the notion that only twenty people would be interested in selling cyberinsurance, that firms would be paying only $2,500 per year for it, the prospect that a security audit would reliably net those firms a 25 percent discount, the suggestion that $250,000 would seem like sufficient coverage to shield companies from the costs of online threats. In 2017, twenty years after AIG launched the first policy, cyberinsurance represented the fastest-growing sector of the insurance industry and there were 471 firms selling cyberinsurance policies that brought in more than $3 billion in premiums.[5] And yet, in many ways, the cyberinsurance industry still faces many of the same problems that Haase highlighted back in 1997: the lack of good data about how often past security incidents have actually occurred and how much they cost, and continued widespread unwillingness on the part of banks and merchants to collect or share that data. By 2017, AIG was no longer alone in offering coverage for computer-related risks, but all of the carriers who had gotten into the business were still taking a gamble to get a piece of the growing market share both in the United States and abroad. They tempered that risk by setting high premiums, carving out careful exceptions to their policies, and fighting to uphold those exceptions in court, narrowing the scope of what their policies actually covered as online threats evolved and policyholders filed claims for new forms of computer-related losses. But even as they tried to carve out exceptions for many computer-related risks, insurers were still using the looming specter of rampant cybersecurity threats and new data security regulations to sell new policies to their customers.

The growth of the cyberinsurance market has been shaped in large part by regulations and regulators, but cyberinsurance itself remains largely unregulated. Unlike other forms of insurance, there are no requirements governing what cyberinsurance policies must cover, who must obtain them, or to whom they must be made available. The passage of state data breach notification laws in the United States and the General Data Protection Regulation in Europe helped drive demand for cyberinsurance and influenced what types of losses those policies covered, as did the decision by the US Securities and Exchange Commission that companies should disclose cyber risks to their shareholders as part of their financial filings. Yet, unlike auto insurance, cyberinsurance is not required by law, unlike flood or terrorism insurance it is not underwritten by the government, and unlike health insurance the actual content of policies and what costs they must cover is not regulated by any legislation at either the state or federal level. That lack of oversight is understandable given the small size of the market for cyberinsurance and the fact that it has historically covered a fairly narrow set of relatively niche threats, like retailer data breaches of the sort envisioned by Haase when he designed the original ISL policy. Historically, however, as new insurance products have grown in popularity or encountered challenges of the sort presently facing cyberinsurers, regulators have often stepped in to stabilize the market, protect consumers, and provide much-needed data or financial support. As the cyberinsurance market continues to grow, therefore, it is worth tracing its development alongside that of other types of insurance products, to better understand the roles that regulators can play in emerging insurance markets as well as the impact public policy has already had on shaping early forms of cyberinsurance. This chapter offers brief overviews of pivotal moments in the history of car, flood, and life insurance in the United States as well as some lessons from these narratives for insuring cyber risks, followed by an in-depth analysis of the early years of the cyberinsurance market and the cybersecurity-related policies that influenced its development.

THE DEVELOPMENT OF AUTO INSURANCE

Perhaps the clearest example of a new technology that introduced new risks to society and subsequently spawned an enormous, robust insurance industry is the car. But while car accidents are largely dealt with using private insurance today, the path to that stable, widespread insurance sector was convoluted and, at times, fraught, suggesting that cyberinsurers may still have considerable work ahead of them to develop an analogous set of products for computer-based risks. In the late nineteenth century, the development of automobiles was closely followed by the emergence of auto insurance, but like early cyberinsurance policies those first insurance policies for auto accidents were relatively uncommon and rarely exercised. The first recorded car accident in the United States occurred in New York City in 1896,[6] and the first automobile bodily injury liability policy was issued to Truman J. Martin of Buffalo, New York, by Travelers two years later, on February 1, 1898.[7] Six years after that, in 1904, the first large claim under an auto policy was settled by the Boston Insurance Company, which paid $9,500 to William Wallace when his car's gas tank exploded while he was driving from Boston to Worcester.[8]

Adoption of auto insurance in the following decades was driven primarily by state regulations. In 1925, nearly three decades after the first auto insurance policy was issued, Connecticut passed the first financial responsibility law, mandating that drivers who had been involved in an accident could retain their licenses only if they posted a bond or purchased liability insurance. Two years later, in 1927, Massachusetts became the first state to pass a law requiring drivers to purchase personal auto coverage.[9] But after this initial surge of enthusiasm in a handful of states, regulatory efforts to promote coverage subsided. In 1957, thirty years after the Massachusetts law went into effect, only two other states had passed similar requirements into law, indicating just how gradual the regulatory process had been.[10] Though mandatory car insurance laws were good for business, insurance carriers opposed them for fear they would invite more regulation that could prevent them from charging sufficiently high premiums and would lead to more claims.[11]

Early auto liability policies operated under the "personal responsibility system" in which whoever was deemed to have caused an accident was liable for any resulting injuries, and victims could seek compensation from those responsible parties or their insurers. Under this system, the drivers responsible for accidents received no benefits or compensation even if they were injured (unless they had purchased separate health insurance or medical coverage policies), and there were no limits on how much victims could seek in compensation for their own losses. This model was derived directly from other types of liability and casualty insurance. In fact, the 1898 policy that Travelers issued to Martin was written on a form that "formerly had been used to insure the liability connected with the use of teams of horses or mules" to draw carriages.[12]

Travelers had been founded only a few decades earlier, in 1863, as the Travelers Insurance Company of Hartford and it had sold its first accident policy in the United States the following year, in 1864, to James Bolter for a premium payment of $0.02 to insure him against accidents on the two-block walk from his house to the Hartford post office.[13] When the company began writing auto insurance policies at the turn of the century, Travelers therefore drew from its existing policies covering travel and accidents to formulate an auto liability policy that adhered to the same principles. "In promoting an auto accident compensation system based on personal responsibility, policymakers were simply extending traditional American legal principles, embodied in the tort system, to a new technology—the automobile," explains Harvey Rosenfield.[14] Similarly, when insurers began offering early forms of cyberinsurance, many of these initial products drew on existing errors and omissions (E&O) coverage that focused on offering personal liability protection to web developers and online content providers during the dot-com boom in the late 1990s.[15]

By 1905, less than a decade after the first US policy was issued to Martin, distinct insurance policies for car were widely available in the United States. Annual premiums for those policies totaled $64 million in 1921, and nearly tripled in sales between then and 1930, but while that growth had helped drivers manage the costs of car accidents it had done little to reduce the rate of accidents or resulting casualties.[16] In fact, the number of motor vehicle deaths had been rising rapidly in the United States alongside this expansion of the auto insurance market. In 1932, a group of academics assembled to form the "Committee to Study Compensation for Auto Accidents" presented a report to the Columbia University Council for Research in the Social Sciences proposing that the United States change its system of auto insurance. The report was motivated by the growing number of car accidents in the United States—at time of the report, the committee wrote, "deaths in motor vehicle accidents form the largest single field of accidental deaths in the United States."[17] At the same time, even with regulatory requirements for private passenger and commercial vehicles to be insured, in 1929 only 27.3 percent of all motor vehicles registered in the United States were insured for public liability, the report estimated, meaning that the owners of more than nineteen million vehicles had purchased no coverage and many victims of car accidents therefore received no compensation whatsoever.[18]

As in the case of cyberinsurance nearly a century later, auto insurance did not, in the early decades of its development, keep pace with the adoption of cars or the growing risks they posed, nor did it manage to noticeably reduce those risks. The Columbia report proposed that the dramatic increase in car-related risks—and deaths—might call for an entirely new form of coverage: no-fault insurance. Under the suggested compensation plan, if a car accident caused an injury—or death—then the owner of the car involved would be liable for compensating the injured parties, regardless of who was at fault, and every owner of a registered vehicle would be required to purchase insurance that could cover those costs.[19] This system was not intended to drive down the number of car accident fatalities, but rather to acknowledge how widespread they were and eliminate the need for victims to engage in lengthy and expensive litigation in order to be compensated for their losses. This would mean insurers could pay out less money for legal fees (which were at one point estimated by the Department of Transportation to comprise 23 percent of auto insurance premiums) but also that, as part of the no-fault insurance system, victims would have to give up their ability to sue for damages, at least up to a certain amount.[20]

The no-fault concept laid out in the 1932 report was modeled on workers' compensation programs, which had similarly been intended to ensure that accident victims received compensation quickly, without having to engage in extended litigation to determine who was at fault.[21] The report highlighted this comparison to emphasize the practicality of the committee's proposal, and the need to try something new in the realm of car insurance even if it meant abandoning deeply entrenched notions of personal responsibility that had been the underpinnings of casualty insurance up to that point. The report noted, "Workmen's compensation laws were adopted in this country not because of a theoretical preference for the principle of liability without fault, but because it had become imperative to discard a system which worked very badly and to try in its place a new system which gave promise of success." In particular, the committee emphasized, the litigation required for employees to prove fault and claim payments from their employers prior to worker's compensation programs "cast a heavy burden of loss entirely upon injured employees and their families."[22] It is interesting to consider the burdens cybersecurity incidents place on victims in light of this logic, especially since there are often multiple different kinds of victims affected by a single such incident, all of whom face largely undefined liability regimes. For instance, in the aftermath of a breach of personal data, the payment card networks and banks that have to cover any resulting fraudulent charges, as well as individual victims whose information has been stolen, can—and often do—sue the breached company for damages. That company is, itself, another victim of the breach, and often, in turn, blames third-party vendors, software vendors, standards-setting bodies, and government agencies for failing to secure its data and networks or give it adequate guidance on how to do so. The outcomes of these lawsuits have varied considerably depending on how sympathetic different courts have been to the types of harm that individuals suffer due to the loss of their personal information as well as how negligent the breached companies have been in securing that information. These outcomes have ultimately provided no clear guidelines for how to determine who is at fault for security breaches.[23] While this system undoubtedly places a heavy burden on all of the victims involved, it rarely yields any decisive determination of who was at fault—other than the perpetrators.

In considering a no-fault model for auto insurance, the United States trailed behind several other countries, including Sweden, Denmark, France, and Finland, that had already adopted a "liability without fault" approach in motor vehicle cases by the 1930s.[24] In 1946, Canada adopted many of the recommendations of the Columbia report with its Saskatchewan Plan, which mandated insurance for all vehicle owners in the country and provided compensation to victims of all car accidents regardless of fault.[25] In the United States, by contrast, the first state to adopt a no-fault law—Massachusetts—did not do so until 1970. Between 1970 and 1976, twenty-six states passed no-fault insurance laws but many states and insurers would later change their minds about the wisdom of this approach, either repealing those laws or weakening them significantly.[26] "Although no-fault looked as if it might sweep the nation, the no-fault bandwagon stalled as quickly as it started," Meier writes, noting that many of the states that passed no-fault laws "simply added no-fault coverage on top of regular automobile insurance without any restriction on tort suits," in some cases even making the addition of no-fault coverage optional.[27]

Part of what made the no-fault system so controversial and problematic in the United States was that it diverged profoundly from existing models of insurance and claims litigation centered on personal responsibility and finding fault with the responsible party. The workers' compensation laws, which provided employees who suffered injuries at work with salary and medical benefits, regardless of whether their employers had been responsible for their injuries, were similarly controversial when they were introduced. In 1911, the New York Court of Appeals ruled that one such law was unconstitutional because of its no-fault basis. The court wrote:

> If the legislature can say to an employer, "you must compensate your employee for an injury not caused by you or by your fault," why can it not go further and say to the man of wealth, "you have more property than you need and your neighbor is so poor that he can barely subsist; in the interest of natural justice you must divide with your neighbor so that he and his dependents shall not become a charge upon the State?" . . . If it is competent to impose upon an employer, who has omitted no legal duty and has committed no wrong, a liability based solely upon a legislative fiat that his business is inherently dangerous, it is equally competent to visit upon him a special tax for the support of hospitals and other charitable institutions, upon the theory that they are devoted largely to the alleviation of ills primarily due to his business. In its final and simple analysis that is taking the property of A and giving it to B, and that cannot be done under our Constitutions.[28]

Ultimately, New York had to amend its state constitution to overcome this objection—an indication of just how anathema the no-fault concept was to US law and audiences, long before it served as an inspiration for auto insurance reform efforts.[29]

The concerns raised by the New York Court of Appeals that a no-fault approach to one area might quickly lead to no-fault approaches to everything were also voiced by many proponents of the personal responsibility approach to auto insurance, who pointed out that the existing system of liability insurance, slow and onerous as it might be, had worked well enough for many other types of accidents and injuries. Advocates of no-fault insurance argued, in turn, that radical changes to this system were justified for car accidents because car accidents were unlike risks the insurance industry, and court system, had dealt with before. The authors of the 1932 Columbia report acknowledged that many other types of casualty insurance, besides auto insurance, also required people to undergo lengthy and expensive litigation in order to claim compensation. But they argued that "motor vehicle accidents form a peculiar class, because they form such a large proportion of accidental injuries and are increasing with alarming rapidity, and because they are caused by a distinct group of highly dangerous instruments introduced for the benefit or convenience of the owners, to which we are already accustomed to apply special laws and regulations."[30]

Much of the logic used by the report's authors to justify reinventing existing models of insurance for cars is strikingly applicable to computers, which can also be viewed as "highly dangerous instruments introduced for the benefit or convenience of the owners, to which we are already accustomed to apply special laws and regulations." The timeline of the development of auto insurance also hints at just how long it can take to fashion insurance policies suited to a particular type of risk, however. From the first US auto insurance policy being issued in 1898, to the first requirements for auto insurance being passed into state law in the 1920s, to the first no-fault insurance law being passed in Massachusetts in 1970, to the abandonment of federal no-fault policy efforts by Congress in 1978, the process has been an undeniably gradual one. It was shaped, every step of the way, by policymakers and regulations addressing not just no-fault insurance but also issues such as automobile safety and collecting statistics on car accident fatalities and injuries. Moreover, the risks associated with cars continue to change even today, particularly with the incorporation of more software and autonomous driving systems into modern vehicles, intersecting with issues of cyber risk insurance and complicating existing systems of liability and responsibility for car accidents.

The history of car insurance is not a ringing endorsement of the no-fault insurance model but it does suggest that some technologies present risks so new, so frequent in occurrence, so significant in size, and so different from those that insurers and courts have dealt with before that they require a radical reimagining of the existing insurance frameworks and mechanisms for assigning responsibility and blame. From that perspective, the reasons that the 1932 report offers for what makes car accidents different from other types of risk are particularly poignant. The report states:

> The principle of compensation without regard to fault could of course be applied to all accidental injuries caused by one person to another. However that may be, the Committee is satisfied that, because of the great number of cases involved and the peculiar difficulties of handling them under the existing system, the

problem of dealing with motor vehicle accidents deserves separate consideration. In motor vehicle accident cases, the principle of negligence is peculiarly difficult to apply. In most automobile accidents, a car collides with another car or with a pedestrian. All the action occurs within a few seconds. It is almost impossible for witnesses, even though they have not been participants in the accident, to remember and to reproduce exactly to the jury swiftly succeeding events which they have been neither trained nor prepared to observe. Litigation in such cases results in jury trials which are largely contests of skill and chance.[31]

Many years later, in claims cases involving computer-related risks, negligence and liability would also often turn out to be "peculiarly difficult to apply" not because of how quickly the incidents occurred but instead because of how complicated and interconnected the computer systems involved were and how little clarity many organizations had about what they were supposed to do to protect their networks and data. Not just the witnesses but also the lawyers and judges in these cases often found themselves dealing with evidence they had not been trained to evaluate or understand, leading to confusing and sometimes contradictory rulings that themselves seemed to result from somewhat arbitrary "contests of skill and chance."

FLOOD INSURANCE: "A TOOL THAT SHOULD BE USED EXPERTLY OR NOT AT ALL"

Unlike auto insurance reform, which arose out of the gradual accumulation of a large number of relatively small accidents, policy around flood insurance was shaped primarily by a small number of large-scale incidents, including the 1927 Mississippi floods and Hurricane Betsy in 1965. Both models are instructive for considering the development of insurance products that cover cybersecurity incidents because cyber risks manifest both in frequent, small-scale compromises and in some much larger, less frequent attacks. The history of flood insurance regulation is especially relevant to the emergence of cyberinsurance because it involves an extensive, government-led initiative not just to back insurance policies but also to collect data about flood risks. Few insurance sectors have been more thoroughly overhauled by regulators than flood insurance, which was transformed in the United States by the passage of the National Flood Insurance Act in 1968 and the creation of the National Flood Insurance Program (NFIP). Meier explains that this regulatory involvement was necessary due to the fact that "flood insurance is a product that private industry cannot profitably provide. Because people who live on high ground do not want flood insurance, risks due to flooding cannot be spread among enough individuals to make it economically feasible."[32] Everyone is susceptible to cyber risks and their costs can therefore be spread across a large number of policyholders, but the particular challenges of providing flood insurance and the role of government nonetheless provide some useful insights for managing cyber risks.

Private insurers routinely offered flood insurance policies in the United States from 1895 to 1927, when they began to withdraw from the market following the Great Mississippi Flood, when the Mississippi River flooded 27,000 square miles across ten different states.[33] Attempts to institute a comprehensive flood relief program through the short-lived Federal Flood Indemnity Association, formed by President Eisenhower in the 1950s, were largely unsuccessful, and the government provided compensation for natural disasters on a largely case-by-case basis for several decades until Congress passed the Southeast Hurricane Disaster Relief Act following Hurricane Betsy in 1965.[34] That law led to the creation of the Task Force on Federal Flood Control Policy, which issued a report in 1966 emphasizing the need for more data on flooding to enable any kind of robust insurance program. It tasked the US Army Corps of Engineers, the Federal Water Resources Council, the Department of Housing and Urban Development (HUD), the Department of Agriculture, and the Geological Survey with collecting data on flooding frequency, flood damage, flood plain residences, and urban hydrology, and further recommended that a "new national program for collecting more useful flood damage data" should be created by government agencies.[35] "In order that premium rates may be set with knowledge of actual degree of risk it is necessary to have accurate information concerning area, frequency, and depth of inundation," the report noted.[36]

In addition to those data-gathering initiatives, the 1966 Task Force report also recommended a "five-stage study of the feasibility of insurance under various conditions" to be carried out by HUD. The stages included extensive statistical studies, followed by a limited experimental test program, careful evaluation of the results of that test program, and finally a recommendation about a national program of flood insurance.[37] The theme of policyholders' personal responsibility was no less prevalent when it came to addressing flood insurance and natural catastrophes than it had been when discussing car accidents decades earlier. "Floods are an act of God; flood damages result from the acts of men," the 1966 report asserted, adding, "Those who occupy the flood plain should be responsible for the results of their actions."[38]

By the time Congress passed the National Flood Insurance Act in August 1968, many of the data-gathering initiatives recommended by the 1966 report had been completed. The Army Corps of Engineers had released its *Guidelines for Reducing Flood Damages*, as well as its assessment of the number of "flood-prone" communities in the United States. The Geological Survey had released a nineteen-volume flood study on the frequency and size of floods, and the Water Resources Council had issued a report on standards for assessing flood risk.[39] Those efforts contributed to Congress's willingness to pass the 1968 law which established the Federal Insurance Administration which, in turn, oversaw the NFIP. Previous failed proposals to provide sustained federal flood relief in the 1950s had been unsuccessful in part because there was not sufficient data or technical expertise to support such a program.[40]

The NFIP launched in January 1969, with the federal government subsidizing flood insurance premiums for homeowners who lived in flood-prone areas in partnership with a group of eighty-nine insurers who had formed the National Flood Insurers Association.[41] The NFIP struggled at first, selling only 90,000 policies in its first four years, until Congress passed the 1973 Flood Disaster Protection Act, which required flood insurance for all properties purchased with federally backed mortgages.[42] More recent natural disasters, including Hurricane Sandy in 2012, have prompted further reforms to the rates and requirements for NFIP and as the program has struggled, so too have the research and data-gathering efforts that underpin it. "The knowledge base required to enact and maintain the NFIP is formidable," Knowles and Kunreuther point out, arguing that "the costly floodplain mapping, so critical to risk calculations, has been badly underfunded and deferred over the years. . . . Without accurate flood-hazard maps, it is impossible to sustain the knowledge required to set insurance premiums that reflect risk, or to establish floodplain development rules, building codes, and other tools of flood mitigation."[43]

Floods, like car accidents, are very different from cybersecurity incidents and there is no reason to believe that a federally subsidized program is necessary for cyberinsurance, especially since there is no shortage of potential policyholders who are susceptible to cyber risks. However, the creation of the NFIP offers both a model of how regulators and government agencies can intervene to aid in the collection of data about emerging, large-scale risks that require extensive study and also a cautionary tale of how much maintenance and ongoing work is required to keep that information up to date. Setting premiums for cyberinsurance requires accurate information about the victims, frequency, and costs of cybersecurity incidents, just as setting premiums for flood insurance required first collecting "accurate information concerning area, frequency, and depth of inundation." And in both cases, that data needs to be regularly reassessed and updated to take into account new threats and a changing risk landscape. Moreover, the scale of major floods and other natural disasters offers an important reference point for large-scale cyberattacks, like NotPetya, that can impact thousands of policyholders simultaneously leading to significant accumulated risks and costs for insurers. In the case of flood insurance, it might theoretically be possible to diversify policyholders by insuring property owners in many different regions who would be unlikely to all be affected by the same flood. However, since only people who owned property in floodplains had any interest in flood insurance, this turned out not to be a feasible solution for a private flood insurance market. For cyberinsurers, the challenge is not finding enough customers but rather figuring out how to assemble a diverse portfolio of policyholders such that they are unlikely to all be affected by the same massive cyberattack. Unlike floods, malware programs have no geographic boundaries, nor is there any other clear way to establish whether a group of companies are sufficiently different so as to not be susceptible to the same cyber threats.

"AN IRRESISTIBLE TARGET FOR FINANCIAL KNAVES AND BUCCANEERS"

In the late 1980s, nearly a decade before Haase and AIG introduced the ISL, the US Congress had taken a renewed interest in the insurance industry and whether it was treating its customers fairly. The House Committee on Energy and Commerce charged its Subcommittee on Oversight and Investigations with looking into why so many insurance companies in the United States had failed, often leaving their customers without any way to file claims or use the policies they had purchased. In many cases, state regulators had to step in and help rehabilitate failed firms or negotiate with other insurers to take on their policies. Chaired by Representative John Dingell, the House subcommittee issued a report in February 1990 titled "Failed Promises: Insurance Company Insolvencies" that laid out its findings and concluded that insurers were woefully underregulated and, as such, were able to routinely cheat or renege on their promises to customers.

"The regulatory system must anticipate and deal effectively with the activities of the pirates and dolts who inevitably will plague an attractive industry such as insurance, where customers hand over large sums of cash in return for a promise of future benefits," the report said. It noted that the insurance industry had relatively low barriers to entry because new carriers did not have to invest any significant capital, all they had to do was make "promises" to potential customers of future coverage. "The cash flow is up front, and the payment of insurance claims can be years away," the report points out, noting that despite how easy it may be to sell coverage initially, actually turning that into a sustainable business is no small feat. "The simplicity of the insurance concept is matched by extreme complexity in its implementation. Pricing the promise properly, managing funds, sharing risks through reinsurance, establishing adequate reserves, and handling claims all require sound judgment, good organization and personal talent," the report continues. "When these are lacking due to wrongdoing or incompetence, insurance can also be a very easy business to leave."[44] The primary concern of the Dingell report was a series of property casualty losses that had bankrupted several insurers in the late 1980s, costing the public billions of dollars to either rehabilitate those firms or pay for other coverage for the customers of insolvent insurers. The report lambasted state regulators for failing to sufficiently scrutinize insurers before accrediting them, calling the existing oversight efforts "seriously deficient."[45]

State governments had been the primary authorities regulating insurance in the United States since the late eighteenth century, when individual states first began chartering corporate insurers. At first, those charters applied only to individual insurance firms, but as the industry grew, states began to regulate carriers as a bloc and, in 1851, New Hampshire established the first regulatory agency to focus on the insurance industry.[46] By the mid-nineteenth century, insurers were chafing under the patchwork of different state rules that required them to be licensed to sell insurance in each individual state—and often gave preference to the carriers that were based in whichever state was doing the regulating. In 1866, a group of New

York insurance firms manufactured a legal challenge to these state regulations by appointing a man named Samuel Paul to sell a fire insurance policy to a Virginia resident even though the state of Virginia had denied Paul a license. The insurers sued Virginia on the grounds that the state had violated the Commerce Clause of the Constitution by discriminating against an out-of-state corporation, but in 1869 the Supreme Court ruled in favor of Virginia, on the grounds that selling insurance was not a form of interstate commerce. The court wrote in its ruling:

> Issuing a policy of insurance is not a transaction of commerce. The policies are simple contracts of indemnity against loss by fire, entered into between the corporations and the assured, for a consideration paid by the latter. These contracts are not articles of commerce in any proper meaning of the word. They are not subjects of trade and barter offered in the market as something having an existence and value independent of the parties to them. They are not commodities to be shipped or forwarded from one State to another, and then put up for sale.[47]

The logic of the *Paul v. Virginia* ruling foreshadowed some of the characteristics that would make insurance such a slippery industry to regulate and would draw the attention of Dingell and his colleagues in Congress more than a hundred years later. The idea that insurance policies did not have any "existence and value independent of the parties to them" was perfectly accurate, but it did not mean that insurers should receive less regulatory scrutiny than firms offering tangible products and services. Quite the contrary, as Dingell would point out in his 1990 report, the very fact that insurance was an industry built entirely on promises and contracts, rather than physical goods or concrete services, made it more susceptible to corruption and mismanagement. By designating insurance sales as something other than interstate commerce, however, the Supreme Court had nixed the possibility of the federal government regulating insurers, instead letting that responsibility rest squarely with the states.

In 1944, the Supreme Court changed its mind about insurance. The US attorney general was trying to charge the largest insurance rate-setting bureau, the South-Eastern Underwriters Association, with fixing fire insurance premiums and agents' commissions in violation of federal antitrust laws. South-Eastern countered that the Sherman Act did not apply to them since, per *Paul v. Virginia*, insurance was not a form of commerce. This time, the Supreme Court took a decidedly different view of the question of whether federal laws applied to insurers under the Commerce Clause:

> The modern insurance business holds a commanding position in the trade and commerce of our Nation. Built upon the sale of contracts of indemnity, it has become one of the largest and most important branches of commerce. . . . Perhaps no modern commercial enterprise directly affects so many persons in all walks of life as does the insurance business. Insurance touches the home, the family, and the occupation or the business of almost every person in the United States.[48]

Instead of heralding the start of a period of federal oversight of the insurance industry, however, this ruling raised concerns that regulation might threaten the well-established, sprawling system of state insurance regulation across the country and the associated state jobs and revenue.[49] To counteract any such possibility, Senators Patrick McCarran and Homer Ferguson introduced a bill intended to make clear that the authority to regulate and tax insurers would continue to rest with the states, not the federal government. The 1945 McCarran-Ferguson Act, passed the year after the Supreme Court ruling in the South-Eastern case, exempted insurers from many conditions of federal antitrust law and explicitly permitted states to set rules for the insurance industry that would otherwise violate federal statutes.[50]

When the Subcommittee on Oversight and Investigations authored its "Failed Promises" report, forty-five years after the passage of the McCarran-Ferguson Act, it was clear that the approach of letting states vet and oversee insurers was no longer working. The very nature of insurance—that same intangible quality that had led the Supreme Court to hold that it was not a form of commerce for seventy-five years—meant it required even greater oversight and regulation than most sectors, the report argued. "The business of insurance is uniquely suited to abuse by mismanagement and fraud. Making believable promises is a stock item in every con man's bag of tricks," the Dingell report cautioned.[51] Cyberinsurance came on the scene just a few years after the states and federal government had established a newfound interest in policing insurers to ensure that they were not swindling their customers. It was far too small and niche a product to attract much interest from regulators itself, but all of the warnings issued in the 1990 Congressional "Failed Promises" report about the risks inherent in buying and selling insurance were still relevant to the new, tiny sector of the market. "The prepayment of large, often vast, sums of money with few restrictions lends itself naturally to monumental wasting of assets through greed, incompetence, and dereliction of duty," the report cautioned. "This combination of easy money based on easy promises makes the insurance industry an irresistible target for financial knaves and buccaneers."[52]

EARLY CYBERINSURANCE POLICIES

When Haase launched the first cyberinsurance policy in 1997, it brought in $2 million in premiums in its first two years but many customers were initially hesitant, especially with the looming specter of Y2K haunting their IT systems and budgets. "That really delayed the market for three years," Haase said.[53] Then, in 2000, after the Y2K threat had finally receded, the dot-com bubble burst and Haase lost a third of his clients "overnight," just as his business was starting to gain traction.[54] By then, Haase had left Hamilton Dorsey and launched his own company in Atlanta, called Insure-Trust, to focus on advising clients about cyberinsurance policies and, in some cases, underwriting them. It wasn't until eleven years after its launch that the business finally became profitable, Haase said, referring to it as his "three-million-dollar hobby."[55]

By 2012, adoption of cyberinsurance was increasing rapidly. Haase was finally able to profit off his early ideas about the need for insurance that covers online threats and risks, but by then the types of coverage being offered had already shifted considerably from the initial plans that were sold in the late 1990s and very early 2000s. In those first years of cyberinsurance there were too few customers for insurers to rely on the bulk of their premium sales to cover claims. Without high-quality data on the frequency or average costs of cybersecurity incidents and outages, insurance firms were forced to rely heavily on vetting their small number of customers to be sure they were adequately protected against online threats. This involvement in auditing and monitoring insurance customers' security systems would, by necessity, dissipate in the later years of cyberinsurance sales, as the volume of customers grew and so too did the number of firms selling policies—many of which did not have the necessary expertise to vet potential customers' networks and data security setups.

One of InsureTrust's early clients in the late 1990s was a Dallas-based digital signature company called AlphaTrust Corp. AlphaTrust offered customers a guarantee against fraud for the digital signatures it provided by offering clients up to $250,000 apiece to cover any fraud-related costs. To support those warranties, AlphaTrust purchased a policy from InsureTrust. The CEO of AlphaTrust, Bill Bryce, said of InsureTrust at the time: "We couldn't afford to do business without them."[56] But in order to do business with them, AlphaTrust first had to submit to a "series of tests and assessments" by InsureTrust's own security auditors who then told Bryce "how to rebuild his company's network security to prevent financial loss."[57] That kind of personal attention, and the ongoing security updates and guidance that AlphaTrust received from InsureTrust, would not scale well as the cyberinsurance industry grew. But when cyberinsurance was still a novelty product, purchased by only a small pool of firms, premiums and policies could be linked closely to an individual customer's security implementation—and the boutique firms, like InsureTrust, that specialized in these policies could provide not just underwriting services but also security consultants and auditing to their customers. That scrutiny was intended to protect the insurance carriers every bit as much as their customers—with only a small pool of customers, the carriers could not count on the volume of their premiums to cover claims, so they had to be sure that the clients they did cover could successfully fend off online threats. Some insurers went even further, vetting not just their customers but also the other vendors and companies those customers relied on for IT services and support. Insurer Hiscox, for instance, evaluated not just the security of its potential customers but also the security of those customer's Internet service providers before agreeing to issue a policy.[58]

Because early cyberinsurance policies came with such rigorous security audits, carrying a cyberinsurance policy in the late 1990s and early 2000s served as a sort of signal that a firm's security had been thoroughly vetted. Some early adopters of cyberinsurance purchased policies because they wanted to send a clear message to their customers and business partners that they were serious about security. For instance, the company LockBox Communications, which provided e-storage for financial firms, purchased one of the early cyberinsurance policies but LockBox CFO Christopher Williams, who decided to buy the coverage, dismissed it in a 2000 interview with *Network World* as being "almost an afterthought." He added, "The reason I'm doing it is 70 percent preventative, 20 percent credibility and 10 percent balance-sheet exposure."[59] This trend continued years later in other countries like Sweden, where companies purchased cyberinsurance in the 2010s in part to signal to international firms that they had strong cyber hygiene practices.[60]

The notion that a cyberinsurance policy would impart credibility, especially in 2000 when so few companies had any such coverage, speaks to how intensely insurers were involved in auditing clients' security at the time. After all, there were far too few firms insured against these threats at the time for shareholders or customers to expect that a company would have this kind of coverage. Furthermore, very little regulation had been passed at that point concerning data breaches or data protection so the potential legal liability for having poor security was largely undefined—the first state cybersecurity breach notification law was still three years away. But Williams's sentiment was echoed by Laura Rippy, the CEO of a software company called Handango, who explained in 2000 that she decided to purchase cyberinsurance to cover piracy losses because "having insurance makes people look more seriously at you as a partner."[61] Tom Shipley, the CEO of Executive Shoppe, also told *Network World* that he had purchased cyberinsurance primarily as a way to signal to potential investors that "we take fiduciary responsibility seriously."[62] Having cyberinsurance was not just about covering potential financial losses in the future but also about receiving insurers' feedback on cybersecurity controls and making clear to outsiders that an insurer had vetted and approved of the security practices and procedures in place. That vetting was a significant undertaking for the insurers. John Wurzler, CEO of insurance carrier J. S. Wurzler Underwriting Managers, estimated at the time that "the best-performing insurance companies spend up to 30 cents of each premium dollar helping clients reduce loss probability."[63] The three main areas that insurers looked at to try to assess the security and loss probability of potential customers were: the "around-the-clock logging" and reporting capabilities built into their computer systems, "fine-grained authorization" rules dictating who was able to access and use which types of data stored in their computer systems, and, finally, user policies and employee compliance with those policies.[64]

But in 2000, many companies—and most insurers—did not have access to people with computer security expertise. Insurance carriers began partnering with technology firms to reduce their customers' loss probability—a trend that would continue in later years as more companies purchased cyberinsurance and a growing number of technology firms came to view insurers as a potential avenue for finding customers. In July 2000, Lloyd's of London announced one of the first such partnerships, a program launched in conjunction with San Jose security firm Counterpane Internet Security that would offer up to $100 million in cyberinsurance coverage to protect companies who used Counterpane's security services against "loss of revenue and information assets caused by Internet and e-commerce security breaches."[65] The Lloyd's policy covered a much broader set of costs than the initial breach insurance model that had been developed by Haase for AIG. Through Lloyd's, customers of Counterpane could purchase insurance that would cover the costs of repairing and replacing software, lost revenue that resulted from a malicious service interruption like a denial-of-service attack, and online extortion costs. In 2000, the cost to a Counterpane customer of such a policy covering up to $1 million in losses ranged from $12,000 to $20,000 in annual premiums, depending on the size of the company, or $75,000 for a $10 million policy.[66]

Prices for cyberinsurance policies in 2000 were all over the map, with annual premiums for $25 million in coverage ranging from $25,000 to $125,000, according to one analysis by the Gartner Group.[67] "You don't see a 500 percent range in traditional premiums," Gartner Group vice president Richard Hunter said about the firm's findings. "That tells me insurance companies don't know how to assess the risk." If anything, these early cyberinsurance policies seem overbroad and underpriced, at least in comparison to more recent policies sold since 2012. But there was also, as Hunter points out, very little consistency across them, either in terms of the costs they covered or their pricing. Christopher Keegan, the vice president of Marsh, another early provider of cyberinsurance, observed in a 2000 interview with *Network World*, "There is an element of feel to these rates."[68] Interestingly, in an analysis of 6,828 observed prices for cyber coverage sold by twenty-six different insurers, Daniel Woods, Tyler Moore, and Andrew Simpson found that, overall, prices for cyber liability coverage trended downwards from 2007 to 2017.[69] This finding may reflect that as carriers collected more data and became less uncertain about the risk landscape, insurance prices fell for these policies. It could also reflect growing competition in the cyberinsurance market, with carriers being forced to lower their prices to lure customers away from other insurers, or even basing their prices for cyber policies on what their competitors were charging.

Inevitably, there was some feeling out to be done when it came to setting rates for a relatively new product without access to reliable, actuarial data about how frequently cyber losses occurred or how large they were. Part of adjusting rates in those first few years involved offering discounts to insurance customers who availed themselves of particular, trusted security services. Just as Haase's original plan with AIG had offered customers a 25 percent discount on their annual premiums if they had their systems certified by the National Computer Security Association, Lloyd's of London also experimented with offering modest discounts to customers who implemented certain security software. In October 2000, Lloyd's announced that cyberinsurance customers who purchased security software manufactured by Portland firm Tripwire would receive a 10 percent premium reduction.[70] The partnership came about after Tripwire reached out to Lloyd's, and Tripwire's president and CEO Wyatt Starnes was, unsurprisingly, pleased that Lloyd's would promote his product to their customers, telling reporters at the time, "This will be great for us."[71] Starnes even launched a subsidiary in 2000, Tripwire Insurance Services, which was intended specifically to market security products to insurers for their customers. But Starnes's projections for the cyberinsurance industry were way off base. He said in 2000 that he expected cyberinsurance premiums to be "in the $1 billion range" by 2003, when, in fact, premium sales would not reach that mark until 2013, according to the Betterley Report.[72] Indeed, he was one of many people who overestimated how quickly the market for cyberinsurance would grow and how long it would take for these sorts of policies to become mainstream.

A modest, but noticeable, increase in interest after the terrorist attacks of September 11, 2001, spurred even loftier projections than Starnes's, with the Insurance Information Institute estimating that premium sales would hit $2.5 billion by 2005.[73] In a 2005 interview, Michael Lamprecht, who ran cyberinsurance sales at broker Arthur J. Gallagher, took aim at that oft-repeated estimate, saying, "A lot of people were predicting that it was going to be a $2.5 billion marketplace by 2005. You'll probably find it's only a $200 million marketplace right now."[74] These seem like astonishingly high estimates, considering that, in 2001, premiums for cyberinsurance sales totaled only $75 million. Even the 40 percent increase in inquiries about cyberinsurance that AIG reported following September 11 was unlikely to have spurred growth on the scale that was being projected at the time.[75] But the number of customers was increasing, even if not at these extremely high rates, and the premiums were starting to go up as well. By 2001, premiums for cyberinsurance were already starting to go up in relation to coverage limits, even compared to only a year earlier. In 2000, the highest premiums cited by Gartner for $25 million policies were $125,000, or about half of one percent of the coverage limit. By 2001, cyberinsurance premiums had risen to between 1 percent and 8 percent of the coverage limit.[76]

For some companies, the policies were simply too expensive—a waste of money that could otherwise be invested in beefing up their technical security. In December 2000, online retailer Egghead.com announced publicly that up to 3.5 million customers' payment card information had been compressed into a zip file by an outside hacker and might have been stolen from their systems. In the following months, when the company's executives were grilled about what steps they would take to ramp up security, Egghead CFO John Labbett explicitly ruled out cyberinsurance, telling reporters "we have Norton Anti-Virus and a whole host of security action and intrusion applications. . . . We have secured [the site] rather than going the insurance route."[77] Labbett specifically cited the costs of cyberinsurance, which he estimated at roughly $20,000 for an annual premium, as the reason Egghead had not chosen to pursue coverage.[78] Because of the growing premium costs, cyberinsurance was aimed primarily at large and medium-sized companies in its early years. Keegan, the Marsh vice president, said in 2001 that it was still too early for most carriers—including Marsh—to be crafting custom policies for small businesses, while cyberinsurance was still in its "formative stages."[79]

In late 2001, a small consulting firm called Senetry based out of Denver decided to look into why sales of cyberinsurance had fallen so far short of projections. Senetry identified several reasons that sales had been slow to gain momentum, even after the small spikes in interest around Y2K and September 11, including that the prices for cyberinsurance policies were often "either unclear or unreasonable."[80] In Senetry's survey of business owners, more than 60 percent of respondents said cyberinsurance was too expensive for them to purchase. For respondents who owned businesses with annual revenue under $250 million, that number went up to 80 percent. Senetry concluded that small companies "are not focused on cyber threats at all—they are too focused on business survival." There were other problems, too, besides cost. There was no standard cyberinsurance policy;

each carrier covered different types of costs and incidents and attached different terms to the coverage, making it difficult for customers and brokers to understand and compare the available options. But the biggest problem—the problem from which all these other obstacles arose—was a lack of education and understanding when it came to cyber risks, Senetry concluded. Insurance brokers didn't understand cyber risks, customers didn't see why they would be targeted by hackers, executives hadn't studied online threats in school, and the threats simply didn't loom large for most of them. One employee at a transportation company in the Midwest told Senetry that cyber threats weren't a concern for the company because they were in the transportation industry, rather than the tech sector. Senetry noted of the company: "they have a Web site, and every desk has a PC with e-mail and Internet browsing capabilities."[81]

In the early 2000s the realities of online commerce were still becoming clear to many companies. Some firms could not imagine anyone would ever be sufficiently interested in their operations to target them with a virus or other online threat. They did not recognize their computer systems and IT infrastructure as crucial components of their business and operations. "Computers and networks are acknowledged as valuable tools, but there is little regard for the significant disruption that a network outage could inflict on the business," Senetry noted. Some firms believed that their antivirus programs and firewalls would be adequate protection against online threats and relieved them of the need to purchase insurance. Others thought their general business insurance might cover cyber threats, and, in any event, they didn't really understand what cyberinsurance covered—and did not have the funds to purchase yet another policy.[82] Certainly, there were some customers for the insurance carriers filling this niche prior to 2003, but they were mostly larger companies, primarily concentrated in the e-commerce sector, who were often more concerned with sending a strong public signal that their security had been vetted by an outside party than the actual financial coverage for breaches and other cyber-related losses.

And yet, as early as 2001, people and analysts kept predicting that in a matter of a few years cyberinsurance would become mainstream, that it would erupt into a multibillion dollar industry for insurance carriers and be seen as essential for all businesses. Instead, interest in cyberinsurance would grow incrementally, with companies gradually coming around to the idea that it might be useful until sales really began picking up around 2012.

Several factors contributed to that slow but steady growth in premium sales. Undoubtedly, the continued occurrence of high-profile and ever-larger data breaches and other security incidents helped drive interest. But so too did a series of policy and legal decisions issued in the early 2000s that combined to clarify the ways in which companies might be held liable for security failings and cybercrimes and that their existing insurance policies might well not cover the resulting claims. These political and legal influences didn't just drive cyberinsurance sales, they also shaped what those policies would cover, helping refine and, to some extent, standardize the early hodge-podge of cyber coverage plans into clearer buckets corresponding to particular types of cyber threats and legal liability.

DATA BREACH NOTIFICATION LAWS

On April 5, 2002, an intruder gained access to a server at the Stephen P. Teale Data Center in Sacramento, California, that contained the personnel files, social security numbers, and payroll information of all 265,000 California state employees.[83] The state controller's office discovered the breach one month later, on May 7, and informed state employees of the breach two weeks after that, on May 21.[84] During the two-week delay between when the state discovered the breach and when it was made public, hackers in Germany reportedly tried to access at least one employee's bank account and tried to change the address associated with the credit card of another employee.[85] The delay before employees were notified of the breach outraged the California Union of Safety Employees and drew attention to the lack of any legal obligation on the part of the state to report the breach promptly—or, indeed, at all.[86] In June, California State Senator Steve Peace convened a hearing to amend S.B. 1386, a state bill he had introduced earlier that year to clarify that personal information collected by state agencies was not subject to disclosure under the Public Records Act. At the hearing in June, Peace announced a complete overhaul of the initial S.B. 1386 text; instead of dealing with whether personal identifying information was subject to the Public Records Act, it would now try to address the issues raised in the wake of the Teale Data Center breach by focusing on the obligations of state agencies and private companies to report similar such data breaches to the people affected by them.

Peace explicitly called out the state employee data breach as a motivating incident for the new legislation, writing in support of S.B. 1386 in June that, "In the Teale incident, authorities knew of the breach in security almost a month before state workers were told. We can at least be thankful that victims were given the opportunity to take protective measures based upon notice of the event—albeit late notice."[87] Peace continued, explaining the reason for his new proposal:

> All too often events of this sort go completely unreported. How can this be? The embarrassment of disclosure that a company or agency was "hacked," or the fear of lost business based upon shoddy information security practices being disclosed overrides the need to inform the affected persons. In other instances, credit card issuers, telephone companies and internet service providers, along with state and local officials "handle" the access of consumer's personal and financial information by unauthorized persons internally, often absorbing the losses caused by fraud as a matter of "customer service" without ever informing the customer of the unauthorized use of his/her account.[88]

The overhauled S.B. 1386, which was passed in 2002 and went into effect in July 2003, required any companies doing business in California to notify customers about breaches of their personal information (for instance, their name in combination with their social security number, driver's license number, passwords, or banking information). Breaches of encrypted information were exempt from the notification requirement, but otherwise the law—even though it had been passed only by the state of California—applied to pretty much every breach at all major US companies, since it encompassed not just companies headquartered in California but also those with any customers living in the state.

The purpose of S.B. 1386 was to help individuals, like the California state employees whose information had been stolen from the controller's office computers, protect themselves against identity theft and financial fraud in the event that their data was stolen. Peace explained the rationale for the bill specifically in terms of consumer protection, writing, "Customers need to know when unauthorized activity occurs on their accounts, or when unauthorized persons have access to sensitive information, in order to take appropriate steps to protect their financial health."[89] Prior to the passage of S.B. 1386, there was no requirement that companies had to notify customers when breaches occurred, and many incidents therefore went unreported since companies often feared the negative publicity and potential lawsuits that might ensue from making such a voluntary disclosure.

Peace may have been motivated primarily by the 2002 breach of California state employee information, but by many standards that incident—in which the affected individuals were notified within one month of the breach's discovery—was actually a success story of breach notification, despite Peace referring to it as "late notice." In the California Senate Privacy Committee hearings on S.B. 1386, state legislators discussed several other incidents, in private industry, that suggested the need for mandatory breach notification. The legislative discussions in California flagged another high-profile 2002 breach in which someone obtained a code typically used by Ford Motor Company to run credit checks on car buyers and was able to access 13,000 credit reports through Experian by impersonating Ford using its code. "In that case, both Ford Motor Credit and Experian notified the affected consumers, a practice this bill seeks to encourage," California legislators wrote in an analysis of S.B. 1386. "Unfortunately, not all companies are as forthcoming."[90]

Of course, it was difficult for the legislators to point to specific examples of unreported breaches—since, by definition, no one knew about those incidents. But as an example of the severity of the problem, the California Assembly Committee on Judiciary pointed to a breach at Bank One, in which a twenty-one-year-old former employee had sold hundreds (or possibly more) of the bank's customers' financial records to an identity theft ring. When the bank discovered the breach, it did not notify any customers until eight months later, when one of the victims of the breach received a call from the Secret Service about a possible case of identity theft—someone had purchased a Jaguar in his name. That victim then contacted a local television station, which ultimately unraveled the story of the Bank One breach. An article about the Bank One incident that was cited in the Judiciary Committee analysis of S.B. 1386 alleged:

> In fact, it's common that consumer victims aren't told about a break-in, as companies try to avoid the potential embarrassment and cross their fingers that no crimes will actually be committed with the stolen data. Bank One played that kind of Russian roulette with its customer data and lost. But Bank One is hardly alone.[91]

In 2002, when S.B. 1386 was being discussed, no one knew how many other Bank Ones were out there, playing a similar game of Russian roulette, hoping no one would find out that they had failed to protect their customers' data. One of the consequences of the passage of S.B. 1386—and the many other data breach notification laws that were passed by other states in the years that followed—was that it suddenly became possible to start counting these breaches. No one valued that data more highly than insurance carriers trying to sell cyberinsurance policies and model the risks and costs associated with online threats. Since companies now had to notify customers about breaches by law, media outlets were able to investigate and report on these incidents more regularly. These reports, in turn, raised awareness among other companies about data breaches and the possible consequences of falling victim to one—as well as, potentially, the value of a cyberinsurance policy.

Companies could no longer just sweep any future data breaches under the rug, so more of them had to think through the consequences of such incidents becoming public and how cyberinsurance might help mitigate those consequences. Lamprecht, the cyberinsurance lead at broker Arthur J. Gallagher, said in 2005, two years after the passage of S.B. 1386, that "in the past, and even to some extent today, companies that had a security breach had gone out of their way not to report it. . . . In some cases, they even sought legal opinion about exactly why they weren't required to report it."[92] According to Lamprecht, the passage of S.B. 1386 helped drive sales of cyberinsurance by "raising awareness quite a bit" about the risks of not reporting security breaches.[93] For the first time, the loss of personal customer information had to be routinely reported to the public and could lead to a range of possible consequences from class action lawsuits to Federal Trade Commission investigations. The prospect of dealing with—and paying for—those consequences helped spur companies in some sectors, particularly retailers handling customer payment data, to invest in data breach insurance.

For an industry that had been plagued by a dearth of concrete data, mandated reports were a godsend. The state breach notification laws provided a wealth of new, publicly available data on how frequently breaches were occurring, how many people they affected on average, and which sectors were most heavily targeted. The previous lack of data sources had "made evidence of big losses hard to find for those trying to persuade reluctant risk managers to buy hacker insurance" and "starved cyber-risks underwriters of vital historical loss information, making it difficult for them to get a complete picture of the frequency and severity of cyber-liability losses," according to one 2005 report on the industry.[94] Prior to breach notification regulations, insurers had only their own, very limited, claims data to model cyber threats—hence the wide-ranging premium fees and high deductibles that early customers were subject to. So the mandatory reporting regimes helped insurers model cyber risks by providing larger data sets, but only about a very specific set of risks. State breach notification laws applied to only a certain subset of cybersecurity breaches—those that involved the theft of personal identifying information. All other cybersecurity incidents, from online extortion to theft of intellectual property and denial-of-service attacks, could still go unreported.

While the passage of S.B. 1386 and other state breach notification laws did spur cyberinsurance sales, it also shifted the content of cyberinsurance policies to emphasize data breach insurance. These laws created new costs for companies, such as the costs of notifying breach victims as required by state statutes, thereby creating new coverage opportunities for carriers to sell policies that would, for instance, pay for mailing individual letters to affected customers. As breach notification laws proliferated across different states, often with slight variations that added to the onerous task of complying with a patchwork set of dozens of different notification regimes, they continued to create new financial risks for companies—and new possibilities for underwriters. By 2011, forty-six states had passed their own breach notification laws, many of them modeled on California's S.B. 1386, and the compliance costs had become a major component of data breach insurance. "More and more of the exposures that these policies address come from being out of compliance with notification laws, regulations, rules, or consumer protection laws," Toby Merrill, a vice president at insurer ACE Professional Risk, said in 2011. "That is where, quite frankly, most of these battles are going to be won or lost."[95]

But those notification costs were far from the largest financial risks created by the advent of state breach notification laws or even covered by the subsequent data breach insurance policies. Much of the focus surrounding the breach notification laws and the cyberinsurance policies crafted in their wake centered on how these laws would alter the legal landscape for data breaches, and particularly the question of whether breached companies could be held liable for failing to protect their customers' data. When S.B. 1386 was being discussed in the California State Assembly, the possibility that it could open breached companies up to class action lawsuits brought by their customers was a recurring concern raised by the bill's opponents, including the Information Technology Association of America (ITAA), a consortium of technology firms. In particular, ITAA sought a cap on liability for firms that reported breaches under the S.B. 1386 requirements—a request the California State Assembly declined to grant in the final bill.[96]

There were concerns about at least two distinct types of liability that arose from breach notification laws like S.B. 1386. One was the possibility that a company could be sued for violating the notification laws by failing to inform customers "in the most expedient time possible and without unreasonable delay" (the language California landed on to define the timeframe for mandatory notification). But the other, possibly larger, legal vulnerability that loomed over the passage of these laws was that individuals affected by the breaches might, now that they were receiving notification about them, seize the opportunity to sue the organizations that had failed to protect their data.

Liability had been part of the discussion surrounding the 2002 breach of California state employee information that ultimately spurred the passage of S.B. 1386. One article on the breach quoted an analyst at Giga Information Group Inc., Michael Rasmussen, predicting, "There are going to be landmark cases where people are going to be suing other people. That is what is finally going to get the attention of companies."[97] Early proponents of cyberinsurance, like Haase, had anticipated lawsuits as well, even before state breach notification laws, but their focus had been on lawsuits filed by banks or payment processors who were bearing the costs of fraud and identity theft. Breach notification laws increased the likelihood of those types of lawsuits but they also broadened the scope of legal liability to include individuals affected by these breaches who might otherwise not have known about them or attempted to sue. In other countries, where there was far less fear of litigation surrounding breaches than in the United States, firms were much less likely to want cyberinsurance. Even as late as 2012, US firms accounted for more than 95 percent of the premiums paid for cyberinsurance policies. "In the US there is a real litigation and class action culture," said Graeme Newman, a British underwriter for cyber risk, explaining the prolonged lack of interest in cyberinsurance among European firms.[98]

State breach notification laws helped pave the way for increased litigation and class action suits by alerting customers—and attorneys—to several large and high-profile breaches. Many of those cases would turn out to be tricky for customers to win because of the challenges of showing how, concretely, they had been damaged by data breaches in the absence of clear instances of identity theft, but even just getting them dismissed could be a lengthy and expensive process for breached firms. Kenneth Abraham has argued that insurance and tort liability have evolved in tandem, with legal rulings and insurance packages each serving to influence the other in areas ranging from automobile accident liability to medical malpractice and product-related injuries.[99] So too would the evolution of legal liability surrounding data breaches and other cybersecurity incidents be deeply intertwined with the development of the cyberinsurance industry. It would not be until several years after the passage of S.B. 1386 that lawsuits would become a regular and expected feature of the aftermath of data breaches, but state breach notification laws were a necessary building block for enabling the set of class action lawsuits and government investigations that would follow and would influence cyberinsurance for many years to come.

SEC GUIDANCE ON CYBER RISKS

Data breach notification laws were essential building blocks for the legal landscape that would drive cyberinsurance sales, but there is disagreement about the extent to which the laws themselves actually drove sales of data breach policies. While many people predicted that the state laws would have a significant impact on adoption of cyberinsurance, Herr argues that the timeline for when most states passed these laws, between 2003 and 2007, does not align with the period of time when premium sales for cyberinsurance policies began to dramatically increase at rates of more than 30 percent annually, beginning in 2012 and continuing through 2017.[100] Herr instead links this increase to several factors, including rising costs of breaches (something which may well have been tied to the breach notification laws and resulting legal disputes) and the nonbinding guidance issued by the SEC in October 2011 advising companies to disclose cybersecurity risks to investors in their public financial filings. The recommendations published by the SEC's Division of Corporation Finance urged firms to "disclose the risk of cyber incidents if these issues are among the most significant factors that make an investment in the company speculative or risky."[101] While these recommendations were not a binding rule, they hinted strongly at the

SEC's view that investors ought to weigh cyber threats when considering a firm's financial health and outlook and that firms ought to incorporate these risks into their broader risk management frameworks.

The disclosures recommended by the SEC, including any cybersecurity incidents that a firm had experienced as well as the associated costs, provided exactly the kinds of information insurers might look for when deciding whether or not to sell coverage to a new customer. Moreover, the assessment process that the SEC recommended firms undertake to determine whether or not they should disclose information about their cybersecurity posture seemed almost designed to drive companies toward insurers. The SEC recommended that companies "consider the probability of cyber incidents occurring and the quantitative and qualitative magnitude of those risks, including the potential costs and other consequences resulting from misappropriation of assets or sensitive information, corruption of data or operational disruption."[102] Furthermore, one of the specific elements of recommended disclosures specifically called out in the SEC guidance was a "description of relevant insurance coverage."[103] Herr points to the nearly 300 percent increase in cyberinsurance premiums that occurred between 2012 and 2015 and argues that the 2011 SEC recommendations helped to "align market incentives with cybersecurity risk—granting insurers a means to more effectively profit from the demands of market participants for new vehicles to manage risk and reduce uncertainty."[104]

The actual impact of the SEC cybersecurity guidance, much like the specific impact of the state breach notification laws, is difficult to measure. Certainly, the guidance coincided with the beginning of a significant period of growth in the cyberinsurance market. Whether that growth resulted from companies actually undertaking the extensive cyber risk assessment procedure recommended by the SEC or eschewing it in favor of purchasing insurance is less clear. Actual disclosures filed by most companies in the wake of the 2011 guidance were relatively vague and boilerplate, despite the SEC's explicit request that "registrants should not present risks that could apply to any issuer or any offering and should avoid generic risk factor disclosure."[105] For instance, Yahoo's annual reports to the SEC differed very little in their discussion of cyber risks from 2010, before the SEC guidance was issued, to 2011, after it was issued, to 2012, after Yahoo experienced a breach of the passwords of nearly half a million customers. In all three years, Yahoo noted in its filings that "our operations are susceptible to out-ages and interruptions due to fire, flood, earthquake, power loss, telecom-munications failures, cyber attacks, terrorist attacks," and in all three years, the filings included a section on the potential risk headed, "If our security measures are breached, our products and services may be perceived as not being secure, users and customers may curtail or stop using our products and services, and we may incur significant legal and financial exposure."[106]

Yahoo's elaboration on these cybersecurity risks followed such a similar line in 2010, 2011, and 2012 that the SEC's guidance—and the company's password breach—hardly seem to have made any difference to Yahoo's dis-closure habits. Consider a section of Yahoo's discussion of its online secu-rity risks from its 2011 annual report to the SEC:

> Any breach or unauthorized access could result in significant legal and financial exposure, increased costs for security measures or to defend litigation or dam-age to our reputation, and a loss of confidence in the security of our products and services and networks that could potentially have an adverse effect on our business. Because the techniques used to obtain unauthorized access, disable or degrade service, or sabotage systems change frequently or may be designed to remain dormant until a predetermined event and often are not recognized until launched against a target, we may be unable to anticipate these techniques or implement adequate preventative measures.[107]

Any portion of that passage could just as easily have been applied to nearly any other company's cyber risks. And Yahoo was not alone in using boiler-plate language to describe the online threats it faced—to the extent that the SEC guidance spurred companies to more closely evaluate and consider their cyber risks, that assessment rarely translated to detailed, public disclosures.

Whether or not the SEC 2011 guidance altered companies' disclosures about the cyber risks they faced, it certainly helped raise awareness that the government considered these risks intrinsically tied to firms' finances and even promoted the possibility of purchasing cyberinsurance. Like the state breach notification laws that preceded it, the SEC guidance on cybersecu-rity influenced the market for cyberinsurance indirectly, heightening firms' fears about the potential consequences of being breached by raising the pos-sibility that their customers or shareholders could hold them accountable for failing to secure computer systems or even just failing to notify them about those security lapses. There were no recommendations from the SEC about how to avoid those types of security incidents, just as there had been nothing in the state notification laws about how to prevent data breaches. Both the SEC guidelines and the data breach notification laws are notable for being policy measures that focused on increasing transparency around cybersecurity but stopped well short of making any prescriptive recommendations for what types of security controls companies should implement or what baseline level of security would be expected for companies to avoid being held liable for breaches. In this regard, both could be seen as serving the purposes of cyberinsurers by raising awareness about the types of risks their policies covered without equipping companies with the knowledge or tools they might need to protect themselves.

Auto insurance safety measures developed in a similar way, along a comparably slow timeline. Laws mandating safety features like seatbelts for cars did not arrive in the United States until 1968, many decades after a robust market for auto insurance had already developed and insurers had become de facto regulators of what safety precautions were and were not required of or recommended to drivers and car manufacturers. Auto insurance, like cyberinsurance, also predated the existence of any such regulations. Placed alongside the timeline of the evolution of auto insurance, the development of the cyberinsurance market does not appear so far behind, even two decades after Haase's Breach on the Beach party to launch the first policy. But the history of auto insurance and car safety also suggests that direct government intervention, at both the state and federal levels, was ultimately needed to improve car safety—relying on insurers to place pressure on their customers and manufacturers was not sufficient to drive down the rates of auto accidents and injuries. It's striking, therefore, that so many of the early cybersecurity efforts by policymakers, like the state breach notification laws and the 2011 SEC guidance, did nothing to address the fact that insurers had sole responsibility to determine the appropriate safeguards and technical controls that should be linked to their customers' premiums. And even when regulators turned their attention directly to the cyberinsurance industry, many of them viewed this freedom on the part of private carriers to make these determinations as a feature not a bug.

On March 19, 2015, at a moment of rapid growth in the cyberinsurance industry, the Senate Commerce Committee's Subcommittee on Consumer Protection, Product Safety, Insurance, and Data Security held a hearing titled

"Examining the Evolving Cyber Insurance Marketplace." Kansas Senator Jerry Moran invoked the analogy to car insurance in his opening remarks, lauding cyberinsurance as a potential "market led approach to help businesses improve their cybersecurity posture by tying policy eligibility or lower premiums to better cybersecurity practices." He continued:

> An example of this relationship is an automobile insurer offering good driver discount to a customer who avoids accidents or driving violations, providing an additional incentive to a driver to be more cautious and attentive. The insurance company also wins. Even though the premium they receive may be lower, in the end, they have fewer claims to pay out.[108]

Over the course of the hearing, however, it became clear that the insurers in attendance were not granting any discounts to businesses using widely accepted government cybersecurity guidelines, such as the cybersecurity risk assessment framework published by the National Institute of Standards and Technology. Not only that, but the hearing further suggested that the auditing process for new cyberinsurance customers had been both drastically diminished and largely outsourced since the earlier days of careful and ongoing security monitoring by carriers, and that it no longer carried with it any of the discounts that had been used to entice buyers in the days of the earlier Counterpane or Tripwire partnerships.

Perhaps because they no longer had to work as hard to attract customers, perhaps because there was more competition from other carriers, perhaps because there were just so many customers now and not enough time to vet each one, insurance carriers seemed to have gotten less interested in pegging premium prices to customers' security setups. Instead of having to be sure that they were covering well-secured clients, carriers could now rely on the volume of their cyberinsurance customers and the associated premiums to cover claims, rather than relying on the strength of each individual customer's security. It was a hearing that often evoked the concerns raised in Dingell's report on the insurance industry some twenty-five years earlier about the failed promises of insurers and the need for more stringent regulation to ensure they lived up to the policies they sold and didn't swindle their customers into paying money up-front for an uncertain or ambiguous payout later on. For instance, Moran questioned one of the speakers at the hearing, business owner Ola Sage, about her cyberinsurance coverage, prompting the following exchange:

MORAN: Can you tell from your policy that if something happens, it is either included or excluded in coverage?

SAGE: Chairman, the answer is no. It is very difficult, and not just the cost of the policy, but legal assistance to help us understand the policy, so now you have costs on top of the policy itself to understand what your policy covers and does not cover.

MORAN: What do you think your policy covers? What events, what might happen to your company that you feel pretty certain are covered and ones you have doubt about?

SAGE: I think some of the costs associated with let's say there was an attack and there was equipment potentially that was compromised, those costs might be covered. I believe costs associated with notification and things like that might also be covered. What is more unclear is what is not covered. We keep hearing, well, it is claim-specific. Well, you do not know what your claim is going to be until you have that, and hopefully you never have that.[109]

Dingell wrote in 1990, "The simplicity of the insurance concept is matched by extreme complexity in its implementation." Perhaps no insurance product was more complex and difficult to understand than cyberinsurance which, by 2015, promised coverage for all sorts of first- and third-party costs, but often in terms so vague and generic that they could have been plucked directly from Yahoo's SEC filings. Like Yahoo, cyberinsurance carriers hinted at dark possibilities and grave risks but were reliably light on the specifics of what would happen in the event those ominous predictions actually came to pass.

II

CYBERSECURITY CLAIMS UNDER NON-CYBER COVERAGE

"THE HACKERS DID THIS": DATA BREACH LAWSUITS AND COMMERCIAL GENERAL LIABILITY INSURANCE

In April 2011, Sony's popular PlayStation Network was compromised and intruders stole information about seventy-seven million PlayStation users' accounts, including their names, addresses, email addresses, birthdays, usernames, passwords, security questions, and credit card numbers. It was one of the largest data breaches ever reported at the time and Sony customers quickly filed a series of lawsuits against the company for failing to protect their personal data, and several of those lawsuits were combined into a class action complaint. Although many of the class action plaintiffs' claims were dismissed in 2012 by district judge Anthony J. Battaglia because Sony had warned customers explicitly in its privacy policy that "there is no such thing as perfect security,"[1] the class action suit ultimately cost Sony nearly $18 million, including a $15 million settlement reached in July 2014 and $2.75 million in legal fees.[2] Faced with these mounting legal fees, Sony looked beyond its data breach insurance to its commercial general liability (CGL) insurance to help cover its legal costs. CGL policies in the United States date back to 1940 and offer coverage for both legal fees and damages related to lawsuits brought against the policyholders for bodily injury or property damage.[3] In the decades following their initial development, CGL policies expanded to cover additional types of risks, such as liability for advertising and privacy harms related to issues including slander, copyright infringement, or misappropriation of someone's name or likeness. Sony hoped that it might be able to claim the 2011 breach as a type of privacy harm through its CGL policy with Zurich American Insurance. Zurich and Sony's other insurers, including the Mitsui Sumitomo Insurance Company of America, vehemently disagreed, pointing to the wording of Sony's policy, which had clearly been drafted with a very different sort of privacy harm in mind. Ultimately, that language would help Zurich and other insurers prevent policyholders like Sony from exercising CGL policies to cover legal costs related to most data breaches. This, in turn, contributed to the trend of carriers shifting cyber risks into their own cyber-specific policies rather than integrating them into existing product lines and categories of risk.

More was at stake in the dispute between Sony and Zurich than just the question of who would end up covering Sony's legal fees. The case raised complicated questions about cybersecurity liability and who was at fault when a data breach occurred—the hackers who instigated the breach or the business that failed to defend itself against intrusion. Those questions were also central to the class action suit against Sony that played out in parallel to the company's dispute with Zurich, and the two cases put Sony in the complicated position of arguing simultaneously that it was entirely at fault for the breach (and therefore justified in exercising its CGL policy) and that it was not to blame in the least because it had been the unfortunate victim of malicious hackers. Beyond its implications for who bore the most responsibility for data breaches, the fight between Sony and its insurers also mattered because it was the first lawsuit that dealt with the question of whether CGL policies covered liability related to data breaches. Most CGL policies were relatively standardized across insurers because their language had been drafted by the Insurance Services Office, so if the language in Sony's policy from Zurich was interpreted as covering data breach liability, that would likely mean that many other CGL policies would be similarly applicable to breaches. On the other hand, if CGL policies did not cover data breaches, that would make it all the more urgent for companies to invest in separate, breach-specific policies of the sort that had begun to be sold in the late 1990s and early 2000s but had not by any means become routine purchases by 2011, when the Sony breach occurred. Sony, in fact, did have data breach insurance at the time of its breach—but the coverage was presumably less than the company felt it needed to pursue litigation and cover the potential damages. If it turned out they could supplement that coverage with their CGL coverage, it might be enough to see them through. Otherwise, the lesson for them and others would be not just to purchase breach insurance, but to buy lots of it.

For insurers, the case was therefore important not just as a way to protect the limits of their existing CGL coverage, but also as a way to potentially expand the market for a new product that could generate more customers and revenue. Both insurers and insurance customers had long understood that creating a market for a new class of insurance would require insurers to carve coverage for those types of risks out of their existing policies. Indeed, in a piece about cyberinsurance in the *Long Island Business News* in 2001, a decade before the Sony breach, Ty Sagalow, the chief operating officer of AIG's eBusiness Risk Solutions group, is quoted as warning businesses that "any company that does business via computers may not be covered by traditional business insurance" and that they should buy a cyber-specific policy.[4] Later that same year, an article in *Forbes* about computer risk insurance noted, "What's pushing companies into these policies is the fear that insurers will begin specifically striking hack-related coverage from general property and casualty policies once claims begin escalating, just as they did in the 1990s with sexual harassment, discrimination and pollution liabilities." The article quotes a risk manager at a bank who was, at the time, negotiating the purchase of $75 million of "hacker coverage" from Chubb, predicting "what I see coming down the road is a sort of Internet exclusion."[5]

NEGLIGENT CYBERSECURITY AND LIABILITY FOR DATA BREACHES

While breach notification laws had made it easier to sue companies for failing to protect their customers' personal information, the liability regimes governing these incidents were still far from clear in 2011, when the Sony PlayStation breach occurred. The dismissal of several data breach class action lawsuits, including one brought against Barnes & Noble for a 2013 breach of customer payment card numbers at sixty-three stores, illustrated that just because individuals were now being notified of breaches affecting their personal information did not mean breached companies were all of a sudden facing massive new liabilities. But neither could companies be confident that they wouldn't be held liable for these incidents. There was no clear set of security standards or requirements that they could point to and say they had complied with to absolve themselves of responsibility for breaches—in other words, nobody was certain what constituted negligence when it came to cybersecurity. On top of that, many data breaches and other types of cybersecurity incidents involved multiple different, interconnected entities. Software and hardware manufacturers, website designers and hosts, payment processors and Internet service providers might all play some role in enabling breaches by leaving vulnerabilities in code, for instance, or failing to detect and block criminals operating on their infrastructure. Deciding who to blame was far from straightforward and depended a great deal on the particular details of any given incident.[6]

For the software and hardware industry, the liability issue was very straightforward—they had been absolved of any liability for vulnerabilities or security issues in their products under the Computer Fraud and Abuse Act (CFAA) passed in 1986. Lobbyists had argued over and over to Congress that it was impossible to develop bug-free code and any attempt to hold tech firms liable for those bugs would destroy the industry altogether, prompting the liability protections in the CFAA. But firms that were not hardware or software companies had no such liability shield when it came to their failures to protect data or computer networks. Still, the risks of being held liable for such breaches did not seem to dissuade firms from collecting and storing digital data on their customers. In fact, the impossibility of implementing perfect security provided firms with a possible means of defending themselves from liability for security breaches: they could just say, truthfully, that there was no sure-fire way of preventing such incidents.

The consolidated class action complaint filed against Sony in California in 2012 alleged that Sony had not even maintained "reasonable, adequate and industry-standard security measures," and that the PlayStation Network "lacked basic security measures such as updated software, adequate encryption and firewalls." Though these measures were not specifically required by law, the plaintiffs claimed they had been deceived by Sony's privacy policies, which promised that the company took "reasonable measures to protect the confidentiality, security, and integrity" of customers' personal information, even as it cautioned users that "there is no such thing as perfect security." The problem was not Sony's failure to perfectly secure its networks, the plaintiffs alleged, but instead the company's failure to live up to the promises of its own privacy policy that personal information would be "stored in secure operating environments that are not available to the public" and that the company would "use industry-standard encryption" to protect "sensitive financial information" such as credit card numbers. In reality, the story was more complicated. The company had encrypted customer credit card numbers, but it had failed to encrypt other information about its customers, including their passwords, which were protected with a cryptographic hash function that left them scrambled but less effectively than full encryption would have. And there even were firewalls for the PlayStation Network, but a former Sony engineer told the plaintiffs they were installed "on an ad-hoc basis" after the company "determined that a particular user was attempting to gain unauthorized access."[7] Whether these protections constituted "reasonable, adequate and industry-standard security measures" was open to debate, in large part because there was no clear, codified industry standard for cybersecurity. Undoubtedly, Sony had made some missteps and could have provided stronger security to its customers but, at the same time, the plaintiffs' allegations that the company failed to update software, encrypt data, or use firewalls were not entirely accurate, either.

In a further attempt to show that Sony knew its protections for customer data were inadequate, the plaintiffs pointed out that the company had invested significantly more resources in protecting its own proprietary intellectual property and data with "firewalls, a debug unit and IP address limitations." These stronger security measures on another part of the company's networks made the relatively weaker security for customer data all the more egregious in the eyes of the breach victims. "While Sony knew that these basic security measures were necessary to protect its proprietary systems, it chose to cut corners when it came to its customers' Personal Information and failed to implement similar safeguards" for the PlayStation Network that stored customer data, the complaint alleged. But here, again, it was not clear whether Sony's stronger security for proprietary company data was an indication of its negligence in protecting customer data less rigorously or merely a routine—even sensible—decision to prioritize protection of the company's highest-value assets.

Similarly, the plaintiffs' contention that Sony should have been aware that a security breach was imminent was tenuous. Earlier in 2011 Sony had sued a nineteen-year-old named George Hotz who had figured out how to modify PlayStation consoles so they could be used to play games that were not manufactured by Sony. The copyright infringement lawsuit that Sony filed against Hotz was controversial and it had attracted attention from hacker group Anonymous which, two weeks prior to the 2011 PlayStation breach, sent Sony an ominous message: "You have abused the judicial system in an attempt to censor information on how your products work. . . . Now you will experience the wrath of Anonymous. You saw a hornet's nest and stuck your penises in it. You must face the consequences of your actions, Anonymous style. . . . Expect us." The class action complaint stated, "Despite this direct threat to imminently breach the Network, Sony unreasonably and unfairly failed to implement adequate safeguards to protect its Network, including failing to take steps to protect Plaintiffs' and the other Class members' Personal Information stored on its Network."[8] But it's difficult to see what, exactly, Sony should have known or been expected to do upon receiving such a threat.

In its response to the complaint, Sony dismissed the plaintiffs' claim of negligence as "wholly conclusory," writing that "pointing by hindsight to the fact that an intrusion occurred does not establish, or permit an inference, that security was not reasonable. Nor does parroting unidentified commentary from blogs about firewalls make it plausible that a firewall was somehow involved in the intrusion." To fight the class action lawsuit, Sony had to take the stance that it had had reasonable security protections in place and had not been negligent in its security—that the harm to the individual victims had come from the perpetrators. To fight the later denial of coverage by its CGL insurers, however, Sony would have to make exactly the opposite case. But in 2012, Sony's priority was trying to get the class action lawsuit dismissed rather than rounding up insurance coverage for the associated costs. So, in keeping with a pattern that had been relatively successful in other breach lawsuits, Sony motioned for the class action suit to be dismissed on the grounds that none of the plaintiffs alleged "any actual harm from exposure of his or her accountholder information." To support its motion, Sony pointed out that "numerous courts have held that allegations of mere exposure of a plaintiff's personal information . . . are insufficient to state a claim for negligence."[9] Despite Sony's best efforts, in an October 2012 ruling, Judge Battaglia allowed the class action complaint to move forward, ruling that the loss of the PlayStation customers' personal data was sufficient injury to grant them standing to sue Sony.

ZURICH V. SONY: PANDORA'S BOX

On February 21, 2014, five months before the $15 million Sony class action settlement agreement was reached, lawyers for Sony and Zurich, as well as several of Sony's other insurers, squared off in a courtroom in Manhattan before Justice Jeffrey K. Oing. The two sides disagreed about whether the CGL policies that Sony had purchased from Zurich and other insurers covered any of the costs incurred by the breach—most notably the mounting legal fees. Sony's CGL insurance included coverage for "personal and advertising injury," which was defined broadly in the policy itself as:

injury including consequential bodily injury arising out of one or more of the following offenses . . .

(A) false arrest, detention or imprisonment.
(B) malicious prosecution.
(C) the wrongful eviction from wrongful injury into or invasion of the right of private occupancy of a room, dwelling or premises that a person occupies committed by or on behalf of its owner, landlord or lessor.
(D) oral or written publication in any manner of material that slanders or libels a person or organization or disparages a person's or organization's goods, products or services.
(E) oral or written publication in any manner of the material that violates a person's right of privacy.
(F) the use of another's advertising idea in your advertisement.
(G) infringing upon another's copyright, trade, dress or slogan in your advertisement.[10]

The fight in the New York courtroom hinged on paragraph (E) of that definition, specifically on whether or not the breach of seventy-seven million Sony PlayStation customers' personal data counted as the "oral or written publication in any manner of the material that violates a person's right of privacy." Zurich's lawyer Kevin Coughlin and Mitsui's lawyer Robert Marshall argued that it didn't because the stolen data had not been "published" and because, even if it had, Sony had not performed that publication itself—rather, outside hackers had. On the other side, Richard DeNatale, a lawyer representing Sony, insisted that the CGL policy was intended to cover "a wide variety of privacy torts" and pointed out to the judge that the relevant clause in paragraph (E) had "no limitations or restrictions that depend upon who makes the disclosure, how the material is disclosed or to how many people the material is disclosed."[11]

Coughlin emphasized that "the Zurich policy as well as the Mitsui policy was never intended to cover cyber losses," highlighting the extent to which insurers regarded these costs as a separate category and one they were eager to exclude from their existing policies. Coughlin's language also made clear that he was arguing for an exclusion of not just data breach–related claims and liability but, more broadly, a whole class of "cyber losses" that Zurich did not intend their policies to cover when they wrote them. But the crucial question for resolving what the CGL policy did or did not cover did not lie in its authors' intentions but rather in the language of the policy itself. Indeed, in court, Justice Oing dismissed Coughlin's point, responding that "whatever your intent is, the bottom line is that I'm restricted to what the policy terms are."

Aside from the insurers' intent, there was also much disagreement in the courtroom about whether what had happened in the Sony case actually constituted a "publication." Coughlin argued that, in the case of the breach, "there is a total absence of publication." Indeed, while Sony had confirmed that their customers' data had been stolen, that data had not been publicly posted or published anywhere (in fact, the allegations of harm raised in the class action lawsuit focused primarily on the possibility that the data might be sold in underground online forums at some future date). Marshall insisted that "the plaintiffs are only alleging that they have a fear that the hackers may [publish the stolen information]. But, there is no allegation that the hackers themselves published anything."

DeNatale countered these arguments by invoking several previous cases that deemed "situations of passive access to information or inadvertent access to information" to be instances of publication. For instance, he cited a West Virginia case in which a hotel installed surveillance cameras that could be viewed from the manager's office and a court later found that "the fact that there were people who could inadvertently see those clients and see the recordings . . . was a publication." He also referenced a case in which baby monitors installed in confidential counseling sessions in Oklahoma were held to constitute a publication, and another in which a LensCrafters glasses store in California allowed someone to sit in on customer's eye exams and had access to customers' confidential information in a manner that was later deemed a "publication" by a court. Marshall countered with his own, loosely related precedent, citing a case in which someone hacked into a company called Prodigy Services, created a fake email account and then sent obscene emails from that account and the recipient sued the company. In that case, a New York court found that the security breach did not involve a "publication" but, as Oing pointed out, it was not a perfect parallel to the Sony breach. "That's hacking into a system to send a message," Oing told Marshall. "This is different. This is hacking into a system and getting information out."

For his part, the judge seemed sympathetic to the view that a potential future publication by the hackers could constitute a publication in line with the particulars of Sony's CGL coverage. "I look at it as a Pandora's box," Oing said in court. "Once it is opened it doesn't matter who does what with it. It is out there. . . . And whether or not it's actually used later on to get any benefit by the hackers, that in my mind is not the issue. The issue is that it was in their vault." However, where Oing did side with the insurers, ultimately, was in ruling that the CGL policy covered only acts of publication performed by Sony itself rather than by third parties like hackers. "This would have been a totally different case if Sony negligently opened the box and let all of that information out," he said. "This is a case where Sony tried or continued to maintain security for this information. It was to no avail. Hackers got in, criminally got in. They opened it up and they took the information. . . . I am not convinced that that is oral or written publication in any manner done by Sony. That is an oral or written publication that was perpetrated by the hackers."

While Sony tried to convince the court that the inclusion of the words "in any manner" in the phrase "oral or written publication in any manner" in their CGL coverage implied that it covered all forms of publication, including those by third parties, Oing took that to mean that the coverage applied only to publication through any medium (e.g., fax or email) not by any party. Even though that particular clause of the CGL policy did not specifically state that the policyholder had to be the one to publish the information, the rest of the policy strongly suggested that was the case, Oing found. "This entire policy . . . it's very policyholder oriented," Oing pointed out. He continued:

> Everything talks about the policyholder has to do this, the insured has to do that; this, that. Now, we get down to this one area here where you are saying, no, that does not mean insured only. It means anybody. So that you're asking me in that sense now to carve-out this little island for you. . . . When you point to E you say that has to be treated differently, like the tail wagging the dog. . . . E can only be in my mind read that it requires the policyholder to perpetrate or commit the act. It does not expand. It cannot be expanded to include 3rd party acts. As we are going back and forth, back and forth, the policy could be read this way and that way, the bottom line is it is written the way it is written.

The crux of Oing's ruling in favor of Zurich and Sony's other CGL insurance providers was that CGL policies only applied to damages policyholders were legally obligated to pay due to affirmative measures they had taken rather than intrusions or liability caused by third parties (in this case, the hackers). In the cases of the hotel installing surveillance cameras or LensCrafters allowing someone to be present at eye exams, the company in question had made a conscious decision to violate their customers' privacy, or as Marshall put it in court, "every case cited by Sony in support of the proposition that negligent security can be equated with publication, again, involved affirmative conduct by the insured." To the insurers—and Oing—these examples of "affirmative conduct" were quite unlike the PlayStation breach where Sony was at fault for providing negligent security only insofar as it had failed to make conscious decisions to better protect its customers' data.

That failure to protect data, or rather, Sony's decision to provide its customers with negligent security, was what Sony was counting on to justify its use of CGL coverage. In fact, when Oing pressed DeNatale on the question of whether he really believed that CGL policies could cover the acts of third parties, DeNatale acknowledged that the coverage was for actions committed by the insured party. "But, it covers you for acts of negligence," DeNatale added. "CGL policies traditionally cover you for acts of negligence. If someone falls on your premises you haven't pushed them over." In other words, Sony's argument hinged on the idea that they were very much at fault for the breach because they had been negligent in failing to protect their customers' data—in much the same way that a company might be negligent for failing to shovel the snow off the sidewalk in front of their premises and causing someone to fall. Across the country in California, the class action lawsuit that Sony was fighting at the same time against its own customers affected by the breach required them to make exactly the opposite argument: that they had not been at all negligent in their data security practices, merely the unlucky, unsuspecting victims of sophisticated adversaries and were therefore not liable for the harm that had befallen their customers.

Coughlin pointed out the hypocrisy of Sony trying to make both of these arguments simultaneously in parallel court cases. He told the court, "they were arguing in the consolidated class action that we didn't do anything wrong. We didn't disclose anything. We didn't publish anything. We did nothing. We are a victim." And, indeed, that argument that Sony was pushing in the class action case was the interpretation of the breach that Oing seemed to most agree with, telling Sony:

> the totality is . . . that your security features weren't sufficient to prevent hackers from coming in and getting access. While the plaintiffs have to say that you guys breached the duty to them, I mean, they are not going to sue the hackers because they cannot find the hackers. They can find the guy that had all of the information. That's you. . . . So, Sony is the victim here.

It's a view that would have been most welcome to Sony had it come from Battaglia, the judge presiding over the consolidated class action complaint filed by Sony's customers—that Sony was the victim, and its customers were only suing because they didn't know who the responsible hackers were and therefore couldn't sue them. In that case, however, Battaglia had been willing to let the class action suit move forward, otherwise Sony would probably not have needed to try to exercise its CGL coverage in the first place.

The striking parallels and contradictions between the two cases tied to the Sony breach playing out simultaneously on opposite coasts speak to the challenges that both Sony and its customers faced in trying to navigate the unclear liability regimes governing cybersecurity incidents in the early 2000s. In one case, Sony was exploring the limits of the personal and advertising injury coverage in its CGL insurance in light of a relatively new type of threat and in the other it was exploring the limits of its responsibility for protecting its customers from that same threat. Oing told the court in 2014:

> in this case it is without doubt in my mind, my finding is the hackers did this. The 3rd party hackers took it. They breached the security. They have gotten through all of the security levels and they were able to get access to this. That is not the same as saying Sony did this.

But later considerations of liability for cybersecurity breaches would complicate that clear-cut distinction between cases where the attackers were responsible and ones where the defenders were at least partly to blame.[12]

The liability considerations around security breach class action suits would become more complicated over time, as courts developed more nuanced interpretations of how the loss of personal information could harm people and regulators around the world developed more stringent sets of digital privacy rights. But the precedent set by Oing's ruling on the applicability of CGL policies to data breaches and other types of "cyber losses" would remain straightforward and highly influential. In the years following Oing's ruling, other companies that tried to exercise their CGL coverage in the face of cybersecurity incidents found that it was often no help at all. The confusion, uncertainty, and technical issues surrounding data breach liability echo some of the reasons insurance reformers proposed the no-fault model for auto liability insurance, in recognition of the fact that "in motor vehicle accident cases, the principle of negligence is peculiarly difficult to apply."[13] While breaches may not occur with the same frequency or suddenness as car accidents, it is also often difficult to reproduce exactly the chain of events that led up to an incident, given the challenges of digital forensic investigation, and juries and judges are often ill-equipped to understand many of the technical details that arise in the course of these investigations. The argument that auto liability litigation "results in jury trials which are largely contests of skill and chance," as the Columbia report put it, could equally well be applied to many of the data breach liability suits, and there is a significant burden on victims to pursue these suits and justify the injuries they have suffered, though that burden is distributed much more widely since data breaches typically involve far more victims than car accidents. If it were possible to more clearly delineate a set of baseline cybersecurity measures and practices for firms, it's conceivable that some principles of no-fault insurance might be applicable to breach liability insurance as a means of compensating victims quickly and reducing the amount of energy and effort expended on deciding who is at fault in these circumstances where, so often, many different parties are deserving of some degree of blame.

INNOVAK INTERNATIONAL INC. AND INDIRECT PUBLICATION

The 2014 ruling in *Zurich American Insurance Co. v. Sony Corp. of America et al.* set the stage for other insurers to fight their customers' attempts to use CGL and other non-cyber-specific policies to cover online intrusions and security breaches. For instance, in 2016, in a very similar dispute, accounting and payroll services provider Innovak International Inc. turned to its CGL policy provider, the Hanover Insurance Company, when it faced a data breach class action lawsuit. The class action complaint, filed in Alabama, alleged that Innovak had been aware of software vulnerabilities in its systems since 2014 and had failed to patch them, enabling the subsequent breach. Furthermore, the plaintiffs alleged, they had learned about the breach of their personal data not from Innovak but instead from the IRS, which sent letters informing them that their social security numbers, birthdates, addresses, and telephone numbers had been compromised. The loss of their personal information had caused "psychic injuries," the plaintiffs alleged, and some of them also said that their stolen information had been used to file fraudulent tax returns. As a result of those emotional and financial losses, caused by Innovak's negligent security, the plaintiffs demanded that Innovak pay compensatory and punitive damages, as well as attorney's fees.[14] Innovak moved swiftly to dismiss the suit, but that motion was denied on August 4, 2016, by district judge W. Keith Watkins.[15]

It wasn't the outcome Innovak was hoping for, but the company had already begun to prepare for the possibility that the class action litigation might move forward. On July 19, 2016, a few weeks before Watkins issued his order allowing the class action suit against Innovak to move forward, Innovak had filed its own lawsuit in Florida against Hanover. Innovak was seeking a declaration from the Florida court that Hanover was "contractually obligated" to cover the breached payroll company's legal fees in the class action suit in Alabama under the CGL policy it had sold to Innovak.[16]

Because CGL policies are so standardized across the industry, Innovak's CGL policy from Hanover was very similar to the one Sony held with Zurich and covered liability losses resulting from personal and advertising injuries in almost exactly the same terms as the Sony policy, including injuries arising out of "oral or written publication, in any manner, of material that violates a person's right of privacy."[17] But there was one notable difference between the two CGL policies—a difference that suggested Innovak might have more luck fighting Hanover in court than Sony had had with Zurich and its many other insurers. Two years after the Sony decision—perhaps even in part because of it—Innovak also had specific provisions for data breaches in its CGL policy. The Data Breach Form portion of Innovak's CGL policy with Hanover stated:

> We will provide Data Breach Services, Data Breach Expense Coverages and Additional Expense Coverages . . . if you have a "data breach" that:
>
> a. Is discovered during the coverage period of this Data Breach Coverage Form; and
>
> b. Is reported to us within 30 days of your discovery of the "data breach."

However, the Data Breach Form also explicitly noted that it would not cover "any fees, costs, settlements, judgments or liability of any kind arising in the course of, or as a result of a claim for damages, lawsuit, administrative proceedings, or governmental investigation against or involving you." Instead, the Data Breach Form—rather peculiarly for a CGL policy—seemed to focus exclusively on first-party breach costs, such as notification, public relations consulting, or forensic investigation.

On June 13, 2016, at the start of the class action lawsuit and one month before Innovak went to court to try to compel its insurer's support in the class action suit, Hanover issued a denial of coverage letter to Innovak that echoed the arguments Zurich had made so successfully against Sony. "Here, third party hackers, not the Insured, caused the data breach," Hanover pointed out. The carrier also ruled out coverage under the Data Breach Form because that section of the CGL policy explicitly excluded coverage for costs related to legal services or liability litigation and also noted that Innovak had failed to notify them of the breach within the thirty-day period required by the Data Breach Form.

In court, Innovak conceded that it would not try to claim coverage under the bodily injury or property damage provisions, or even the Data Breach Form, but, like Sony, the company argued that the circumstances of its breach qualified as a "publication" that violated its customers' right of privacy. Bolstered by Zurich's success in 2014, Hanover essentially repeated all of the same arguments that Sony's insurers had made in court two years prior. Hanover argued first that there had been no publication of the stolen data, only "appropriation" of the information "by third party hackers," and then argued that even if the court did consider the stolen data to have been published, that publication was done by a third party, not Innovak. Finally, Hanover's lawyers said, even if Innovak was found to have, in some sense, "published" the stolen data through its negligence, the CGL policy *still* would not apply because it covered only "intentional acts by the insured," and Innovak's failure to implement strong data security could hardly be viewed as an intentional act.

Innovak, understandably, mimicked Sony's arguments less closely, choosing a new precedent on which to base its argument. Innovak focused on a 2013 California case between Hartford Casualty Insurance Company and one of its customers, a business called Corcino & Associates, that had provided a job applicant with some confidential medical information supplied by Stanford Hospital and Clinics and asked the applicant to "perform certain tasks with the data" as part of her application, including converting the spreadsheet into bar graphs and other charts. The applicant, apparently unable to complete those tasks, turned to the Internet for assistance, posting the data and associated tasks on a website called "Student of Fortune," where students asked for help with homework and assignments. The data that the job applicant posted, along with the request for help, included the names of nearly 20,000 patients of Stanford Hospital's Emergency Department as well as their medical records, diagnosis codes, dates of their admission to and discharge from the hospital, and billing charges. The patients whose information was revealed later sued, and Corcino turned to Hartford Casualty Insurance Company, the provider of its CGL coverage, for support in the suit. Hartford filed a suit claiming the breach was excluded from its CGL coverage but Judge Gary Allen Feess dismissed the suit on October 7, 2013.[18]

Though Feess's decision hinged on whether or not the privacy violation for the affected patients derived only from statutory privacy protections, Innovak attempted to repurpose the ruling to show that third-party leaks of information could trigger CGL coverage. If the job applicant's actions were covered under Corcino's CGL policy, then why shouldn't the actions of the hackers who breached Innovak's online portal also be covered? Judge Mary S. Scriven, who presided over the Innovak decision, was unimpressed by this logic. "Corcino is wholly inapposite," she wrote in her November 17, 2017, ruling rejecting Innovak's attempts to force Hanover to provide coverage. Scriven continued:

> Notably, Corcino involved allegations that private information was actually posted by the insured, through one of the insured's job applicants, to a public website, which connotes a "publication" of information. Here, the Underlying Claimants [who filed the class action suit against Innovak] do not allege that their [personal private information] was ever made publicly accessible by Innovak.[19]

Scriven's assertion that Corcino "actually posted" the private information is striking since, in fact, Corcino did not post the information; an applicant for one of its positions did. Unlike an employee of Corcino, the job applicant could hardly be seen as acting as a legal agent of Corcino when she posted the confidential data in an attempt to get help with her application. However, Corcino did deliberately turn over the data to that applicant, unlike Innovak, which did not intentionally provide its customers' data to the hackers who stole it. If it had, perhaps it would have been in a better position to exercise its CGL coverage—a somewhat confusing conclusion from a cybersecurity perspective since turning over the data would, to some extent, imply even laxer security than a series of failed defenses.

Corcino could perhaps have been said to have indirectly published the information from Stanford Hospital's Emergency Department, a line of reasoning that Innovak also tried to invoke in court, arguing that it had, in some sense, indirectly published the stolen information by failing to protect it. But Scriven was also unwilling to entertain that notion, primarily because the class action complaint brought against Innovak did "not contain any allegations of indirect publication by Innovak." She said of the class action lawsuit, for which Innovak was seeking coverage, that the plaintiffs "repeatedly contend that Innovak failed to protect their [personal private information] by failing to implement sufficient data security measures" and concluded that this "is not an allegation of indirect publication; it is not an allegation of publication at all."[20] In this regard, Scriven seemed to take an even sterner line than Oing in interpreting the constraints of a CGL policy's relevance to data breaches, contending that the parties affected by the breach must themselves allege publication—or indirect publication—in order for the breached firm to invoke its CGL coverage. In the Sony suit, by contrast, Oing appeared relatively unconvinced by the argument that a data breach was not a form of publication. He indicated that he viewed a breach as tantamount to publication in many ways with his reference to Pandora's box and statement that "Once it is opened it doesn't matter who does what with [the stolen data]. It is out there."[21]

The discrepancy between Oing's and Scriven's perspectives on what constitutes publication in the context of a data breach is important because many—if not all—of the risks associated with breaches stem from the possibility that the stolen data will be made available to parties who will be able to use it for harmful or malicious purposes, ranging from financial fraud and identity theft to extortion and espionage. Scriven's ready dismissal of the possibility that a data breach could be considered a form of publication, or even indirect publication, suggests a relatively narrow interpretation of the term "publication" as meaning "public dissemination" and a short-term view of the consequences of a data breach. This interpretation of what it means to publish data would render CGL policies inapplicable to most breaches, with the possible exception of those that explicitly aim to publish stolen data in as public a manner as possible, like the 2014 Sony Pictures breach.

Despite their divergence on the question of whether a data breach can function as a form of publication, and how that question should be answered, there is no doubt that Scriven's ruling was heavily influenced by Oing's earlier one. Scriven noted that "case law on the subject is scant," but referenced the Sony case as the one instance in which a "court has addressed this issue in the data breach context." Scriven cited Oing's decision that the CGL policyholder must "perpetrate or commit the act" of publication and that, in the case of a breach, that publication is perpetrated by the hackers. "The Court concurs in that reasoning and finds that the only plausible interpretation . . . is that [Innovak's policy] requires the insured to be the publisher," Scriven wrote. Scriven's ready dismissal of the arguments that Innovak's CGL policy might apply to a data breach class action lawsuit speaks to how influential Oing's ruling was already in 2016 as the only case that had dealt with the question of whether CGL insurance covered breach lawsuits. Scriven suggested, in declining to equate a data breach with an act of publication, that she might be willing to go even further than Oing in blocking data breaches from being considered covered forms of personal or advertising injuries. Oing's reasoning, therefore, acted in some sense as a moderating influence in the Innovak decision, allowing Scriven to stop short of the most extreme opinions she hints at in her ruling about the inapplicability of CGL coverage to data breaches.

ROSEN HOTELS & RESORTS AND COVERAGE FOR BREACH NOTIFICATION COSTS

Both the Sony and Innovak disputes with the carriers of their CGL policies involved pending class action lawsuits brought by their customers, who were attempting to hold the companies liable for the loss of their data. Those suits and the looming liability they posed made CGL policies in some sense the obvious focus of the breached companies, but CGL claims regarding data breaches were not limited to incidents that led to class action lawsuits. In at least one case, a CGL insurance carrier took steps to avoid covering breach costs even in advance of any such lawsuit being filed— emboldened no doubt by the success of Zurich and Hanover in fighting off breach-related claims. On February 3, 2016, Florida hotel chain Rosen Hotels & Resorts Inc. received the first reports from payment card networks that a pattern of fraudulent activity had been tied to customers of its hotels. Rosen paid an independent firm $150,000 to examine its systems and the investigation revealed several periods of long-lasting breaches of the hotel chain's payment card information beginning in September 2014 and continuing all the way through February 2016.

Following this investigation, on March 4, 2016, Rosen notified the affected customers of the breach. The notification process cost Rosen more than $100,000, with $50,000 going to pay the company's lawyers, another $15,000 to a crisis management firm, and a final $40,000 in costs for issuing the notifications themselves. But those costs were trivial compared to the fines that Visa, MasterCard, and American Express levied against Rosen upon learning of the breach. Rosen had signed card service agreements with each of the major payment networks to process payment cards belonging to the networks, and all three networks determined that Rosen, in failing to protect its customers' data, had been in violation of those agreements and had caused major payment fraud losses to the payment networks and issuing banks responsible for covering fraudulent charges. MasterCard and Visa each issued fines of more than $1 million to Rosen, and American Express fined the company an additional $128,830 in connection with the breach.[22]

On December 29, 2016, at the end of a tumultuous (and expensive) year, Rosen Millennium, a wholly owned subsidiary of Rosen Hotels & Resorts that provided data security services for the hotel chain, sent a brief Notice of Claim letter to its insurer, St. Paul Fire & Marine Insurance Company: "Credit card systems breach. Loss dates range from Sept 2014 thru Feb 2016." Rosen's insurance broker later informed St. Paul that Rosen would be seeking coverage for damages resulting from the breach under its CGL policy with St. Paul. On March 2, 2017, St. Paul issued a coverage denial letter stating that it would provide no coverage for the breach under Rosen's CGL policy, but allowing that Rosen might provide additional information that could influence that determination. Later that month, on March 24, 2017, St. Paul sued Rosen in Orlando, Florida, asking the court to make a declaratory judgment that the CGL policy St. Paul had sold to Rosen did not cover any of the damages associated with the data breach.[23] More than a year later, on June 8, 2018, with the suit still pending in court, Rosen sent a letter to St. Paul demanding payment for the breach costs.

The standard-form CGL policy Rosen had purchased from St. Paul had limits of up to $1 million per event, $1 million for advertising injury per person, and $1 million for personal injury per person, as well as an overall $2 million aggregate limit. Since Rosen's costs for the breach totaled roughly $2.4 million, according to St. Paul's complaint, the policy could potentially have covered a significant portion of those losses had Rosen been able to classify them as resulting from personal or advertising injuries. The personal and advertising injury offenses specified in the policy included "Making known to any person or organization covered material that violates a person's right of privacy." The policy included no definition of what it means to make material known, but both parties later agreed the requirement was synonymous with "publication," though, as in the Sony and Innovak cases, they disagreed on whether the breach involved any such publication of the stolen data.[24]

St. Paul relied heavily on the logic of the 2014 Sony ruling and 2016 Innovak ruling to make the case that Rosen itself would have had to make the stolen credit card information known in a manner that violated its customers' privacy in order for the policy to provide coverage. Rosen, in turn, couched itself as responsible for the breach in its demand letter, writing that it had "made private information known to third parties that violated a credit card holder's right of privacy."[25] This language both mirrored the personal injury definition in the CGL policy and also framed Rosen as the perpetrator of the breach. The penalties issued by Visa, MasterCard, and American Express, which comprised the bulk of the costs Rosen faced, St. Paul also regarded as falling outside the covered classes of injury. Those fines were further excluded from coverage, in St. Paul's view, because of a clause in the CGL policy stipulating, "We won't cover injury or damage for which the protected person has assumed liability under any contract or agreement."[26] Rosen disagreed, claiming that the personal injury provisions of its CGL policies applied to the breach notification costs, and also arguing that the need to replace stolen credit cards—for which the payment networks fined Rosen—should be covered as "property damage" under the policy.[27]

In keeping with the Sony and Innovak rulings, the deciding district judge in the Rosen dispute, Carlos E. Mendoza, concluded that St. Paul was not liable for any of Rosen's breach-related costs because the "alleged injuries did not result from Millennium's business activities but rather the actions of third parties."[28] Rosen, like Sony and Innovak before it, attempted to find relevant precedent in earlier insurance cases unrelated to data breaches, invoking one case in which a company accidentally posted patient records online, and another in which a firm published a customer's DNA test results on its website without consent. In both of those cases, courts had ruled that the insurers had a duty to defend the companies in questions under CGL policies—but, as Mendoza pointed out, neither one involved disclosure by a third party. They also involved more unambiguous examples of "publication" than the Rosen case did.

Perhaps hoping to squash any debate over whether its breach could be considered an act of publication, Rosen invoked a more surprising case, involving spyware. The spyware insurance dispute stemmed from a couple named Crystal and Brian Byrd who, in July 2010, leased a laptop from a store called Aspen Way. On December 22, 2010, a manager from the store showed up at their home to reclaim the computer because he believed, incorrectly, that the Byrds had fallen behind on their lease payments. The manager showed the couple a picture of Brian Byrd at the computer that had been taken with the laptop's camera. The Byrds later learned the photo been taken using a program called PC Rental Agent that can capture a computer's keystrokes, take photos with its camera, and take screen shots. The Byrds then filed a class action suit against Aspen Way in May 2011 alleging that the retailer had violated the Electronic Communications Privacy Act by intentionally disclosing private data to a store employee. The State of Washington also sued the company on similar charges in October 2013, and Aspen Way turned to its insurance provider, Liberty Mutual, to provide coverage for its legal defense in both suits.[29]

Liberty Mutual and Aspen Way's other insurers were ultimately able to get out of covering the retailer's legal defense costs thanks to an exclusion in the policy that explicitly ruled out coverage for "recording and distribution of material or information in violation of law." While that exception did not apply to Rosen's situation, the *Aspen Way* ruling was relevant in another regard to their case because it dealt directly with the question of the circumstances under which data could be considered "published" and did so in a fashion much more charitable to breached entities than the *Innovak* or even *Sony* rulings. In the Aspen Way dispute, Montana district judge Susan P. Watters determined that the meaning of "publication" included "the dissemination of information to at least a third party, if not the public-at-large." Watters explained: "This liberal definition of 'publication' conforms with Montana's strong policy of construing insurance policy terms in the insured's favor."[30] This very generous interpretation of publication—as disclosure to even just one third party—stood in contrast to the narrower definition Scriven had seemed to espouse in the Innovak case and hinted at a possible path for construing a data breach as a privacy injury.

But ultimately, Mendoza—like Oing and Scriven before him—determined that because third-party hackers had infiltrated Rosen's networks and violated its customers' privacy, rather than the hotel chain accidentally publishing its customers' information itself, Rosen's CGL policy did not apply to the incident, regardless of whether or not an act of publication had taken place. The precedent set by the Sony, Innovak, and Rosen cases regarding large-scale data breaches and the resulting massive class action lawsuits speaks to how effective insurers were at explicitly carving out coverage for that type of liability from CGL policies. The privacy injuries described in these policies were so narrowly defined that the definitions applied to only a very narrow set of incidents in which a company publishes customer information itself and thereby excluded all data breaches perpetrated by outside hackers. Those rulings were a victory for insurers on two levels. First, they allowed insurers to avoid paying the legal costs for a string of these class action lawsuits. But perhaps even more importantly, the rulings sent a strong message to businesses concerned about the growing risk of data breaches: if they wanted any protection for such incidents, then they would have to buy an entirely new type of insurance. Underlying that definitive exemption of data breaches from CGL coverage, however, was a much more complicated and unresolved set of liability issues that the insurance disputes barely touched on beyond forcing breached companies like Sony to argue both of their conflicting roles as breach victim and enabler at once, in parallel lawsuits. The CGL disputes over coverage for breach liability laid bare the contradictions and inherent challenges of trying to untangle who was responsible for incidents that had multiple, often overlapping, layers of victims, enablers, and potential defenders.

"THE POINT OF NO RETURN": COMPUTER FRAUD INSURANCE AND DEFINING CYBERCRIME

On December 11, 2008, investor Bernie Madoff was arrested for perpetrating the largest private Ponzi scheme in history, amounting to nearly $65 billion in fraud. Thousands of individuals and organizations who had invested their money with Madoff lost massive sums of money in the scandal, including Nobel laureate author Elie Wiesel and former Dodgers pitcher Sandy Koufax. The Methodist Health System Foundation Inc. (MHSFI), a nonprofit based in Slidell, Louisiana, focused on improving access to primary health care in East New Orleans, lost the full value of its investment with Madoff's firm, which it estimated at $439,467. On September 3, 2009, less than a year after Madoff's arrest, the nonprofit filed a claim for that loss with its insurer, Hartford, under its Crime Shield Insurance policy with the carrier. MHSFI's policy had a $500,000 limit per loss, which the Louisiana foundation hoped would cover its entire Madoff investment, less a $5,000 deductible.

In its claim, MHSFI pointed to the Computer and Funds Transfer Fraud portion of the Crime Shield policy, which defined computer fraud as the loss of money or other property "following and directly related to the use of any computer to fraudulently cause a transfer of that property from inside the 'premises'" to a person or place outside those premises. Since the fraudulent trading slips and month-end account statements that Madoff had provided to account holders were created on computers and "central to Madoff's scheme," the Ponzi scheme was an act of computer fraud and therefore should be covered under its policy, MHSFI argued. The organization explained its reasoning for labeling the financial fraud a computer crime:

> But for Madoff's use of a computer to obtain and manipulate data that made its trading slips and month-end account statements appear accurate, and created a false perception of a successful history of investment and trading, MHSFI's money would not have been transferred to Madoff. MHSFI's loss was therefore

"directly related" to Madoff's use of computers to fraudulently cause the transfer of MHSFI's money from banking premises and/or financial institutions to Madoff, and Hartford is therefore obligated to cover that loss under its Crime Policy.[1]

As further evidence of the essential role computers had played in Madoff's scheme, MHSFI pointed to the fact that federal prosecutors had filed charges against two computer programmers working for Madoff who had written programs that generated fictitious trading data for his client accounts.

On October 20, 2009, Hartford sent MHSFI a letter denying their claim on the grounds that Madoff's Ponzi scheme, despite involving computers, was not an act of computer fraud. Hartford pointed out that MHSFI had voluntarily given its money to a fund called Meridian that later invested it with Madoff's firm. "Madoff did not use computers to fraudulently cause a transfer of Methodist's funds," Hartford pointed out. The insurer continued:

> At no point did the transferors open their online statements and learn in shock that transfers had occurred without their knowledge. Rather, the transfers flowed from decisions made by the transferors to speculate in the stock market. . . . These decisions were informed by a hope that its investments would increase in value and did not "flow immediately" from any use of a computer by Madoff. Any role played by a computer in Methodist's loss theory is, at most, incidental. . . . This is not computer fraud within the meaning of the Hartford Policy.[2]

MHSFI sued Hartford, contesting the claim denial, but US district judge Helen Berrigan granted summary judgment to the insurer on July 1, 2011. Berrigan dismissed the case because MHSFI's investment decision was "too many steps removed from Madoff's fraud" to qualify for coverage under the Hartford policy. Since MHSFI had voluntarily made those investments, "the Madoff Ponzi scheme was not a direct cause" of MHSFI's losses, Berrigan explained. Because of that, she did not even address in her ruling the question of whether Madoff's actions constituted computer fraud, but almost certainly the answer would have been that it did not.

In March 2009, years before the MHSFI suit was resolved, Madoff pleaded guilty to eleven counts of fraud, money laundering, perjury, and theft, and he was later sentenced to 150 years in prison, but at no point was he charged with any computer crimes. Of course, he had used computers in the course of operating his Ponzi scheme—by the early 2000s, it would have been nearly impossible to operate a Ponzi scheme or really any form of white-collar crime without the use of a computer—but that, in itself, did not make him a cyber-criminal. And yet, as the MHSFI case hinted, defining what, precisely, was and was not computer fraud was not an entirely straightforward undertaking when so many crimes involved computers in at least some capacity. As computers became increasingly involved in financial transactions, computer fraud transformed from something that had initially seemed like a very specific type of crime to a much broader and murkier class of crimes that relied on or involved computers in a range of capacities, from sending fraudulent emails to initiating unauthorized financial transfers. Because insurers were selling policies geared specifically toward covering computer and electronic crimes, this evolution of the nature of cybercrime and its variations prompted significant disputes about what those policies covered and, more fundamentally, what constituted a computer crime, as opposed to a crime that just happened to involve computers. Canonical examples of computer crimes included someone stealing or guessing an employee's password and using it to transfer funds to themselves from another account or a hacker exploiting a vulnerability in a company's software to initiate an unauthorized transfer—the types of crimes that were executed entirely, or almost entirely, through computers. On the other end of the spectrum, Madoff's Ponzi scheme seemed to be a fairly clear example of a crime where computers played a peripheral, supporting role, but other incidents would prove to be much murkier. As computers became increasingly embedded in both business and criminal activity during the late 1990s and early 2000s, insurers and policyholders repeatedly scuffled over what exactly constituted computer fraud as carriers experimented with different definitions and language in their coverage.

While insurers were largely successful in their efforts to deny any cyber-related claims under CGL policies, they met with much more mixed success in court when it came to denying coverage under computer fraud policies for crimes they deemed insufficiently computer-centric, in part due to the fact the language in these policies defining computer fraud varied much more than the language defining personal and advertising injuries in standard-form CGL policies. Different policies offered different definitions of what counted as computer fraud and courts, in turn, had very different opinions about just how clear that language was, what it meant, and how directly a crime had to be executed via computer for it to count as computer fraud. Some courts took a fairly narrow view that for a crime to qualify as computer fraud it could not involve any human intervention on the victim's part. Other courts were more open to the idea that something like phishing emails containing faked invoices might play an enabling role in computer fraud even if the victims themselves were responsible for ultimately acting on the fraudulent information in those emails to initiate financial transfers. These disputes often centered on the question of whether computers had to *directly* cause financial fraud for an incident to be considered an act of computer fraud or whether it was sufficient for the perpetrators to use computers to mislead employees into initiating fraudulent financial transfers through spoofed emails or other forms of computer-enabled manipulation. This requirement for the computers to directly cause the fraud stemmed from insurance policy language that often defined computer fraud in similar terms to the MHSFI policy as losses "directly related to the use of any computer to fraudulently cause a transfer." But the specific language varied from policy to policy as the threat landscape evolved and insurers' understanding of computer fraud shifted. For policyholders, these different definitions and interpretations of computer fraud coverage led to significant uncertainty about what such policies actually applied to, especially as computer crimes continued to evolve and change, and carriers continued to experiment with new language in their computer fraud policies.

INTERVENING EVENTS AND IMMEDIATE CAUSES:
BRIGHTPOINT V. ZURICH

On January 23, 2003, the wireless device company Brightpoint received a purchase order for 200,000 prepaid telephone cards at its branch in the Philippines. The fax appeared to come from long-time Brightpoint customer Enrico Genato, who ran a business that regularly purchased large numbers of prepaid phone cards from Brightpoint. Because Genato purchased such large volumes of phone cards, Brightpoint required him to include postdated checks with his purchase orders, as well as bank guarantees certifying that his accounts held sufficient funds to cover those checks. Genato would fax Brightpoint copies of the checks and guaranties along with his purchase orders, and Brightpoint would then pick up the original checks, guaranties, and purchase orders when they delivered the phone cards, which they purchased directly from telecom companies. Everything appeared to be in order for the purchase order that arrived on January 23, 2003; it included both the postdated check and bank guaranties, as did the fax from Genato that arrived the following day, January 24, which contained a purchase order for another 150,000 phone cards.[3]

On both January 23 and 24, Brightpoint employee Jay-Jay Moralde went to the office of Globe Telecom, a major Philippines telecom provider, and purchased enough prepaid phone cards for each of Genato's orders. In the parking area just outside the Globe office where he made the purchases, Moralde then turned them over to Reena Aldeguer, who had received orders for Genato in the past, and who gave Moralde the original postdated checks and bank guaranties for the orders. But the checks, totaling 82,350,000 Philippine pesos, or roughly $1.5 million, turned out to be forged. So, on April 11, 2003, Brightpoint submitted a claim for the money they had spent on the stolen prepaid phone cards to its insurer, Zurich, citing Form F of its Crime Policy which covered computer fraud and wire transfer crimes and defined computer fraud as "theft of property following and directly related to the use of any computer to fraudulently cause a transfer of that property." Brightpoint's policy explicitly stated that fraudulent transfers falling under this definition could be initiated via "written, telephonic, telegraphic, telefacsimile, electronic, cable, or teletype instructions."[4]

On October 16, 2003, Zurich denied Brightpoint's claim, writing that "there is nothing . . . that proves that a computer was used to fraudulently cause a transfer of the phone cards." Brightpoint sued Zurich, looking to the *American Heritage Dictionary* to help prove that it had, in fact been the victim of computer fraud. Form F of the Zurich coverage defined computer fraud as theft "directly related" to the use of a computer, so Brightpoint looked up both words in the fourth edition of the *American Heritage Dictionary*, which defined "related" as meaning "connected" or "associated" with something, and "direct" as meaning "characterized by close logical, causal, or consequential relationship." Thus, Brightpoint argued, "the theft of the phone cards had a 'close logical, causal, or consequential' connection or relationship to the use of a computer" because "the first step taken in the scheme each day was to fax purchase orders to Brightpoint for approval. . . . And the only means by which Brightpoint received the fraudulent purchase orders was by fax. So the use of the fax here was not a 'remote cause' . . . it was an integral part of the theft."

Zurich did not dispute that the fax machine played a role in the scam or the dictionary definitions Brightpoint had looked up, but it contended that the faxes, central though they may have been to the fraud, could not be considered the "efficient proximate cause" of Brightpoint's losses, that is "the risk that sets others in motion." Zurich maintained that it was the physical checks and bank guaranties that Aldeguer had handed to Moralde in the Globe parking lot—not the faxed copies of them—that were the true "predominating cause" of the fraud. In its response to Brightpoint's suit, Zurich argued that Aldeguer's and Moralde's "'face-to-face' event of physically exchanging the cards for original checks and guaranties was the cause of Brightpoint's loss. . . . As such, Brightpoint's alleged loss was not 'directly related' to the receipt of faxed purchase orders, checks and Bank Guaranties."

On March 10, 2006, Indiana district judge Sara Evans Barker ruled in favor of Zurich. She was not just skeptical about designating the Brightpoint incident as an act of computer fraud, she was even skeptical about calling a fax machine a computer, writing in her ruling that "the common and ordinary meaning of computer as widely used and understood in our society and around the world is severely stretched by the inclusion of a facsimile machine." But her decision to support Zurich's denial of the Brightpoint claim ultimately stemmed from the argument Zurich had made that Moralde's and Aldeguer's face-to-face exchange of the physical phone cards for the paper checks and bank guaranties was the true direct cause of Brightpoint's losses. "The facsimile transmission caused Brightpoint to purchase the cards from its supplier, not to transfer them to its purchaser, and the use of the fax thus cannot be viewed as having directly or proximately caused the theft," Barker wrote in the ruling.

Brightpoint had argued that just because there were multiple different causes of the fraud didn't mean that the faxes weren't every bit as central as the hand-off of the physical copies. The faxes containing copies of the forged purchase orders, checks, and guaranties could be viewed as a proximate cause of the fraud, even if the actual hard copies of those documents were also a proximate cause, Brightpoint contended. Since many crimes, including Madoff's Ponzi scheme, have some computer-based component, Brightpoint's reasoning, in which a computer could be one of many different causes of a crime, had the potential to significantly expand the scope of what kinds of incidents were considered computer fraud.

But Barker was not convinced by this argument. She pointed to the language in Brightpoint's Form F coverage requiring that a covered theft be "directly related to the use of any computer" and, eschewing the *American Heritage Dictionary* definitions that Brightpoint had cited, looked to the definition of the word "directly" in *Black's Law Dictionary* as meaning "in a straight line or course" or "immediately." Even if there were multiple causes of the Brightpoint fraud, "the loss to Brightpoint that occurred here did not flow immediately from the use of the facsimile," Barker concluded. Underlying the logic of her decision was a clear concern that broad interpretations of the meaning of computer fraud could quickly spiral out of control and allow policyholders to label every crime that involved even the slightest technological component—from counterfeiting to Ponzi schemes—as computer fraud. Barker highlighted this risk in her ruling:

> Brightpoint's approach in isolating words and relying upon dictionary definitions of terms such as "following" and "directly related," leads to bizarre constructions of the contract. For example, applying this approach, Form F could be read to provide coverage where a customer sends an e-mail indicating that he is coming over to Brightpoint's offices to make a cash purchase of 50 mobile phone units and completes the transaction by using counterfeit money. If coverage were permitted, it would reflect an interpretation other than a plain and ordinary interpretation of the policy at issue; any reasonable person would not give the Form F provisions regarding coverage for computer fraud or wire transfer that "spin." Obviously, in both the contrived example and in this case, intervening events or circumstances became the direct, proximate, predominate and immediate cause of Brightpoint's loss.

The most significant element of the *Brightpoint* ruling for influencing future cases over computer fraud insurance disputes was Barker's contention that, in order to be considered the result of computer fraud, a loss must "flow immediately" from the use of a computer, without any "intervening events or circumstances." But the nature of those intervening events would change significantly as computer crimes evolved. And, adding to the confusion, different insurers would define computer fraud in different ways, further complicating the question of what kinds of crime each different policy applied to. For instance, the rise of social engineering techniques like phishing would lead to many crimes that were not entirely automated but did not rely on the face-to-face exchange of physical forged documents either.

Some insurers created specific social engineering coverage under cyber risk policies for such incidents, but not all customers purchased those more specialized policies, and many of those who didn't continued to feel that their computer fraud coverage should provide them with some protection from computer-based manipulation—a sentiment that some courts turned out to share, as well. Barker's reference to what "any reasonable person" would consider to be computer fraud would be important for these cases as well since computer spoofing schemes would be understood by many reasonable people as falling within that category.

HACKING, UNAUTHORIZED ACCESS,
AND *PESTMASTER V. TRAVELERS*

In August 2009, a pest control company headquartered in California called Pestmaster Services hired a contractor to administer its payroll services. The contractor, Priority 1 Resource Group, was owned by a woman named Dawn Branzuela, who agreed to pay payroll taxes and prepare and deliver payroll checks on Pestmaster's behalf. So that Priority 1 could perform these services, Pestmaster authorized Priority 1 to initiate automated clearing house (ACH) transfers from Pestmaster's bank accounts in order to cover employee paychecks. Each payroll period, Priority 1 would send Pestmaster invoices for the amounts owed for employee salaries and taxes, and after Pestmaster approved the invoices Priority 1 would then initiate ACH transfers to move the approved amounts from Pestmaster's account to their own. In June 2011, Pestmaster CEO Jeffrey Van Diepen was notified by the IRS that five quarters of the company's federal payroll taxes, totaling $335,304.87, had gone unpaid. Instead of actually paying Pestmaster's payroll taxes, it turned out Branzuela had been spending that money on her own expenses. As a result, the IRS told Van Diepen, the company now owed the government $373,136.[5]

On June 13, 2011, Pestmaster filed a claim under its crime liability policy with insurer Travelers for the losses it suffered as a result of Priority 1's fraud, citing specifically the policy's Computer Crime Insuring Agreement, which provided coverage for losses "directly caused by Computer Fraud," where computer fraud was defined as "the use of any computer to fraudulently cause a transfer of money, securities or other property." On January 4, 2013, Travelers denied the claim, and on June 11, 2013, Pestmaster filed a complaint against Travelers in Los Angeles Superior Court. The California district judge who presided over the case, John Walter, was unconvinced by Pestmaster's argument that it had been the victim of computer fraud. In particular, he was struck by the fact that nothing Branzuela had done resembled computer hacking. "'Computer Fraud' occurs when someone 'hacks' or obtains unauthorized access or entry to a computer in order to make an unauthorized transfer," Walter wrote in his July 17, 2014, ruling in favor of Travelers. He continued, "Pestmaster does not argue—nor could it—that Priority 1 was an unauthorized user or hacker or that Priority 1 somehow subverted Pestmaster's computer in the actual transfer of funds into Priority 1's account. . . . Therefore, Priority 1's conduct does not constitute 'Computer Fraud' as defined by the Policy because the transfer of funds was at all times authorized and did not involve hacking or any unauthorized entry into a computer system."[6] The most striking thing about the language Walter used to describe computer fraud as hacking is how closely it echoes the CFAA, especially in its emphasis on authorization. The CFAA, commonly regarded as the US anti-hacking law, makes it illegal to access computers without authorization or in excess of authorization. Although Pestmaster's policy with Travelers made no mention of access, authorization, or hacking in its definition of computer fraud, Walter seized on the idea that computer fraud was synonymous with hacking which, in turn, required unauthorized access to a computer.

The *Pestmaster* ruling extended Barker's logic in the *Brightpoint* case about "intervening events" to apply even to incidents of fraud that didn't involve any physical copies of forged materials but relied entirely on electronic transfers and invoices. Those transfers, so long as they had been approved by the policyholder and not through unauthorized hacking, were still sufficient intervening events to show that "Pestmaster's claimed losses did not 'flow immediately' and 'directly' from Priority 1's use of a computer," Walter wrote in the ruling, quoting Barker's language from *Brightpoint*. Once again, the crucial question was how directly the computer fraud— and, by extension, the computers—had caused these losses because of the language in the policy limiting coverage to losses "directly caused" by computer fraud. It was a significant victory for Travelers, not least because the actual definition of computer fraud in the policy it had issued to Pestmaster made no mention of hackers of unauthorized access, a point Pestmaster emphasized in its appeal. But on July 29, 2016, the Ninth Circuit affirmed

Walter's analysis of the policy's computer fraud provision and his contention that computer fraud was inextricably linked to the issue of authorization. The Ninth Circuit explained its reasoning:

> We interpret the phrase "fraudulently cause a transfer" to require an unauthorized transfer of funds. When Priority 1 transferred funds pursuant to authorization from Pestmaster, the transfer was not fraudulently caused. Because computers are used in almost every business transaction, reading this provision to cover all transfers that involve both a computer and fraud at some point in the transaction would convert this Crime Policy into a "General Fraud" Policy. While Travelers could have drafted this language more narrowly, we believe protection against all fraud is not what was intended by this provision, and not what Pestmaster could reasonably have expected this provision to cover.[7]

However, the Ninth Circuit's willingness to overlook the broad language in the policy Travelers sold to Pestmaster and construe the coverage narrowly, on behalf of the carrier, would not be shared by all courts.

PHISHING, AMBIGUOUS DEFINITIONS, AND *AMERICAN TOOLING V. TRAVELERS*

On March 18, 2015, Gary Gizinski, the vice president and treasurer of Michigan-based company American Tooling Center, sent an email to one of American Tooling's vendors in China, Shanghai YiFeng Automotive Die Manufacture Co. Ltd, asking a YiFeng employee named Jessie Chen to provide any outstanding invoices. American Tooling manufactures metalworking machinery as well as equipment for welding and die cutting and, at the time of the incident, it subcontracted some of its manufacturing work to YiFeng. After completing its orders for American Tooling, YiFeng, and other international vendors, would submit invoices via email to Gizinski, who would then review a spreadsheet of the outstanding accounts payable each week and initiate wire transfers through an online banking portal. For each of these transfers, Gizinski would manually enter the recipient's name, banking information, and the amount to be wired, at which point the assistant comptroller for American Tooling would have to log into the same portal and approve the transfer.[8]

It's unclear what exactly happened to the 2015 email Gizinski sent to Chen, but American Tooling later alleged that "an unidentified third party, through means unknown, intercepted this email" and then responded to it, impersonating Chen by using a spoofed "from" address and submitting invoices that purported to be from YiFeng. On March 27, 2015, the impersonator emailed Gizinski that YiFeng had changed its banking information and American Tooling should send the payments to the new account. Gizinski complied with the request and wired money to the new account, only to receive an email on April 3 informing him that the transfer had not gone through "due to some new bank rules in the province." YiFeng would return the payment, the email said, and American Tooling would need to wire the money to yet another new bank account. On April 8, 2015, Gizinski wired the same sum of money to this new account, before the previous transfer had been returned. On April 9, 2015, he wired an additional payment of $1,575 at the impersonator's request, and then on May 8, 2015, he sent an additional payment of $482,640.41 to yet another account that he had been instructed to use. Overall, American Tooling transferred approximately $834,000 to the impostor's accounts through these four wire transfers before learning from YiFeng that the company had not received any of these payments.[9]

American Tooling's business insurance policy at the time was provided by Travelers, which promptly denied American Tooling's claim. American Tooling sued Travelers for breach of contract, arguing that the incident was covered under the "computer fraud" provisions of the policy's computer crime section, which stated: "The Company will pay the Insured for the Insured's direct loss of, or direct loss from damage to, Money, Securities and Other Property directly caused by Computer Fraud." This was yet another variation on the definition of covered computer fraud—one that relied on the terms "direct" and "directly" even more heavily than Pestmaster's policy.

Travelers argued that the computer fraud clause did not apply to the YiFeng incident because "the loss was not directly caused by Computer Fraud."[10] The circumstances of the American Tooling incident were slightly more complicated than the Pestmaster fraud had been—there was a "hacker" of sorts involved, whoever was sending spoofed emails from Chen. But other courts had already looked to the *Pestmaster* ruling as the basis for not requiring insurers to cover scams triggered by phishing emails. For instance, a 2016 ruling by the Fifth Circuit had vacated a judgment against Great American Insurance Company (GAIC) in a case that closely resembled the American

Tooling incident. One of GAIC's policyholders, a Houston oil company called Apache Corporation, had changed the bank account information it had on file for a vendor, Petrofac, after receiving phone calls and emails from someone purporting to represent Petrofac. The emails had been sent from the domain petrofacltd.com, instead of the actual Petrofac domain, petrofac .com, but by the time Apache realized its mistake it had already transferred approximately $7 million to the fraudulent account. Apache filed a claim under its crime insurance policy with GAIC. When GAIC denied Apache's claim, Apache sued its insurer and a Texas district judge, Alfred H. Bennett, ruled in Apache's favor in 2015, finding that the scam qualified as an act of computer fraud and GAIC was obligated to cover it.[11] But the following year, in October 2016, Bennett's ruling was overturned by the Fifth Circuit Court of Appeals, which cited the Ninth Circuit's recent ruling in the *Pestmaster* case.[12]

John Corbett O'Meara, the Michigan district judge who authored the first ruling in the *American Tooling* case, relied on both the narrow interpretations of computer fraud set out in the *Pestmaster* and *Apache* cases, and also Barker's earlier reasoning in *Brightpoint*, that "intervening events" separating the use of a computer from an actual act of fraud invalidated computer fraud coverage. In his August 2017 ruling that Travelers was not obligated to cover American Tooling's losses under their computer fraud policy, O'Meara wrote:

> Here, the fraudulent emails did not "directly" or immediately cause the transfer of funds from ATC's bank account. Rather, intervening events between ATC's receipt of the fraudulent emails and the transfer of funds (ATC verified production milestones, authorized the transfers, and initiated the transfers without verifying bank account information) preclude a finding of "direct" loss "directly caused" by the use of any computer.[13]

In other words, because of all the intermediate steps involved in the firm's invoicing process that occurred between receiving the spoofed emails and issuing the wire transfers—Gizinski manually entering account information and initiating transfers, for instance, and the assistant comptroller signing off on those transfers—the fake emails could not be said to have "directly" caused the wire transfers, O'Meara found.

He also referenced the *Pestmaster* precedent that computer fraud required "hacking," and O'Meara clearly did not view spoofed emails as meeting that bar. "Although fraudulent emails were used to impersonate a vendor and dupe ATC [American Tooling Center] into making a transfer of funds, such emails do not constitute the 'use of any computer to fraudulently cause a transfer.' There was no infiltration or 'hacking' of ATC's computer system," O'Meara wrote. He concluded: "The emails themselves did not directly cause the transfer of funds; rather, ATC authorized the transfer based upon the information received in the emails."[14]

At the heart of O'Meara's initial ruling in favor of Travelers was that same sentiment the Ninth Circuit had put forward the previous year, arguing against construing "computer fraud" to mean any act of fraud involving computers. Both O'Meara and the Ninth Circuit seemed to be getting at the idea that computer fraud occurs when a fraudulent act is carried out *entirely* through a computer system, not just using a computer peripherally. It's a distinction that Walter also made in his ruling in the *Pestmaster* case, when he wrote that the "use of a computer was merely incidental to, and not directly related to, the misuse of Pestmaster's funds."[15] In *Apache*, the Fifth Circuit had made a similar distinction, finding that "the [fake Petrofac] email was part of the scheme; but, the email was merely incidental to the occurrence of the authorized transfer of money."[16] But distinguishing between when computers are "merely incidental" to acts of fraud and when they are "directly related" to or "directly cause" fraud can be complicated.

Adding to the growing consensus that computer fraud should be construed narrowly, the Eleventh Circuit issued an opinion on a computer fraud insurance claim in May 2018 for a case in which a company called Interactive Communications International Inc. (InComm) was suing its insurer, GAIC. InComm sold reloadable debit card credits and had lost $11.4 million in 2013 and 2014 when fraudsters figured out how to redeem individual InComm credits multiple times. The company sought coverage for the losses under its computer fraud policy, issued by GAIC, but the Eleventh Circuit ruled that their losses were not covered because "although the fraudsters' manipulation of InComm's computers set into motion the chain of events that ultimately led to InComm's loss, their use of the computers did not 'directly'—which is to say immediately and without intervention or interruption—cause that loss."[17]

To justify this analysis, the Eleventh Circuit outlined four distinct steps in the InComm fraud scheme: (1) the fraudsters manipulated InComm's computer system to enable duplicate redemption, (2) InComm received a call to redeem a credit and transferred money to a bank that issued the reloaded debit card with the appropriate credits, (3) the debit card user made a purchase and paid using the reloaded card, and finally, (4) the bank that had received money from InComm in step 2 transferred money to the merchant to cover the purchase made by the cardholder. "InComm insists that its loss occurred at Step 2—and is thus 'directly' the result of the Step-1 fraud. . . . But the facts of the case demonstrate otherwise," the Eleventh Circuit ruled. "InComm retained at least some control over the funds . . . even after the Step-2 transfer, and could prevent their loss by intervening to halt the disbursement of money . . . to merchants at Step 4." Based on that analysis, the Eleventh Circuit concluded:

> the loss did not occur until—at Step 4—Bancorp [the bank] actually disbursed money from the InComm-earmarked account to pay merchants for purchases made by cardholders. That was the point at which InComm could not recover its money. That was the point of no return. That being the case, it seems clear to us that InComm's loss did not "[result] directly" from the initial computer fraud.[18]

It is a striking conclusion partly because the perpetrators in this case did, in fact, "hack" into InComm's computer systems without authorization to allow them to redeem credits multiple times—that was the first step the Eleventh Circuit identified in their breakdown of the fraud. But because it occurred too many steps before the actual fraud was carried out, even the unauthorized hacking in this case was not considered sufficient to rise to the level of computer fraud.

There had clearly been several intermediate steps between American Tooling's receipt of the fraudulent invoices and their issuing the payments (Gizinski entering account information into the system, Gizinski initiating the transfers to those account, the assistant comptroller signing off on those transfers) and at no point had anyone actually hacked into American Tooling's computer systems. If the Sixth Circuit had upheld O'Meara's ruling that the fake emails sent to Gizinski by someone impersonating Chen had not "directly" caused the fraud, and were instead merely incidental to it, such a ruling would have been entirely consistent with other courts' decisions. Instead, just two months after the Eleventh Circuit issued its opinion for *Interactive Communications*, the Sixth Circuit reversed O'Meara's decision in a ruling filed on July 13, 2018, that found that American Tooling had in fact been the victim of computer fraud. The Sixth Circuit did cite the

Pestmaster decision, but rather than focusing on the section of the decision about the risk of converting computer crime policies into general fraud policies through overbroad definitions of computer fraud, the Sixth Circuit instead highlighted the immediately following clause in the *Pestmaster* ruling, which acknowledged that "Travelers could have drafted this language more narrowly," returning to the principal that ambiguities in insurance policies must be interpreted against the insurer.[19]

The Sixth Circuit disagreed with the idea that, absent that narrower definition being spelled out in the insurance policy itself, computer fraud should be restricted to instances of unauthorized hacking of computer systems. The court explained in its *American Tooling* decision, "Travelers' attempt to limit the definition of 'Computer Fraud' to hacking and similar behaviors in which a nefarious party somehow gains access to and/or controls the insured's computer is not well-founded. If Travelers had wished to limit the definition of computer fraud to such criminal behavior it could have done so."[20] The fraudulent emails sent to American Tooling from a spoofed address were enough to render the incident a case of computer fraud, the Sixth Circuit decided, because those "emails fraudulently caused ATC to transfer the money to the impersonator."[21]

As for whether the spoofed emails *directly* caused American Tooling to transfer the money, the Sixth Circuit adopted the approach of the Eleventh Circuit in the *Interactive Communications* case, sketching out a series of steps to the fraud. But the Sixth Circuit identified only two such steps "when framed at the same level of generality as the Eleventh Circuit used." The Sixth Circuit explained:

> ATC received the fraudulent email at step one. ATC employees then conducted a series of internal actions, all induced by the fraudulent email, which led to the transfer of the money to the impersonator at step two. This was "the point of no return," because the loss occurred once ATC transferred the money in response to the fraudulent emails. Thus, the computer fraud "directly caused" ATC's "direct loss."

It is an astonishing twisting of the Eleventh Circuit's logic—it conflates the steps in which American Tooling employees "conducted a series of internal actions" (i.e., checking that the work for which they were being invoiced had been completed, entering the new bank account information into their systems, submitting the transfer, approving the transfer), as well as the electronic transfer itself, into a single step so that the fake emails can be presented as the direct cause of the fraudulent transfer.

The Sixth Circuit went to great lengths to explain how its ruling was consistent with those issued by the Ninth and Eleventh Circuits, arguing that the spoofed emails distinguished *American Tooling* from *Pestmaster* and that there were fewer intermediate steps between the computer action and the subsequent fraud in *American Tooling* than in *Interactive Communications*. But what was really different about *American Tooling* was the Sixth Circuit's willingness to go after the ambiguity of the language in the Travelers policy defining computer fraud. *American Tooling* complicated the growing consensus around what computer fraud meant in the context of insurance policies, but it also made clear that the burden of appropriately scoping those definitions fell to insurers. That shifting of responsibility was in line with the principle that any ambiguity in the terms of an insurance policy should be interpreted in favor of the policyholders. In some ways, what is most surprising about *American Tooling* is not that the court departed from the decisions of so many other courts but rather that it had taken until 2018 for a circuit court to place the onus on insurers to narrowly define computer fraud in their policies. That so many courts had previously given the benefit of the doubt to insurers when it came to interpreting computer fraud policies suggests how concerned judges had been about the scale of computer fraud claims that might result from broader interpretations. But it also speaks to the inability—or unwillingness—of both courts and insurers to think through more specific, narrow definitions and descriptions of the different roles computers could play in financial fraud and what it meant for them to play a "direct" role.

"ARMED WITH A COMPUTER CODE": *MEDIDATA SOLUTIONS V. FEDERAL INSURANCE COMPANY*

In July 2018, the same month that the Sixth Circuit issued its ruling in *American Tooling*, the Second Circuit decided a very similar case between a company called Medidata Solutions and its insurer, Federal Insurance Company. In September 2014, Medidata had made a $4,770,226 transfer to someone claiming to be an attorney named Michael Meyer, after a series of forged emails that appeared to come from Medidata's president had authorized the transfer. Federal Insurance denied Medidata's claim under its computer fraud policy, but a New York court ruled in July 2017 that Medidata's losses were covered by the policy because the spoofed emails constituted an act of hacking. Federal Insurance had argued "that the emails did not directly cause Medidata's loss, because no loss would have taken place if Medidata employees had not acted on the instructions contained in those emails." They had also tried to persuade the court that spoofed emails did not fall under the definition of computer fraud in Medidata's policy, which specified that such an incident must involve the "direct loss" of money resulting from "the fraudulent: (a) entry of Data into or deletion of Data from a Computer System or (b) change to Data elements or program logic of a Computer System, which is kept in machine readable format."[22] Here was yet another variation on the definition of computer fraud, using different policy language that was less predicated on how directly a computer caused the fraud and more focused on how exactly the computer and the data stored on it were being manipulated.

The New York district judge who ruled on the case, Andrew L. Carter Jr., considered an email with a spoofed "from" address to be a kind of hacking because that email "accessed" Medidata's email system by landing in an employee's inbox. "The fraud on Medidata was achieved by entry into Medidata's email system with spoofed emails armed with a computer code that masked the thief's true identity," Carter wrote in his ruling. He referenced the Medidata insurance policy's language about "entering" and "changing" data, adding that "the thief's computer code also changed data from the true email address to Medidata's president's address to achieve the email spoof."[23] Carter's language, particularly his reference to "spoofed emails armed with computer code"—a phrase he used twice in the ruling—hints at just how important judges' technical understandings of computers and the Internet were to their decisions about what was and was not computer fraud.

Going by the definition of computer violations in Medidata's insurance policy, the fake email would have involved the "entry of data into . . . a computer system"—but so does everything done using a computer. It's a very broad definition, in some sense, for an insurer to be relying on to delimit computer fraud. Carter's lengthy description of how email works made the process of spoofing a from address sound considerably more complicated than it actually was. Carter explained:

The thief constructed messages in Internet Message Format ("IMF") which the parties compare to a physical letter containing a return address. The IMF message was transmitted to Gmail in an electronic envelope called a Simple Mail Transfer Protocol ("SMTP"). Much like a physical envelope, the SMTP Envelope contained a recipient and a return address. To mask the true origin of the spoofed emails, the thief embedded a computer code. The computer code caused the SMTP Envelope and the IMF Letter to display different email addresses in the "From" field. The spoofed emails showed the thief's true email address in the SMTP "From" field, and Medidata's president's email address in the IMF "From" field. When Gmail received the spoof emails, the system compared the address in the IMF "From" field with a list of contacts and populated Medidata's president's name and picture. The recipients of the Gmail messages only saw the information in the IMF "From" field.[24]

As for the idea that the intervening steps of Medidata employees authorizing the transfer, after they received the forged emails, would disqualify the incident from being directly caused by computers, Carter rejected that as well. "Medidata employees only initiated the transfer as a direct cause of the thief sending spoof emails posing as Medidata's president," he wrote. Here, the particular language in Medidata policy was especially relevant since it did not emphasize the directness of a computer's link to fraudulent activity to the same extent as the American Tooling or Pestmaster policies, requiring only that the policyholder suffer a "direct loss . . . resulting from computer fraud" rather than a loss "directly related" to the use of a computer.

The next year, just days before the Sixth Circuit's decision reversing the lower court's *American Tooling* ruling, the Second Circuit affirmed Carter's opinion that the Medidata email scam was covered by its computer fraud policy with Federal Insurance. "The chain of events was initiated by the spoofed emails, and unfolded rapidly following their receipt," the Second Circuit wrote, dismissing Federal Insurance's appeal that the emails themselves did not cause the fraudulent transfer. "While it is true that the Medidata employees themselves had to take action to effectuate the transfer, we do not see their actions as sufficient to sever the causal relationship between the spoofing attack and the losses incurred," the ruling continued. Like Carter, the Second Circuit viewed email spoofing as sufficient to render the incident an act of computer fraud, writing that "the attack represented a fraudulent entry of data into the computer system, as the spoofing code was introduced into the email system."[25]

At the heart of these disputes between insurers and their customers over what constitutes computer fraud is the question of how directly linked to a computer the actual act of fraud must be. Part of what makes these definitional issues about computer fraud and unauthorized access to computers difficult to resolve is the variety of different ways that computers feature in everyday life—and crime—as well as the large spectrum of technical skills and manipulations required to use and exploit them. The ubiquity of computers in business settings makes it easy to understand the Ninth Circuit's concern in *Pestmaster* that a broad interpretation of the meaning of computer fraud might allow companies to transform these into "general fraud" policies. These concerns have been exacerbated by how confused and, in many cases, nonspecific policy language defining computer fraud has been, contributing to continuing legal disputes and uncertainty for both insurers and their customers about what those policies actually cover.

OVERLAPPING COVERAGE AND *NATIONAL BANK OF BLACKSBURG V. EVEREST*

On Saturday, May 28, 2016, hundreds of ATMs across North America began dispensing cash from National Bank of Blacksburg accounts without the account owners' knowledge or authorization. The unauthorized withdrawals continued through the weekend, ending early in the morning of Monday, May 30. All told, the fraudulent disbursements, including related fees, amounted to $569,648.24. National Bank couldn't figure out what had happened—how someone had gotten access to so many of its customers' accounts or why all of its automatic safeguards, such as daily withdrawal limits to prevent individuals from taking out large sums of cash at once and blocks on withdrawals for overdrawn accounts, had been overridden.

National Bank hired digital forensics and security firm Foregenix to investigate the theft. Foregenix determined that the incident had likely originated with a phishing email sent to National Bank employees, which enabled the criminals to install malware onto a computer within National Bank's network. From that initial toehold in National Bank's system, the attackers were then able to access and install malware on another machine, Foregenix believed, and that second server had access to the STAR Network, a debit payment network that National Bank used to provide "bank card processing services" to its customers so that they could use their bank cards at ATMs and retailers. Certain National Bank employees were able to access the STAR Network through a web portal that allowed them to change several parameters and security settings for their customers' accounts. For instance, it was possible for National Bank to block or activate customer accounts as well as to "remove or alter anti-theft and antifraud protections such as 4-digit personal identification numbers (PINs), daily withdrawal limits, daily debit card usage limits, and fraud score protections" through their access to the STAR Network.[26] By stealing credentials for the National Bank employees who had administrator-level access to the STAR Network, the perpetrators of the 2016 breach were then able to "actively monitor customer accounts and remove or modify numerous security measures on accounts belonging to National Bank customers." So, during the last weekend of May 2016, when the theft occurred, the perpetrators had been able to continue dispensing funds past the standard limits by logging into the STAR Network and removing blocks on overdrawn accounts and returning customer accounts to active status even after they had been maxed out, Foregenix reported to National Bank. But how exactly the criminals had managed to initiate so many withdrawals across the continent or collect the cash they stole without attracting attention remained a mystery. Even following the investigation by Foregenix, National Bank concluded that "the exact mechanics of this criminal enterprise are still not fully known."[27]

Then, in January 2017, National Bank suffered another, nearly identical intrusion, likely perpetrated by the same group in Russia that had been accused of breaching their systems in 2016. National Bank hired Verizon to investigate this second incident. Verizon determined that the 2017 breach, like the 2016 one, had begun with a phishing email sent to National Bank employees. This time, the phishing email that initiated the theft included an attached Word document that contained malware, in the form of a macro, which the intruders used to steal more employee credentials. As in 2016, the intruders were able to leverage this malware to gain access to other computers at National Bank, including one that had access to the STAR Network as well as to the bank's Navigator software, which was used to manage customer banking transactions. With their access to Navigator, the perpetrators were able to fraudulently credit $2,070,000 to National Bank customer accounts. Then, returning to their previous pattern, at the beginning of the first full weekend in January 2017, the intruders used their access to the STAR Network to disburse funds from these accounts to hundreds of

ATMs beginning on Saturday, January 7, 2017, and continuing through the morning of Monday, January 9, 2017, when National Bank was alerted to the withdrawals. This time, the fraudulent disbursements and related fees totaled $1,833,984.58—thanks to the fraudulent deposits of more than $2 million, the perpetrators had managed to significantly increase how much money they were able to withdraw from the targeted accounts.

On July 27, 2017, National Bank filed a claim with Everest National Insurance Co. for the 2016 and 2017 incidents, which had cost the bank $2.4 million, under its Computer and Electronic (C&E) Crime Rider. National Bank's C&E Crime Rider, which had a single loss limit of liability totaling $8 million and a $125,000 deductible, covered losses "resulting directly from an unauthorized party (other than an Employee) acting alone or in collusion with others, entering or changing Electronic Data or Computer Programs within any Computer System . . . operated by the Insured . . . provided that the entry or change causes: (1) property to be transferred, paid or delivered, (2) an account of the Insured, or of its customer, to be added, deleted, debited or credited, or (3) an unauthorized account or a fictitious account to be debited or credited." The May 2016 theft, as described by National Bank in its complaint, certainly seemed to fit these criteria—it did involve changing electronic data in such a way as to cause money to be paid from National Bank accounts. On June 13, 2018, almost a year after National Bank filed its claim, Everest denied coverage for both incidents under the C&E Crime Rider. Instead, Everest said, the losses associated with the two incidents were covered exclusively under the Debit Card Rider in National Bank's policy, which had a single loss limit of liability totaling $50,000 and a $25,000 deductible. The Debit Card Rider covered losses "resulting directly from Debit Transactions, or automated mechanical device transactions, due to the fraudulent use of a lost, stolen or altered Debit Card or Counterfeit Debit Card used to access a cardholder's deposit account through an electronic payment device or automated mechanical device."

In its coverage determination, Everest raised two exclusions in National Bank's policy that they argued made clear there was no coverage for the incidents other than that provided by the Debit Card Rider. The first relevant exclusion, Exclusion K, excluded coverage for losses "resulting directly or indirectly from the use or purported use, of credit, debit, charge, access, convenience, or other cards . . . (1) in obtaining credit or funds, or (2) in gaining access to automated mechanical devices which, on behalf of the Insured, disburse Money, accept deposits, cash checks, drafts or similar Written instruments or make credit card loans." The second exclusion Everest cited, Exclusion L, excluded coverage for losses "involving automated mechanical devices which, on behalf of the Insured, disburse Money, accept deposits, cash checks, drafts or similar Written instruments or make credit card loans." The lack of clarity around the specific circumstances of the theft made it difficult to parse exactly how relevant these exclusions were to the 2016 and 2017 incidents. It did not appear from Foregenix's account of what happened that there was necessarily any use of "credit, debit, charge, access, convenience, or other cards," as required for Exclusion K to apply, though clearly there were automated mechanical devices—ATMs—involved in disbursing money on behalf of National Bank.

National Bank sued Everest, and it seemed, at first, like exactly the kind of incident that would fit even the narrowest definition of computer fraud. When Judge Berrigan had dismissed MHSFI's claim that its losses in the Madoff Ponzi scheme were the consequence of computer fraud, she had pointed out, "At no point did the transferors open their online statements and learn in shock that transfers had occurred without their knowledge." But in the case of the National Bank scam, people actually had opened their online statements and learned in shock that withdrawals had occurred without their knowledge. The lawsuit was complicated, however, by the differences in the relevant policy language and the fact that neither party seemed to be entirely certain exactly how the theft was perpetrated. In their complaint, National Bank described the incident as follows:

> The hacking allowed unidentified criminal actors, through coordinated unauthorized intrusions into National Bank's computer systems and network, to change customer account balances, monitor network communications, remove critical security measures such as anti-theft and anti-fraud protections, conduct keystroke tracking, and otherwise enter or change electronic data and computer programs on National Bank's computer systems, which allowed them to illegally withdraw funds from the accounts of National Bank customers, post fake deposits, and remove illegal transactions from customer accounts. . . . Critical to this Court's analysis of National Bank's claims, none of the losses arise from a National Bank customer's debit card being stolen, or from their debit card information being stolen directly from a National Bank customer's possession without their knowledge or permission (e.g. use of a "skimmer" or of a counterfeit or fraudulently obtained debit card).

The relatively vague description of what actually happened offered by National Bank—"unauthorized intrusions" that enabled the perpetrator to "change customer account balances" and "enter or change electronic data and computer programs"—suggested that the bank was not entirely clear how the stolen credentials were used to steal $2.4 million. This is not unusual in the aftermath of cybersecurity incidents. Depending on how carefully companies log changes in their networks and computer systems, how long those logs are stored, and how quickly a breach is noticed, it may not always be possible for them to completely reconstruct every step of an intrusion and how it happened. In the case of National Bank, however, this uncertainty about the mechanics of the breach also contributed to the controversy over which of the two riders in its crime coverage was most directly applicable to the incident in question.

The two riders appeared to cover distinct threats—stolen, lost, or counterfeit debit cards, on the one hand, and malicious manipulation of the bank's computer systems, on the other—but, in fact, there was considerable potential for overlap between the two as the National Bank incidents demonstrated. Even if fraudulent or stolen debit cards were used to make the withdrawals, and it is not clear that they were, it was quite possible— probable, even—that the information for manufacturing those cards came from the perpetrators' access to the bank's computer network. And certainly, the perpetrators' ability to withdraw large sums of money from those accounts using ATMs was directly caused by the fraudulent deposits that the intruders had made using their remote access to the computer network. Conceivably, both riders could have been applicable to the National Bank incidents, assuming it was possible to show that stolen or fraudulent debit cards played some role in the theft. However, only the Debit Card Rider— and not the C&E Crime Rider—referenced coverage of losses that involved an "automated mechanical device," such as an ATM. That appeared to be Everest's rationale for determining that the Debit Card Rider was the sole relevant coverage for National Bank's claim since ATMs, unlike debit cards, were indisputably involved in the theft.

On January 23, 2019, National Bank and Everest settled their case at a closed meeting overseen by a magistrate judge.[28] The terms of the settlement were confidential and therefore offered little insight into a central challenge of cybercrime-related claims that the case had raised, namely that many cybersecurity incidents fall under multiple types of coverage because computers and cyber risk can be tied to so many different types of losses. In the case of National Bank, Everest was able to use these overlapping policies against its customer to try to significantly reduce how much the bank would be reimbursed under its policy by classifying the incident—which combined elements of computer crime and debit card fraud—solely under the portion of National Bank's insurance with the lowest coverage. The confusion around cybercrime coverage arose not just from disagreements over how computer fraud should be defined, but also, in part, from situations like the one National Bank found itself in where an incident of computer fraud overlapped with other potential kinds of fraud and therefore with other coverage.

Computer fraud, and cybercrime more generally, has proven a challenging category of risks for insurers to define clearly, both because there is a wide variety of mechanisms for executing fraud through computers, and these mechanisms are constantly changing, and because cybercrimes often overlap with other types of theft. Adding to these challenges, the victims of cybercrimes aren't always able to retrace every detail of how these crimes were committed, making it even more difficult to know how exactly computers were involved. Many of the policies governing computer fraud have relied on language about fraud resulting "directly" from the use of computers but the variations on that language, and the different interpretations of it by different courts, suggest a need for much greater specificity and clarity in defining what types of crime carriers view as resulting directly from computers and how cybercrimes that overlap with other types of fraud are covered. Policyholders—and insurers—would benefit from more standardization of the language used to define computer fraud in these policies and perhaps even from breaking down computer fraud into several different, more specific types of cybercrime instead of trying to find language broad enough to encompass the diversity of computer uses and crimes but still narrow enough so as not to include every crime involving a computer in any way.

"INSURRECTION, REBELLION, REVOLUTION, RIOT": NOTPETYA, PROPERTY INSURANCE, AND WAR EXCLUSIONS

In June 2017, the multinational food company Mondelez International was hit by the NotPetya virus. NotPetya exploited a vulnerability in the Microsoft Windows operating system to encrypt the contents of infected computers' hard drives and demanded a ransom payment of roughly $300 worth of Bitcoin before it would turn the contents of the computers back over to their owners. NotPetya infiltrated more than eighty companies worldwide during the summer of 2017, including Mondelez, which had to shut down 1,700 servers and 24,000 laptops due to NotPetya infections. In the aftermath of the incident, Mondelez filed a claim with its insurer, Zurich American Insurance, under its global property insurance policy which covered "physical loss or damage to electronic data, programs or software, including physical loss or damage caused by the malicious introduction of a machine code or instruction." Zurich initially agreed to pay out $10 million to Mondelez to cover its losses but then changed its mind and refused to cover any of the costs on the grounds that NotPetya was a "hostile or warlike action" perpetrated by a "government or sovereign power," and thereby excluded from coverage. Mondelez filed a $100 million lawsuit against Zurich in October 2018 and the case (unresolved at the time of writing) serves as a reminder of how cyber risks—and, by extension, the types of costs that companies look to their insurers to help cover—have changed since the early days of data breach liability insurance policies.[1]

Early cyberinsurance policies focused on coverage for breaches of personal data, both because those were the incidents about which insurers had the most information, thanks to breach notification laws, and because they were the incidents that businesses—especially retailers—were primarily concerned would cost them money, again because of the mandatory notification in most states. However, as the landscape of online threats broadened, businesses in all sectors began to face a new set of costly and serious risks, ranging from ransomware to cloud service outages to economic espionage.

As the threat environment continued to evolve, businesses also began real-izing the limitations of their existing CGL and commercial crime insurance policies and began clamoring for more coverage of threats beyond straight-forward data breaches. Since 2015, a whole host of specialized cyberinsurance offerings have emerged to meet this demand, from personal cyberinsurance for high-net-worth individuals to online extortion insurance, coverage for business interruptions due to third-party vendor outages, and even policies that cover renting temporary equipment and services to withstand denial-of-service attacks. Embedded in these new, specialized cyberinsurance poli-cies, however, is a set of fairly boilerplate exceptions, many of which are drawn from other areas of insurance, including CGL and property insur-ance. While these exceptions may be more routine or immediately under-standable when applied to other types of risk, they often present unique problems and complications when it comes to dealing with cyber risks, both because of the nature of these risks and the patchwork nature of cyberinsur-ance coverage.

The "warlike action" exclusion in Mondelez's property coverage raises difficult questions about what constitutes war (or "warlike" activity) in the online domain. Since the lines distinguishing online espionage, sabotage, and warlike attacks are often blurrier online than in the physical domain, classifying an incident like NotPetya as "warlike" is far from straightfor-ward. While war is typically not a regular occurrence or routine concern for insurance holders, cyberattacks perpetrated by nation-states are no lon-ger uncommon and excluding them from coverage could place a significant burden on policyholders. Moreover, the lengthy and sometimes conten-tious process of determining who is behind a cyberattack and whether it can be definitively attributed to a nation-state adds to the challenges of interpreting this exception and applying it to online threats.

PROPERTY INSURANCE AND OPEN-PERIL COVERAGE

Modern property insurance coverage derives from two of the oldest forms of insurance, maritime and fire insurance. Forms of insurance for both marine expeditions as well as fire damage date back centuries and William Reynolds Vance describes the emergence of both in his 1904 *Handbook of the Law of Insurance*, tracing the start of early mutual insurance contracts for ships and their cargo back to the early thirteenth century in the maritime states of Italy. According to Vance, Italian merchants introduced the practice in England and prominent British insurer Lloyd's got its start in these contracts arranged among maritime merchants in the late seventeenth century. Edward Lloyd owned a London establishment called Lloyd's Coffee House where merchants would gather and arrange their insurance contracts, with individuals who wanted to insure particular voyages writing their names or initials beneath descriptions of the expedition written on slips of paper. It was through this process that insurers came to be known as "underwriters."[2]

The seventeenth century also witnessed the beginning of the business of fire insurance, according to Vance, who cites the Great Fire of London of 1666 as the motivation for many British insurance brokers to begin issuing fire coverage, followed closely by the establishment of the first fire insurance company, Sun Fire Office, in 1710.[3] Insurance policies covering fire damage were less well received in England than those for maritime expeditions because of a concern that fire insurance would cause more incidents of arson. Indeed, this appeared to be the case for a period during the mid-nineteenth century when fire insurance grew rapidly in popularity, accompanied by a significant increase in the overall number of fires, the number of fires per household and per capita, and the percentage of fires in England determined to be "of suspicious origin," which rose from 34.5 percent of fires in 1852 to 52.5 percent of fires in 1866.[4] In the United States, however, fire insurance met with much greater success following the formation in 1752 of the first US fire insurance company, the Philadelphia Contributionship for Insuring Houses from Loss by Fire, for which Benjamin Franklin served as one of the directors.[5]

While both early marine and fire insurance policies dealt with protections for loss of or damage to property, they developed according to very different models. John Gorman points out that "in the early days of insurance, the greatest single hazard to property on land was fire, whereas the hazards to property being transported by sea were inexhaustibly many."[6] Therefore, fire insurance was tied to a particular type of risk—fire damage—whereas marine insurance was typically written or designed to cover "all the perils of the sea." The latter model is sometimes referred to as "all risks" or "open peril" coverage, as opposed to "specified peril" or "named peril" insurance, such as fire policies, that specify precisely what type of risk they cover. The distinction is an important one for cyberinsurance coverage because of how difficult it can be to pin down specific cyber risks for this type of coverage—even a relatively straightforward risk like "computer fraud" is open to a variety of different interpretations and variations—and how wary many insurers are of taking an all risks approach to covering such a complicated and constantly changing set of threats. The development of modern property insurance in the twentieth century centered largely on the development of all risk or open peril commercial and homeowner policies that appealed to insurance customers because they offered broad coverage against direct losses to their property.[7]

Open peril property insurance grants policyholders protections for all "direct physical loss to property" except for certain types of losses that are specifically excluded. As Kenneth Abraham points out, "this approach places great pressure on the exclusions and limitations to coverage. If a particular form of direct physical loss to property is not excluded, it is covered."[8] This is also the case with CGL policies, but the exclusions in CGL insurance and property insurance policies follow two converse principles. Abraham explains, "In property insurance there is no coverage unless the peril causing damage comes from the outside-in, so to speak. In contrast, in CGL insurance there is no coverage unless the damage for which the insured is held liable comes from the inside-out."[9] This distinction helps explain why Sony was denied coverage for its 2011 data breach under a CGL policy—the damage came from outside the company, hence Justice Oing's insistence that what really mattered was that outside hackers had perpetrated the breach, not whether Sony had been negligent. It also hints at the reasons why property insurance might be a more attractive tool than CGL for policyholders seeking coverage for cyber-related damages perpetrated by outside attackers. Property insurance wouldn't help with coverage of third-party liability costs, of course, but especially as computer systems become increasingly connected to various forms of physical property, the first-party costs of cyberattacks were becoming increasingly significant, especially since first-party insurance could include coverage for notification costs and business interruption, which were significant components of many cybersecurity incidents.

Even before the growth in cyber-physical systems, some insurance customers were already looking to their property insurance to cover certain types of computer-related costs. In the late 1990s, many large companies were scrambling to update their computer systems in order to avoid any Y2K-related failures when the two-digit year field for the date reset to "00" on January 1, 2000. For the most part, these efforts were successful at preventing significant damage or interruptions but the maintenance and updating work required was extensive and expensive. Several organizations later filed claims to recoup portions of those costs under their property insurance "sue and labor" provisions. Sue and labor clauses typically provide coverage to policyholders who take steps to prevent imminent losses or damages that, had they occurred, would have been covered by those same property insurance policies.[10] Many of those Y2K claims were denied, prompting a series of lawsuits in 2000 brought by companies including Kmart, The Gap, Mandalay Resort Group, and Nike.[11]

These suits were largely unsuccessful; several courts ruled that the losses these companies had averted by updating their computer systems would not have been covered under their property insurance policies in the first place, and therefore the sue and labor provisions did not apply to the mitigation costs. For instance, in a 2004 ruling, the Third Circuit Court of Appeals found that telecommunications firm GTE could not claim coverage for remediating its computers systems to address Y2K glitches. GTE's property insurance through Allendale Mutual Insurance Co. included a standard sue and labor clause that covered situations where the policyholder faced "actual or imminent loss or damage" to their property from a risk that the policy covered. Under those circumstances, GTE would be permitted to "sue, labor, and travel for, in, and about the defense, the safeguard, and the recovery of the property" and Allendale would "contribute to the expenses so incurred according to the rate and quantity of the sum herein insured."[12] In other words, if GTE could show that the damage that would have resulted from not fixing the Y2K problem would have been covered under their property insurance then they might also be able to use that policy to cover the costs of preemptively mitigating that damage.

Although the Y2K glitch would have been unlikely to cause significant physical property damage, GTE's decision to file a claim with its property insurer stemmed from a common provision in its policy that included coverage for "loss resulting from necessary interruption of business conducted by the Insured and caused by loss, damage, or destruction by any of the perils covered herein." Those perils included not just physical losses but also "any destruction, distortion or corruption of any computer data, coding, program or software except as hereinafter excluded."[13] This type of property insurance coverage for business interruption losses would be especially important for later cases, including the Mondelez one, in which cybersecurity incidents like ransomware or denial-of-service attacks prevented businesses from conducting their normal operations, even if they did not result in any outright theft or physical damage.

GTE's policy, like all open peril insurance, also included several exclusions. The Third Circuit ultimately ruled that two of those barred the potential Y2K damages from being covered under the policy and thereby barred the mitigation work from being covered under the sue and labor clause as well. The two exclusions in GTE's property insurance that the Third Circuit focused on were the defective design and inherent vice exclusions. The former precludes coverage for "the cost of making good defective design or specifications" and the Third Circuit, agreeing with a previous district court ruling, determined that the Y2K problem was one of defective design and therefore excluded from coverage under the property policy. "The essence of the Y2K problem is that the two-digit date design precludes the system from functioning properly on or after January 1, 2000. The problem in this case was not that a program or system malfunctioned, or some external threat caused damage to GTE's systems," the court ruled. "Rather, the system performed in exactly the manner it was designed to operate—the problem is that the system as designed and specified did not permit recognition of dates in the 21st century."[14]

Additionally, the Third Circuit found that even if the Y2K bug had not been a matter of defective design, any damage it caused would still have been excluded from coverage under GTE's property insurance because of the "inherent vice" exclusion which applied to "any existing defects, diseases, decay or the inherent nature of the commodity which will cause it to deteriorate with a lapse of time." The Third Circuit cited another Y2K property insurance lawsuit, brought by the Port of Seattle against its insurer, Lexington Insurance Co., and decided two years earlier in 2002, also in favor of the insurers. In that case, Judge Susan R. Agid of the Court of Appeals of Washington had determined that "but for the two-digit date field code programmed into the Port's software, the arrival of January 1, 2000, would not result in loss. Thus, the Port's Y2K problem is an excluded inherent vice because the date field is an internal quality that brought about its own problem."[15] The Third Circuit agreed and similarly disqualified GTE's claim that Y2K-related damages would have been covered under their property insurance policy.

The Y2K cases also coincided with the insurance industry beginning to craft specific exclusions aimed at cyber losses, perhaps in part because of the attention Y2K had brought to the potential for digital problems to cause significant losses. In 2001, Lloyd's Underwriters' Non-Marine Association (NMA) developed two exclusions, Electronic Data Endorsements A and B (also referred to as NMA 2914 and NMA 2915), that excluded coverage for the "loss, damage, destruction, distortion, erasure, corruption or alteration of electronic data," though they did allow for coverage of fires or explosions caused by computer malfunctions.[16] Those exclusions were widely adopted by property insurers in the early 2000s, spurred in part by rumors that reinsurers were planning to include NMA 2914 or 2915 in their reinsurance policies beginning in 2002.[17] Then, in 2003, the insurance industry developed the Institute Cyber Attack Exclusion Clause, also known as CL380, which excluded losses "arising from the use or operation, as a means for inflicting harm, of any computer, computer system, computer code, computer virus or process or any other electronic system." The CL380 coverage exemption clauses also became popular with property insurers, enabling them to deny coverage for malicious cybersecurity incidents.[18] The development and adoption of these early cyber-focused exclusions in property insurance policies spoke to carriers' heightened awareness about cyber risk in the aftermath of Y2K and the resulting claims disputes—despite the fact that insurers were triumphant in most of those disputes because courts generally held that policyholders had created the Y2K software problems themselves, internally.

Ten years later, when Justice Oing ruled in the Sony data breach case, he would disqualify Sony's claims under its CGL policy for exactly the opposite reason: the breach had been caused by external factors, rather than by Sony bringing about its own problem. This reflects Abraham's point about the converse nature of property and CGL insurance exclusions such that the former covers only damage that "comes from the outside-in" and the latter only applies to liability resulting from damage that "comes from the inside-out." In the case of NotPetya, however, the damage to Mondelez, and many other firms, clearly originated from the outside—later reports attributed the malware to the Russian government, but even before victims understood who was behind the incidents, there was no question that some outside third party had initiated the widespread ransomware attacks. So Zurich could not rely on the defective design or inherent vice exclusions wielded by insurers to such great effect following Y2K. Instead, to avoid covering the most expensive cyberattack in history, Zurich would have to look to one of the many other exclusions in the Mondelez property policy.

"WAR IN THE ONLY SENSE THAT MEN KNOW AND UNDERSTAND IT": WAR EXCLUSIONS AND PEARL HARBOR

The exclusion Zurich pointed to in Mondelez's property insurance covered losses or damage directly or indirectly caused by "hostile or warlike action in time of peace or war." The practice of excluding war risks from open peril insurance policies dated back more than one hundred years before NotPetya. Originally, in the eighteenth and nineteenth centuries, maritime insurance policies had included coverage for losses at sea caused by wars—an issue of particular concern to ship owners since wars often affected marine voyages. However, in 1898, Lloyd's added a "free of capture and seizure" (FC&S) clause to its general marine cargo clause that excluded coverage for any losses caused by war. As FC&S clauses became standard practice, some insurers, including Lloyd's, also started offering coverage specifically for war risks, but the scale and unpredictability of losses caused by wars made it difficult for insurers to reliably model such policies or be certain they could cover the resulting claims. In particular, the potential for wars to result in highly correlated risks posed significant challenges to insurers and continues to make these risks difficult for insurers to model and cover today. Accordingly, in 1913, a committee established by the British government determined that private insurers could not meet the demand for war insurance and the government subsequently agreed to reinsure 80 percent of the war risks insurers underwrote. Similarly, in the United States, Congress passed the War Risk Insurance Act in 1914, establishing the Bureau of War Risk Insurance in the Treasury Department to provide war risk coverage for marine commerce. Thus, by the early twentieth century, war risks were already being excluded from standard forms of all-risk insurance and were understood to be uninsurable by the private market without support from policymakers.

War exclusions evolved from their roots in marine insurance to become a common feature of other types of coverage, including property insurance and life insurance. Following the attack on Pearl Harbor in 1941, a series of lawsuits, mostly brought by the beneficiaries of life insurance policies for people killed during the attack, tested the meaning and limitations of this type of exclusion. In particular, the fact that the attack on the morning of December 7, 1941, occurred one day prior to the United States' declaration of war against Japan, complicated the question of whether Pearl Harbor could be considered an act of war, for insurance purposes. For instance, when Navy seaman Howard A. Rosenau died at Pearl Harbor, his parents, Arthur and Freda Rosenau filed a claim with Idaho Mutual Benefit Association, where their son had purchased a $1,000 life insurance policy prior to his death and named them as beneficiaries. Idaho Mutual denied the claim because Rosenau's policy included an exclusion for "death, disability or other loss sustained while in military, naval, or air service of any country at war."[19]

Because the United States was not yet at war with Japan at the time of the Pearl Harbor attack, an Idaho court ruled in favor of the Rosenaus, ordering Idaho Mutual to pay them the full $1000 due under their son's policy. The insurer appealed this decision to the Idaho Supreme Court, arguing that the United States was already at war when Howard Rosenau died at Pearl Harbor, and his death was therefore excluded from coverage. To support this argument, Idaho Mutual cited the preamble of the resolution that Congress adopted the day after Pearl Harbor, on December 8, 1941, titled "Joint Resolution declaring that a state of war exists between the Imperial Government of Japan and the Government and People of the United States." The preamble of that document stated, "the Imperial Government of Japan has committed unprovoked acts of war." It concluded, "The state of war between the United States and the Imperial Government of Japan, which has been thrust upon the United States is hereby formally declared." These references to the Pearl Harbor attack as an "unprovoked act of war" and a preexisting "state of war" between the United States and Japan that was merely codified, not initiated, by Congress on December 8, meant that the Pearl Harbor attack occurred in a "country at war," Idaho Mutual argued.[20]

Arthur and Freda Rosenau disputed this broad interpretation of war that allowed for a country to be considered at war even prior to a formal declaration by its government. If the court accepted the insurer's interpretation of what it meant to be "at war" then that "would mean that the United States has been constantly at 'war' with Japan since the sinking of the gunboat Panay in China in the early 1930's, and it would mean that Russia and Japan are now at 'war' by virtue of the fact that within recent years there have been border patrol clashes and hostilities in some force along the border between Manchuria and Russian Siberia," the Rosenaus' lawyers wrote in response to Idaho Mutual's appeal. Their point—a particularly poignant one for considerations of online warlike acts—was that a broad interpretation of what it meant to be "at war" could quickly expand to apply to many hostile attacks, not all of which led to actual wars that were declared as such by the nations involved. "The Panay incident was a hostile attack, but it was atoned for. The border clashes between Russian and Japanese territory were unquestionably armed invasions of the other's territory. Yet they were atoned for and 'war' did not ensue," the Rosenaus pointed out. "It was possible, no matter how improbable, that the Pearl Harbor attack could have been atoned for and adjusted without 'war' necessarily ensuing."

The majority ruling of the Idaho Supreme Court was sympathetic to this line of reasoning, citing an international law textbook by John Bassett Moore that emphasized war as a "legal condition" such that "if two nations declare war one against the other, war exists, though no force whatever may as yet have been employed. On the other hand, force may be employed by one nation against another, as in the case of reprisals, and yet no state of war may arise." The court majority was unwilling to deviate from this strict, legal definition of war in interpreting Rosenau's life insurance policy, writing in its 1944 ruling:

> It is true, as pointed out by appellant that the word war, in a broad sense, is used to connote a state or condition of war, warlike activities, fighting with arms between troops, etc., but we are here concerned with the meaning and intent of the word as contained in a formal, legal contract of insurance, a class of contracts which the courts are very frequently called upon to consider and construe, and it seems quite obvious that words and phrases in a contract of this nature, are used and intended to be used in the legal sense.

A ruling in favor of Idaho Mutual would mean interpreting the language in the life insurance policy not "in its accepted legal sense" but, rather, as applying to "cases where conditions of war, or conditions which might lead to war, existed," the Idaho Supreme Court determined. If it did that, the majority opinion pointed out, "the court would . . . be making a new contract for the parties, by adding to the contract phrases, terms and conditions, which it does not contain. This, of course, is not one of the functions of a court."

Two justices on the Idaho Supreme Court dissented, arguing that the Pearl Harbor attack had, for all intents and purposes, been an act of war. "Where the armed forces of two sovereign nations strike blows at each other, as occurred at Pearl Harbor on December 7, 1941, and do so under the direction and authority of their respective governments, it is difficult for me to understand why that is not *war*," Justice James F. Ailshie wrote in his dissent. Ailshie's rationale was based on the idea that Pearl Harbor looked like an act of war—not just to him, but also to "the average citizen, who might apply for and procure a life insurance policy." To him, what determined whether a country was at war was not the legal status of that war but, rather, whether a person witnessing a violent or hostile act would recognize it as such. Broadening the definition of war in this way was essential, Ailshie argued, because, according to him, "Our political history demonstrates that most wars have been commenced and prosecuted without any formal declaration of war; and that war dates from its inception rather than from the time on which some formal declaration to that effect is made."

While the Rosenaus were ultimately successful in forcing their son's insurer to pay out his policy in 1944, other beneficiaries met with more mixed results. In 1942, two years prior to the final ruling in the Rosenau case, for instance, the Supreme Court of Massachusetts had ruled against Marcella Stankus, who was seeking a life insurance payout from New York Life Insurance Company following the death of Anthony Stankus in 1941. Anthony, like Howard Rosenau, was a Navy seaman, second class. Unlike Rosenau, though, he did not die at Pearl Harbor—he died two months earlier, on October 30, 1941, when his ship, the USS *Reuben James* was sunk by a torpedo in the Atlantic Ocean. Like Rosenau, Stankus died in possession of a life insurance policy with a war exclusion. The exclusion in Stankus's policy was worded slightly more broadly than the one in Rosenau's to rule out coverage for death resulting "directly or indirectly from war or any act incident thereto."[21] Marcella Stankus, like Rosenau's parents, argued that since the United States had not declared war on October 30, 1941, at the time of Anthony's death, it could not be considered a death resulting from war.

An early judgment by a lower court had agreed with that argument, holding that the insurer must pay out the full claim to Marcella, but when New York Life Insurance appealed that decision, the Supreme Judicial Court of Massachusetts sided with them, reversing the initial decision. Justice James Joseph Ronan authored the 1942 opinion, writing that "the existence of a war is not dependent upon a formal declaration of war. Wars are being waged today that began without any declaration of war. The attack by the Japanese on Pearl Harbor on December 7, 1941, is the latest illustration."[22] Two years later, in his dissent in the Rosenau case, Ailshie seized on that line as evidence that the attack on Pearl Harbor should also count as an act of war because the Massachusetts court had already deemed it so when deciding *Stankus*. Ultimately, the Massachusetts court reached exactly the opposite conclusion of the Idaho court, deciding "the clause exempting the defendant from liability where death is caused by war is not restricted in its operation to a death that has resulted from a war being prosecuted by the United States."[23] In his dissent, Ailshie alluded to the fact that war was ongoing in Europe well before the United States' official declaration, raising the question of whether an officially declared conflict between some countries would suffice to satisfy the war exclusion, even if the resulting damage occurred in a different country. This line of reasoning would be relevant for NotPetya as well, since the ongoing conflict that the malware was designed for was between Russia and Ukraine, but the damage inflicted by it spread well beyond the borders of those two countries.

The disagreement among courts about the meaning of war continued in the years following the contradictory *Stankus* and *Rosenau* rulings. In 1945, the year after the *Rosenau* decision, the Supreme Court of Hawaii came to a decision similar to that of the Idaho court, ruling in favor of Gladys Ching Pang, who was suing Sun Life Assurance Company of Canada for refusing to pay out the life insurance policy of her husband, Tuck Lee Pang, a Honolulu Fire Department employee who had died at Pearl Harbor. "On December 7, 1941, we not only were maintaining diplomatic relations with Japan but a special Japanese envoy was then in Washington ostensibly for the purpose of patching up the strained relations then existing between his country and ours, and not until December 8, 1941, did the political department of our Government or the Japanese Government do any act of which judicial notice can be taken creating 'a state of war' between the two countries," the Hawaii Supreme Court concluded, ruling that the Pearl Harbor attack did not fall within the war exclusion in Pang's life insurance policy and Sun Life was therefore required to pay his wife.[24]

Then, the following year, in 1946, the Tenth Circuit Court of Appeals came to the opposite conclusion, following the model of the Supreme Court of Massachusetts in the *Stankus* case by reversing a judgment for the beneficiaries of the life insurance policy belonging to Captain Mervyn S. Bennion, a naval officer from Utah who died at Pearl Harbor on the battleship *West*

Virginia. Bennion's life insurance policy, also issued by New York Life Insurance, contained exactly the same exception as Stankus's—word for word—and the Tenth Circuit determined that the exception applied to "any type or kind of war in which the hazard of human life was involved," including Pearl Harbor.[25]

The difference between the outcomes in favor of the insurers in the *Stankus* and *Bennion* cases and the rulings for the insurance beneficiaries in *Rosenau* and *Pang* stems from a fundamental disagreement between the deciding courts about how narrowly and colloquially the language of an insurance policy should be interpreted—particularly, the term "war." The Idaho and Hawaii courts in *Rosenau* and *Pang* were in favor of a very narrow, legalistic interpretation of war. Meanwhile, the Tenth Circuit and Supreme Court of Massachusetts were instead focused on how people commonly understood war and the idea that, to many people, Pearl Harbor would *look* like an act of war, even if war between the United States and Japan had not yet been officially declared at the time of the attack. The Tenth Circuit insisted that "mankind . . . does not stand on ceremony or wait for technical niceties" in its "definitive search" to understand what war is.[26] In a similar vein, the Massachusetts court argued that "the words of an insurance policy . . . must be given their usual and ordinary meaning." That "ordinary meaning," the court held, was determined by "ordinary people" and what they would consider to be war. Ronan explained: "The term 'war' is not limited, restricted or modified by anything appearing in the policy. It refers to no particular type or kind of war, but applies in general to every situation that ordinary people would commonly regard as war."[27] This "ordinary person" test presents significant challenges when applied to emerging notions of cyberwar, where there is little consensus or common understanding of when an online threat crosses the threshold of a warlike act even among experts, much less among ordinary people.

The evidence provided by the Massachusetts court in *Stankus* relies heavily on the historical context of the moment when Stankus died—the hints that the United States was gearing up for military conflict in 1941, if not yet directly engaged in war. Ronan cited a September 11, 1941, address by President Roosevelt in which he declared, "From now on, if German or Italian vessels of war enter the waters the protection of which is necessary for American defense, they do so at their own peril," as well as the passage of the Lend-Lease Act in March 1941 as indicators that the United States was already effectively engaging in war-related activities at the time of Stankus's death. Ronan wrote:

> The President . . . had stated that German or Italian vessels of war entered these waters at their peril. The sinking by German or Italian submarines of ships belonging to a belligerent nation, or of ships of another nation conveying war materials and supplies to a belligerent nation, is the usual result of waging war by one nation against another, and the torpedoing of the Reuben James while convoying vessels engaged in such traffic was an act that arose out of the prosecution of such a war.[28]

It's striking that the president's statements carried so much weight with the Massachusetts court and hints at just how significant the public-facing language and political context of conflicts can be for determining when an event does or does not qualify for an insurance policy's war exception. After all, much stronger statements made by both the president and Congress following Pearl Harbor were quickly dismissed by the Idaho court in the *Rosenau* case, dealing with an incident that occurred much closer to the official declaration of war in the United States. This uncertainty around the weight of public statements about the warlike nature of certain events also has important implications for cybersecurity incidents, particularly since terms like "cyberwar" are thrown around freely for political purposes with relatively little consistency or clarity about what they actually mean.

The very different rulings in the *Stankus* and *Bennion* cases as compared to the *Rosenau* and *Pang* disputes also make clear just how important the specific language of the actual exclusion written into an insurance policy can be. In the *Rosenau* ruling, for instance, the majority justified its decision to diverge from the rationale used to decide the *Stankus* case by stating that the war-related provisions in Stankus's life insurance coverage were "quite different" from those included in Rosenau's policy. Unlike the Stankus and Bennion policies, which excluded deaths that "resulted from war or any act incident thereto," the Rosenau policy specifically excluded injuries "sustained while in military, naval, or air service of any country at war." The Idaho court focused particularly on the phrase "at war," arguing that it "very clearly" meant the exclusion applied only during a time when war had been legally declared. Similarly, they distinguished the *Rosenau* case from an even earlier life insurance dispute brought after Alfred G. Vanderbilt died on May 7, 1915, aboard the RMS *Lusitania*, when it was sunk by a German submarine. In that case—which the beneficiaries of Vanderbilt's life insurance lost against his insurer, Travelers—the war exclusion had ruled out coverage for deaths "resulting, directly or indirectly, wholly or partly, from war or riot." The absence of that crucial reference to a "time of war" differentiated the Vanderbilt policy from the Rosenau policy, the Idaho Supreme Court decided, giving Travelers more leeway to interpret the sinking of the *Lusitania* as an excluded act than Idaho Mutual had to interpret Pearl Harbor as occurring "in time of war."

In other words, the majority in the Rosenau ruling did not hold that Pearl Harbor was any less an act of war than the torpedoing of the *Lusitania* or the USS *Reuben James*, but rather they found that Idaho Mutual had crafted the language of their war exclusion more narrowly to apply only to deaths that occurred "in time of war." Indeed, one of the lessons for insurers following Pearl Harbor, was that they should rewrite their war exclusions more broadly. Sun Life, for instance, changed the wording of its policies after Pearl Harbor. Pang's life insurance policy issued by the company had excluded death "resulting from riot, insurrection, or war," but shortly after Pearl Harbor the company modified that exclusion in new policies, inserting, after the word "war," the words "whether declared or not."[29]

These early war exclusion disputes shaped the language of those exclusions for years to come, pushing insurers to broaden their descriptions of war to include undeclared war or warlike acts. This broadening of the terms of war exclusions was not unique to life insurance, it spread into other insurance products, too, including property insurance. For instance, the policy Mondelez had purchased from Zurich before the NotPetya ransomware attacks excluded property loss and damage "directly or indirectly caused by or resulting from . . . hostile or warlike action in time of peace or war."[30] This language had been deliberately crafted to apply to a much broader swath of circumstances than the narrower war exclusions that had appeared in the life insurance policies belonging to Vanderbilt, Rosenau, Bennion, Stankus, and Pang many decades earlier.

Almost a century before the NotPetya attacks, in June 1920, the Supreme Court of New York ruled in favor of Travelers in the Vanderbilt life insurance dispute. The foundation of that ruling, disqualifying the claim on Vanderbilt's life insurance, was an assumption that any conflict between the governments of two countries constituted war, whether or not it had been officially and legally declared. The New York court cited an even older maritime law case, decided in 1800, in which the US Supreme Court had ruled that "every contention by force between two nations in external matters under authority of their respective governments is not only war, but public war."[31] Going by that logic, the New York Supreme Court determined in the Vanderbilt life insurance case:

> The concessions of the parties that the Lusitania was sunk in accordance with instructions of a sovereign government by the act of a vessel commanded by a commissioned officer of that sovereign government, being then operated by that said officer and its crew, all of whom were part of the naval forces of the said sovereign government, and that war was then being waged by and between Great Britain, the sovereign controlling the Lusitania, and Germany, the sovereign controlling the submarine vessel, control the conclusion which must be reached that the casualty resulted from war and that the consequences of the casualty come within the excepted portions of the policy.[32]

Twenty-six years later, the Tenth Circuit would use a similar rationale in deciding the *Bennion* case and determining that Pearl Harbor was an act of war, asserting that "when one sovereign nation attacks another with premeditated and deliberate intent to wage war against it, and that nation resists the attacks with all the force at its command, we have war in the grim sense of reality. It is war in the only sense that men know and understand it."[33]

This too is a line of reasoning with significant implications for cyberattacks, which are regularly directed by one sovereign government against another. Indeed, it was, in many ways, the crux of Zurich's argument that the NotPetya attacks were not covered under Mondelez's property insurance policy. The ransomware attacks were not violent, they did not look like what an ordinary person might consider to be war, they did not occur at a time when the United States had officially declared war on the perpetrator, but that perpetrator was credibly believed by many to be Russia—a sovereign government. However, most of the victims, including Mondelez, were private entities, so NotPetya was not exactly a "contention by force between two nations." This was yet another way in which cyberattacks complicated traditional interpretations of war and war exclusions—the entanglement of public and private actors under circumstances that insurers and earlier insurance disputes had not anticipated and for which insurers had not devised clear rules.

"A MOST UNUSUAL AND EXPLICIT CONTRACT":
TERRORISM AND OVERLAPPING COVERAGE

Pearl Harbor and the sinking of the *Lusitania* may not have been unambiguous acts of war, but they both certainly came much closer to situations "that ordinary people would commonly regard as war" than NotPetya—a computer virus of ambiguous origin, at the time of its spread, that caused no direct casualties or violence and targeted mostly private companies. A series of more recent insurance disputes dealing with circumstances further removed from war than the *Lusitania* or Pearl Harbor sheds some light on how war exclusions might apply to situations like NotPetya, as well as the role of these exclusions in property insurance policies, like the one Mondelez had purchased from Zurich. These cases reveal how much remains uncertain and unclear in the interpretation of insurance policy war exclusions, particularly when it comes to distinguishing between acts of war and acts of terrorism.

On September 6, 1970, Pan American Flight 093 was hijacked by two passengers, forty-five minutes after the Boeing 747 had departed from Amsterdam, heading to New York. The two hijackers, armed with guns and grenades, ordered the pilot to fly to Beirut, Lebanon, and announced to the passengers and crew that they were working on behalf of the Popular Front for the Liberation of Palestine (PFLP). After the hijackers threatened to blow up the plane in midair, Lebanese officials permitted the flight to land in Beirut on the condition that it refuel and then leave. On the ground in Lebanon, more PFLP members boarded the plane with explosives, and one—a demolition expert—stayed on the plane when it took off again, this time bound for Cairo. Egyptian officials permitted the plane to land after the hijackers lit the fuses of the explosives while the plane was still in the air. The hijackers informed the crew that they would have only eight minutes after the plane landed to evacuate everyone before the plane blew up, and the passengers were all successfully evacuated in Cairo. The explosives detonated on schedule and the plane was destroyed. Pan Am filed a claim with its insurers for the value of the aircraft, totaling $24,288,759.[34]

Pan Am had purchased comprehensive insurance coverage from several different insurers. From Aetna Casualty and Surety Co., as well as other insurers, the airline had purchased all-risk insurance that covered one-third of the value of their fleet in the event of "all physical loss of or damage to the aircraft." Despite its name, that insurance came with a long list of exclusions, including any losses or damage resulting from:

1. capture, seizure, arrest, restraint or detention or the consequences thereof or of any attempt threat, or any taking of the property insured or damage to or destruction thereof by any Government or governmental authority or agent (whether secret or otherwise) or by any military, naval or usurped power, whether any of the foregoing be done by way of requisition or otherwise and whether in time of peace or war and whether lawful or unlawful . . . [hereinafter "clause 1"]
2. war, invasion, civil war, revolution, rebellion, insurrection or warlike operations, whether there be a declaration of war or not [hereinafter "clause 2"];
3. strikes, riots, civil commotion [hereinafter "clause 3"].[35]

In order to ensure they would still be covered in the event of these excluded circumstances, Pan Am also purchased war risk insurance from Lloyd's. That coverage had an upper limit of $14,226,290.47 in coverage and covered the three clauses of excluded risks in the all-risk policy, verbatim. Since American underwriters did not offer war risk coverage, Pan Am obtained the rest of its war risk coverage, beyond what Lloyd's was willing to insure, from the United States government for an additional $9,763,709.53 of coverage that only applied to damage caused by the perils in the first two clauses of the all-risk insurance exclusions. This coverage Pan Am obtained from the Secretary of Commerce who is authorized under the Federal Aviation Act of 1958 to issue insurance for risks that are excluded from commercial policies under "free of capture and seizure" clauses, like the first two clauses in Pan Am's all-risk policies exclusions. Because the US government was authorized only to cover risks excluded under "free of capture and seizure" clauses, this insurance could not apply to the clause 3 exclusions—strikes, riots, and civil commotions—in Pan Am's all-risk insurance. So, in July 1970, just a few months before the hijacking, Pan Am came to an agreement with Aetna and its other all-risk insurers to make an additional premium payment of $29,935 in order to delete the third clause of its exclusion that had previously ruled out coverage for "strikes, riots, [and] civil commotion" and cover damage caused by those risks up to $10,062,393.

At the time of the hijacking, Pan Am therefore had a complicated patchwork of insurance coverage, and the question of which of its many insurers was responsible for covering the damage to the airplane depended on which of the three clauses of the exclusion the hijacking fell under. If the hijacking was deemed to be a clause 1 peril ("capture, seizure . . . or any taking . . . by any military . . . or usurped power") or a clause 2 peril ("war . . . civil war, revolution, rebellion, insurrection or warlike operations"), then Aetna and the other all-risk insurers would be off the hook for it and coverage would be paid by Lloyd's ($14,226,290.47) and the US government ($9,763,709.53), totaling $23,990,000. On the other hand, if the hijacking was deemed to be a clause 3 peril ("riots, civil commotion"), then Pan Am would be owed $10,062,393 from Aetna as well as an additional $14,226,290.47 from Lloyd's, totaling $24,288,683.47. Finally, if the hijacking was determined not to fall into any of the excluded categories of risks described in the three clauses, then Aetna and the other all-risk insurers would be responsible for the entire $24,288,759 claim for the destroyed plane.[36] This arrangement of dividing up different types of large-scale risks into a set of consistent categories that can then each be covered by the appropriate entities, whether private-sector carriers or governments, offers certain lessons for cyberinsurance, as well. If insurers and policymakers were able to agree on what cyberwar was, then it might be possible for each to offer certain types of complimentary coverage that would enable policyholders to be confident that whatever a court determined about the nature of a particular incident, they would still be covered.

Unsurprisingly, all of the insurers claimed that the Pan Am hijacking was a type of risk covered by someone else's policy, leading to an extended legal battle. Aetna and the other all-risk insurers argued in court that the hijacking fell under the clause 1 and 2 exclusions—the ones it had no responsibility to cover—because it was perpetrated by a "military . . . or usurped power" and was an example of "revolution, rebellion, insurrection or warlike operations." Lloyd's and the US government argued that the hijacking did not fall under any of the exception clauses, all of which were covered by their war risk policy, and was therefore entirely the responsibility of the all-risk insurers. Pan Am itself took this position as well, arguing that the hijacking was not an excluded risk, hence their decision to sue Aetna. Pan Am further argued that, if the hijacking was an excluded risk, then it fell under the clause 3 exclusion as a "riot" or "civil commotion." Not coincidentally, these were the two interpretations (that the hijacking was not excluded or that it was an excluded clause 3 peril) that would lead to the largest payouts for the company given the complicated coverage situation.[37]

New York District Judge Marvin Frankel ruled in 1973 that the Pan Am hijacking did not fall under any of the exclusion clauses, in a lengthy decision that discussed the political circumstances surrounding the Middle East and the PFLP at some length. Aetna had argued that "the Arab-Israeli Conflict was the efficient cause of the hijacking operation" and that the hijacking should therefore be considered a war risk. They also noted the hijackers' attempt to use the plane loudspeaker system to read a handwritten note to the passengers explaining that they were hijacking the plane "because the government of America helps Israel daily . . . [and] gives Israel Fantom airoplanes which attack our camps and burn our village." Aetna argued that the "seizure and destruction of the aircraft were announced by the group as a blow and as retaliation against the United States," and concluded that "these facts alone would be sufficient to place the loss under the broadly drawn war risk language." Frankel rejected these arguments for relying on an overbroad definition of war. Aetna's justification for why the hijacking of the Pan Am plane qualified for the war risk exclusion "would apply equally to the bombing of stores in Europe, by children or adults, the killing of Olympic athletes, the killing of an American military attaché in Amman . . . or other individual acts of organization-sponsored violence," Frankel pointed out.[38] Nor did he allow that the larger Arab-Israeli conflict was to blame for the hijacking or could be said to have "proximately caused" the incident.

Several courts ruling on computer fraud insurance cases in later years would focus on the question of whether a computer had directly or immediately caused an act of fraud, determining in many of those cases that the computer-based stages were too far removed from the actual theft for them to be considered acts of computer fraud. Similarly, Frankel felt there was too much distance—both literal and metaphorical—between the conflict in the Middle East and the Pan Am hijacking for the latter to be viewed as an act of war or even a direct consequence of war. "It would take a most unusual and explicit contract to make the self-determined depredations of a terrorist group, thousands of miles from the area of the 'Conflict,' acts of 'war' for insurance purposes," Frankel wrote in his ruling.[39] And Aetna had not, in Frankel's view, authored a sufficiently explicit (or unusual) contract for this purpose. In fact, the judge noted that, as in the case of the Pearl Harbor disputes, Aetna and the other all-risk insurers had changed the language of their exclusion clauses to respond to the hijacking, adopting "new exclusion clauses applying in adequate and unambiguous terms to operations like the PFLP hijackings." In doing so, Frankel noted, they seemed to concede that "the former clauses lacked the clarity necessary to vindicate" their position in the Pan Am case that the previous language already unambiguously applied to hijackings.[40]

In 1974, the Second Circuit Court of Appeals upheld Frankel's ruling, agreeing with him that war "refers to and includes only hostilities carried on by entities that constitute governments at least de facto in character" and that the hijacking could not be considered a "warlike operation" because "that term does not include the inflicting of damage on the civilian property of non-belligerents by political groups far from the site of warfare." The insurers tried to get around the fact that the PFLP was not a government by arguing that it was a "military . . . or usurped power" in Jordan and was therefore still covered under the exceptions listed in clause 1. But the Second Circuit decided that "in order to constitute a military or usurped power the power must be at least that of a de facto government" and the PFLP did not meet that bar in their view. Going clause by clause, the Second Circuit went on to eliminate each possible category of exception that the incident might have fallen under: the hijacking could not be considered a "warlike act" because "the hijackers did not wear insignia. They did not openly carry arms. Their acts had criminal rather than military overtones. They were the agents of a radical political group, rather than a sovereign government." It was not an "insurrection" because "the PFLP did not intend to overthrow King Hussein when it hijacked the Pan American 747." It was not a "civil commotion" because "for there to be a civil commotion, the agents caus-ing the disorder must gather together and cause a disturbance and tumult." It was not a "riot" because "the hijacking was accomplished by only two persons."[41]

If Aetna and Pan Am's other property insurers had intended for their policies to exclude hijackings then they should have used clearer, more spe-cific language, the Second Circuit ruled. In this regard, the court suggested, the history of property insurance and its roots in early marine policies had not served the insurers well. The Second Circuit dismissed the language of the Pan Am policy exclusions as being based on "ancient marine insurance terms," which, in the eyes of the Second Circuit, "simply do not describe a violent and senseless intercontinental hijacking carried out by an isolated band of political terrorists."[42]

"THE SPECIAL MEANING OF WAR": THE LEGACY OF *PAN AM*

The *Pan Am* ruling that terrorist acts were not excluded from property insurance policies under war exclusions was highly influential in later legal disputes about what did or did not constitute an act of war under property insurance policies. In 1974, the same year that the Second Circuit issued its decision in the Pan Am case, a twenty-six-floor Holiday Inn hotel opened in Beirut, Lebanon. In October 1975, conflict broke out in the neighborhood in West Beirut where the hotel was located between the Muslim Nasserist political party, the Mourabitoun, and the Christian right-wing party called the Phalange. As the fighting continued in late 1975, members of the Phalangist militia occupied the Holiday Inn and the conflict caused considerable damage to the building—windows were shot out, fifteen rooms were damaged by fire, and another thirty-five had burned curtains and broken glass, forcing Holiday Inn to close the hotel to guests in November 1975.

On "Black Saturday," December 6, 1975, the fighting in Beirut escalated significantly and the Holiday Inn became a focal point for the combatants. All of the remaining staff were evacuated as the Phalangists claimed the hotel for themselves, and the building changed hands between the two sides several times over the course of the next few months as the fighting continued. George McMurtrie Godley, who was serving as the American ambassador to Lebanon at the time, described the scene around the hotel: "You had . . . Christians occupying Holiday Inn. You had Moslems wanting to take it. Holiday Inn was right, you might say, on the borderline between the predominantly Christian areas and the predominantly Moslem areas. There you had rather well-organized military factions where men were holding an area and other men were attacking it."[43]

Holiday Inn had insured its foreign properties through Aetna under an all-risk policy similar to the one that covered Pan Am's fleet; it provided coverage for "all risks . . . of direct physical loss or damage . . . from any external cause except as hereinafter provided." Unlike Pan Am's policy, the Holiday Inn policy specifically included damage "directly caused by persons taking part in riots or civil commotion or by strikers or locked-out workers or by persons of malicious intent acting in behalf of or in connection with any political organization." In fact, Holiday Inn had agreed to higher premiums so that Aetna would include civil commotion coverage for their Beirut property. But the Holiday Inn policy still excluded any losses or damage caused "directly or indirectly, proximately or remotely" by "war, invasion, act of foreign enemy, hostilities or warlike operations (whether war be declared or not), civil war, mutiny, insurrection, revolution, conspiracy, military or usurped power." Unsurprisingly, when Holiday Inn filed a claim for nearly $11 million to cover the damage to their Beirut hotel, Aetna contended that the conflict between the Mourabitoun and the Phalangists had been a civil war or insurrection and was therefore excluded from Holiday Inn's coverage. Holiday Inn—like Pan Am before it—sued Aetna, insisting that the conflict was, instead a form of "civil commotion" and therefore covered according to the terms for which it had specifically negotiated and paid extra.[44]

District judge Charles S. Haight Jr., who decided the Holiday Inn case in 1983 in favor of the hotel chain, relied heavily on the *Pan Am* precedent in his ruling. While Aetna had called various journalists to testify that the events in Beirut were widely regarded as a civil war, Haight rejected that testimony in favor of the assertion made by the Second Circuit in its *Pan Am* ruling that, "the specific purpose of overthrowing the constituted government and seizing its powers is a necessary element of both 'insurrection' and 'civil war.'" Based on that definition, Haight found, the events in Beirut could not be considered an insurrection because "the Mourabitoun, in seeking to dislodge the Phalange from the Holiday Inn, were not acting for the specific purpose of overthrowing the Lebanese government. They did not proclaim a casting off of allegiance to that government; they did not proclaim or seek to establish a government of their own." It was not a civil war, according to Haight, because none of "the factions involved in any way with the damage to the Holiday Inn embraced partition of Lebanon as a specific objective." Instead, Haight ruled:

> The Holiday Inn was damaged by a series of factional "civil commotions," of increasing violence. The Lebanese government could not deal effectively with these commotions. The country came close to anarchy. But the constitutional government existed throughout; the requisite intent to overthrow it has not been proved to the exclusion of other interpretations; and there was no "war" in Lebanon between sovereign or quasi-sovereign states.[45]

Thanks to its foresight in negotiating special "civil commotion" coverage for an additional premium, Holiday Inn was therefore covered under its Aetna property insurance policy, and Aetna was ordered by the court to pay the claim. One of the most fascinating elements of the cases that crop up around these war exclusions is this phenomenon of US judges trying to sort out unbelievably complicated geopolitical conflicts, like the one in Beirut, that almost no one fully understood. The process of disputing these denied claims compels the legal system to sort out the most chaotic and uncontrolled stories—terrorist attacks, cyberattacks, civil unrest easing into civil war—and classify them within the tight confines of the language in insurance policies.

"Journalists and politicians invariably referred to these events in Lebanon as a 'civil war.' They do so today," Haight wrote toward the end of his ruling. He went on to explain that regardless of how people commonly used those terms, his job was "to give the words at issue their insurance meaning." Haight's willingness to dismiss the terms that people commonly used to describe the conflict is striking, as is his insistence that terms like "civil war" and "insurrection" could and did have a specific "insurance meaning" quite different from how they might be used and understood by the general public. Unlike the courts that insisted, following Pearl Harbor, that any event that looked to an ordinary person like war should be considered as such for insurance purposes, Haight, following in the footsteps of Frankel and the Second Circuit, was advocating for very narrow interpretations of the war exceptions written into property insurance policies, an approach in line with interpreting ambiguities in the coverage in favor of the policyholder, rather than the insurer. In *Stankus*, the Massachusetts Supreme Court had advocated for interpreting war under its "ordinary meaning," but Haight had no interest in the ordinary meaning of all-risk policy exclusions; he cared only about their insurance meaning.

The idea that war has a very particular meaning and definition in the context of insurance contracts continued to gain traction in courts following the *Pan Am* and *Holiday Inn* rulings and was even extended to other insurance contracts besides all-risk property policies. In July 2019, when the Ninth Circuit Court of Appeals reversed a ruling in favor of Atlantic Specialty Insurance Company, an entire section of the opinion authored by Judge A. Wallace Tashima was titled "The Special Meaning of 'War' in the Insurance Context." That case was brought by Universal Cable Productions, which had been filming a television series called *Dig* in Jerusalem during the summer of 2014 when Hamas launched rockets at Israeli targets from Gaza, forcing the studio to shut down production and move filming to a new location. Universal filed a claim with Atlantic under its television production insurance policy to cover the costs of interrupting and moving production, but Atlantic denied the claim, citing the four war exclusions in Universal's policy, which excluded coverage for losses caused by (1) war (including "undeclared or civil war"); (2) "warlike action by a military force"; (3) insurrection, rebellion, and revolution; and (4) "any weapon of war including atomic fission or radioactive force, whether in time of peace or war."[46]

A district court in California concluded in 2017 that Atlantic was correct in its assessment, and that the Hamas rockets fell under the first two exclusion categories of war and warlike action because "such a conflict easily would be considered a 'war' by a layperson." The district court based its analysis on California state law, which dictated that the terms of an insurance policy must be "understood in their ordinary and popular sense, rather than according to their strict legal meaning"—a provision presumably designed to help the insured rather than the insurers. The Ninth Circuit reversed the district court decision, noting that, in fact, California law actually made an exception to its "ordinary and popular" rule on the interpretation of insurance policies if "a special meaning is given to" those terms "by usage." Citing both *Pan Am* and *Holiday Inn*, the Ninth Circuit determined that this exception applied to war on the grounds that "in the insurance context, the term 'war' has a special meaning that requires the existence of hostilities between de jure or de facto governments." Since Hamas was not, in the court's view, a de jure or de facto sovereign, its "conduct in the summer of 2014 cannot be defined as 'war' for the purposes of interpreting this policy." Nor could the firing of those rockets be considered a warlike action, the Ninth Circuit ruled, because such a determination would conflate war with terrorism. Tashima noted in the ruling that Hamas launched unguided missiles that were "likely used to injure and kill civilians because of their indiscriminate nature." Therefore, "Hamas' conduct consisted of intentional violence against civilians—conduct which is far closer to acts of terror than 'warlike action by a military force,'" Tashima concluded.

A very narrow and particular meaning of war in the context of insurance policies, as well as a sharp distinction between warlike acts and terrorism emerged from *Pan Am* and the cases that followed it, like *Holiday Inn* and *Universal*. Both of those legacies—the narrow definition of war and the separation from terrorism—have significant implications for cybersecurity incidents like NotPetya that appear to originate from government actors but that target civilians. Attribution of cyberattacks can be a slow and tricky endeavor, but at least in the case of NotPetya that process seemed to point unequivocally to the Russian government as the responsible party. In this sense, an attack like NotPetya might seem to come closer to meeting the criteria for the insurance definition of war as "hostilities between de jure or de facto governments" than an attack launched by a nonsovereign group like Hamas, Mourabitoun, or the PFLP.

On the other hand, while the perpetrator of NotPetya may have been a government, the victims were largely civilian and only those that were clearly elements of Ukraine's critical infrastructure, including Ukrainian power companies, transportation organizations, and banks, were clearly intended targets with close ties to the ongoing Russia-Ukraine conflict. Many other firms, both Ukrainian and non-Ukrainian, were affected indiscriminately by the malware, including Mondelez, and in those cases, Russia's use of a far-reaching, untargeted ransomware program suggests something closer to the Ninth Circuit's definition of terrorism as "intentional violence against civilians by political groups." Perhaps most important, for all the extensive damage NotPetya caused, it was not a violent attack. Unlike almost every other incident that has raised legal disputes on the meaning of war exclusions in insurance—from the sinking of the *Lusitania* and the attack on Pearl Harbor to the hijacking of Pan Am flight 093 and the attacks on Israel by Hamas—NotPetya did not directly put anyone's life in danger. To call a piece of computer code, no matter how destructive, an act of war when it resulted in no physical destruction or loss of lives would be to go against most people's common conceptions of what war looks like—and it would go against the special insurance meaning of war that had evolved in prior cases. In 2014, following the breach of Sony Pictures by the North Korean government, President Obama referred to the breach as "an act of cyber-vandalism that was very costly, very expensive," during an interview on CNN, but said explicitly, "I don't think it was an act of war."[47] NotPetya exhibited more elements of warlike activity than the Sony Pictures breach—including more immediate armed conflict between the central two nations involved and targeting of critical infrastructure—but for most of its non-critical infrastructure victims, it fundamentally shut down computers and deleted data (much like the Sony Pictures breach) rather than causing broader physical damage, suggesting it still retained many more elements of an act of cyber sabotage than a violent or warlike act. The key exceptions to this are the critical infrastructure targets of NotPetya, including the Ukrainian power grid, which did result in some clear kinetic consequences, raising the question of whether all victims and consequences of NotPetya should be lumped together for the purposes of classification or whether the attacks on Mondelez might be categorized differently from those on Ukraine's power infrastructure, despite being executed by the same lines of code. This, then, raises an interesting question of whether NotPetya was a single attack or whether each infiltration by the virus of an individual company or computer network should be seen as a separate attack—in which case the attack on Mondelez would seem even less in line with any definition of war.

MONDELEZ, NOTPETYA, AND CYBERWAR

When Mondelez was hit by the NotPetya ransomware in 2017 it had a comprehensive property insurance policy from Zurich that appeared to be explicitly designed to cover any digital disruptions to the company's business. Specifically, the policy covered expenses "incurred by the Insured during the period of interruption directly resulting from the failure of the Insured's electronic data processing equipment or media to operate." Mondelez promptly filed a claim with Zurich, following the attack, and provided its insurer with documentation of the malware and its impacts. On June 1, 2018, Mondelez received a letter from Zurich denying the claim on the grounds that NotPetya was excluded from its policy based on exclusion B.2(a):

This Policy excludes loss or damage directly or indirectly caused by or resulting from any of the following regardless of any other cause or event, whether or not insured under this Policy, contributing concurrently or in any other sequence to the loss: . . .

2) a) hostile or warlike action in time of peace or war, including action in hindering, combating or defending against an actual, impending or expected attack by any:

(i) government or sovereign power (de jure or de facto);

(ii) military, naval, or air force; or

(iii) agent or authority of any party specified in i or ii above.[48]

The war exclusion in Mondelez's policy bore many of the marks of insurers' efforts to broaden the language of their exclusions in light of previous court losses. The reference to warlike actions "in time of peace or war" codified the lesson of the Rosenau family life insurance dispute about Pearl Harbor. In that case, the insurance exclusion phrasing about policyholders "engaged in military or naval service in time of war" had been the insurer's downfall, so insurers like Zurich now made sure to clarify that the war exclusions also applied at times when war had not been officially declared. The use of the term "warlike" was also an attempt to broaden the boundaries of a strict definition of war, just as it had been when used in the Pan Am, Holiday Inn, and Universal insurance policies, and the inclusion of any "agents or authority" of governments or sovereign powers in the scope of whose actions could be considered warlike hinted at yet another way in which Zurich was aiming to broaden the exclusion.

In the life insurance disputes following Pearl Harbor, the central question for the courts to decide was whether one country's attack on another's military could be considered war even absent a formal, legal declaration. In the more recent property insurance disputes about war exceptions involving Pan Am, Holiday Inn, and Universal, the disagreements hinged chiefly on whether those exclusions encompassed violence directed at civilians by groups that were not governments. NotPetya combined elements of both of these issues. Like the attack on Pearl Harbor, NotPetya emerged in the midst of ongoing, escalating conflict between two countries (in this case, Russia and Ukraine), and it appeared to have been developed and launched by a sovereign government, though the attribution to Russia took some months and was strenuously denied by the Russian government. However, as in the *Pan Am*, *Holiday Inn*, and *Universal* cases, NotPetya primarily affected civilian targets rather than military ones, and many of those targets—including Mondelez—were outside Ukraine and fairly far removed from the political conflict between the two governments. And unlike all of these conflicts, of course, NotPetya caused no direct physical damage to the policyholder's property. That didn't invalidate the insurance coverage since Mondelez's policy from Zurich explicitly included coverage for business interruptions and the associated losses that were caused by the failure of computers, but it did make the incident seem, on the whole, slightly less "warlike" than an airplane hijacking or a missile attack.

The strongest evidence in favor of Zurich's assertion that NotPetya was a "hostile or warlike action" lay in the attack being attributed to the Russian government. That process of attribution lasted months and took place during the nearly yearlong period between Mondelez's initial filing of an insurance claim and Zurich's denial of that claim. Beginning immediately after the NotPetya attacks in June 2017, Ukrainian officials and cybersecurity researchers cast blame for the attack on Russia. That same month, Roman Boyarchuk, who ran Ukraine's Center for Cyber Protection, told *Wired* that the attack was "likely state-sponsored" and that it was "difficult to imagine anyone else," besides Russia, who "would want to do this."[49] Ukrainian cybersecurity firm Information Systems Security Partners was also among the first to claim that the NotPetya code closely resembled previous Russian cyberattacks in its design and technical "fingerprints." Later that month, US cybersecurity company FireEye made a similar claim, with its head of global cyber intelligence, John Watters, telling the *Financial Times*, "we are reasonably confident" Russia was responsible for NotPetya, based on analysis of the targets, code, and malware infection vectors. "The best you can get is high confidence," Watters said of the attribution effort, emphasizing that it was not definite Russia was behind the attack, even though "there are a lot of things that point to Russia."[50]

On February 14, 2018, the UK National Cyber Security Centre published a statement saying the Russian military was "almost certainly responsible" for NotPetya. The next day, February 15, 2018, the Australian minister for law enforcement and cyber security, Angus Taylor, issued a similar statement, that "the Australian Government has judged that Russian state sponsored actors were responsible" for NotPetya, as did White House press secretary, Sarah Huckabee Sanders. Sanders's brief statement read, in its entirety:

> In June 2017, the Russian military launched the most destructive and costly cyber-attack in history. The attack, dubbed "NotPetya," quickly spread worldwide, causing billions of dollars in damage across Europe, Asia, and the Americas. It was part of the Kremlin's ongoing effort to destabilize Ukraine and demonstrates ever more clearly Russia's involvement in the ongoing conflict. This was also a reckless and indiscriminate cyber-attack that will be met with international consequences.[51]

Four more countries—Canada, Denmark, Lithuania, and Estonia—quickly followed suit, issuing official statements blaming Russia for the attack within the week in what Australia's ambassador for cyber affairs, Tobias Feakin, later referred to as "the largest coordinated attribution of its kind to date."[52] A spokesman for the Russian government, Dmitry Peskov, denied the coordinated allegations and denounced them as "Russophobic."[53]

It is, of course, difficult to say definitively whether the Russian government was behind the NotPetya malware, but Zurich's case for claiming the incident was the act of a "government or sovereign power" is about as persuasive as it's possible for a cyberattack attribution to be. The evidence pointing to Russia includes similarities between the NotPetya code and previous strains of malware attributed to Russia. While most ransomware encrypts the contents of infected computers and then provides a way for victims to decrypt their files so long as they make a cryptocurrency ransom payment, NotPetya did not encrypt the hard drives of computers it infected. Instead, it overwrote the master boot records of those computers, making it nearly impossible for the files to be restored. Additionally, while NotPetya did appear to demand a (relatively small) ransom payment from victims of roughly $300 in Bitcoin, the ransom demand was unusual in that it required victims to send confirmation of their payments to a particular fixed email address. That address was quickly blocked by the email service provider after the attack began—making it difficult for anyone to prove they had actually paid the demanded ransom according to the attackers' terms.[54]

These signs that the attackers did not actually aim to restore their victims' files and had no real interest in collecting ransom payments hinted that the perpetrators were not financially motivated criminals but instead had some other agenda. This lack of financial motivation ruled out traditional cybercrime organizations and pointed to a state actor, either acting on its own or in coordination with outside agents (in which case the incident might seem less warlike). The attackers' agenda was clarified somewhat by the fact that the perpetrators initially spread NotPetya by embedding it inside a software update from a Ukrainian accounting software company called MeDoc. Because a Ukrainian firm was used as the initial conduit, most of the victims of NotPetya were Ukrainian. In fact, early estimates suggested that more than three-quarters of the affected organizations were based in Ukraine, though the malware quickly spread to other companies outside Ukraine, at least in part through their infected Ukrainian subsidiaries.[55] This focus on Ukraine aligned with earlier Russian cyberattacks that targeted Ukrainian infrastructure, as well as the ongoing military conflict between the two countries dating from Russia's annexation of Crimea in

February 2014—a conflict sometimes referred to as the "Russo-Ukrainian War."[56]

This political context—and even the language used to describe it—is relevant to Zurich's argument that NotPetya was a "warlike action." In July 2019, eight months after Mondelez filed its lawsuit against Zurich, the Ninth Circuit issued its ruling in the *Universal* case stating that "in the insurance context, the term 'war' has a special meaning that requires the existence of hostilities between de jure or de facto governments."[57] The conflict between Russia and Ukraine certainly appeared to meet that bar of hostilities between governments, and the coordinated attribution of NotPetya to Russia by several countries in February 2018, three and a half months before Zurich denied the Mondelez claim, gave Zurich a strong basis for arguing that Not-Petya had been perpetrated by a government party to those hostilities. What was less clear was whether NotPetya itself—or any computer-based attack, for that matter—could legitimately be considered "warlike."

Mondelez thought not. In its lawsuit against Zurich, the company referred to "Zurich's invocation of a 'hostile or warlike action' exclusion to deny coverage for malicious 'cyber' incidents" as "unprecedented." Indeed, no previous legal conflicts that centered on interpretation of insurance war exclusions had dealt with cyberattacks, nor was there any reason to believe that the exclusions had been crafted to apply to computer-based attacks. This supported Mondelez's claim that "the purported application of this type of exclusion to anything other than conventional armed conflict or hostilities was unprecedented." But just because Zurich's interpretation of the war exclusion was unprecedented didn't necessarily mean it was wrong. In fact, much of Mondelez's argument seemed to lie in simply asserting that "incursions of malicious code or instruction into MDLZ's [Mondelez's] computers did not constitute 'hostile or warlike action,' as required by Exclusion B.2(a)." In framing its argument this way, Mondelez implied that malware, at least when it is directed at a private company that operates no critical infrastructure, cannot constitute "hostile or warlike action" rather than that anything about the specific nature of NotPetya or the damage it incurred should be considered unwarlike.[58]

However, Mondelez's contention that "malicious code," or cyberattacks more generally, could not be considered warlike was at odds with the growing trend of recognition by nations and international organizations that cyberattacks were rapidly becoming an integral part of warfare and that "incursions into computers" had the potential to cause serious damage, even physical damage. For instance, in June 2016, a year before NotPetya, NATO secretary general Jens Stoltenberg told the German newspaper *Bild* that the alliance had classified cyberspace as an "official domain of warfare" and confirmed that a sufficiently severe cyberattack on any of its members would be considered an act of war and trigger a military response.[59] At the time, Stoltenberg did not point to any specific examples of known cyberattacks that had reached that level, but some experts later indicated that the use of cyber capabilities by Russia against Ukraine was a prime example of what such warlike actions in cyberspace might look like.

On March 29, 2017, just a few months before NotPetya hit Mondelez, an adviser for the Center for Strategic and International Studies, Olga Oliker, testified before the Senate Armed Services Subcommittee on Emerging Threats and Capabilities that if an earlier attack on the Ukrainian electric grid had been perpetrated by Russia, it was "an example of precisely the type of cyber operation that could be seen as warfare."[60] Looking back at earlier lawsuits over the application of insurance war exclusions, many of which prominently feature public statements from political figures, journalists, and experts about whether the relevant events were akin to war, it's not hard to imagine Zurich building its case on statements like these. For instance, *Wired* reporter Andy Greenberg, who did extensive reporting on NotPetya and in 2020 published a book about it titled *Sandworm*, wrote in one of his widely read articles about the attack: "The release of NotPetya was an act of cyberwar by almost any definition."[61]

It is difficult to predict exactly how much weight such statements will carry in court. Some courts—for instance, the Massachusetts Supreme Court in *Stankus* looking at President Roosevelt's address—have been swayed by public statements and popular coverage of the events at issue in insurance cases. But this is typically only the case for courts that believe that the meaning of war in an insurance context is the same as its common meaning in everyday parlance. The more recent trend of war exception cases, since the *Pan Am* ruling, has been to insist on a narrower definition of war that operates independently of the language and terms used by the broader public. In the *Holiday Inn* ruling, for instance, the deciding judge was quite ready to dismiss the fact that "journalists and politicians invariably referred to these events in Lebanon as a 'civil war'" on the grounds that it was irrelevant to determining whether the conflict was a civil war in the "insurance meaning" of the words.[62] It seems entirely plausible that a court could similarly dismiss references to NotPetya as an act of cyberwar as irrelevant to the question of whether the cyberattack qualified as warlike in an insurance context.

One insurance broker, Marsh, took a strong stand to this effect in August 2018, shortly after Zurich denied Mondelez's claim but before Mondelez filed its lawsuit. In a short article titled "NotPetya Was Not Cyber 'War,'" Matthew McCabe, Marsh's assistant general counsel for cyber policy, made the case that NotPetya was not a warlike action and should therefore not be excluded from insurance coverage under war exceptions. "For a cyber-attack to reach the level of warlike activity, its consequences must go beyond economic losses, even large ones," McCabe wrote. Furthermore, he pointed out, "the most prominent victims of NotPetya operated far from any field of conflict and worked at purely civilian tasks like delivering packages, producing pharmaceuticals, and making disinfectants and cookies."[63] As the representative of an insurance broker—an organization that helped customers purchase insurance policies—McCabe clearly had an interest in representing the interests of its clients and persuading them that continuing to purchase these types of policies was worthwhile and not a waste of money. But even if his motives may have been influenced by his employer's business interests, McCabe's concluding call for greater clarity in war exclusions is an important one: "if insurers are going to continue including the war exclusion on cyber insurance policies, the wording should be reformed to make clear the circumstances required to trigger it."[64]

Perhaps the strongest piece of Mondelez's argument is that the language of exclusion B.2(a) is "vague and ambiguous," and that "Zurich's failure to modify that historical language to specifically address the extent to which it would apply to cyber incidents" means it "therefore must be interpreted in favor of coverage."[65] The *Pan Am*, *Holiday Inn*, and *Universal* rulings in favor of the policyholders rather than their insurers all supported this argument—that absent specific language excluding a certain scenario, courts were generally inclined to interpret the exclusions fairly narrowly. On the other hand, in a certain light, NotPetya could be viewed as fitting even that narrow definition because, unlike the Pan Am, Holiday Inn, and Universal incidents, the perpetrator appeared to be a sovereign government engaged in hostilities with another country. When the Second Circuit determined that the hijacking of Pan Am flight 093 was not a warlike act it based that decision largely on the fact that the hijackers' "acts had criminal rather than military overtones. They were the agents of a radical political group, rather than a sovereign government." Similarly, the *Holiday Inn* ruling rested in part on the fact that "there was no 'war' in Lebanon between sovereign or quasi-sovereign states." Neither of those rationales quite fits the NotPetya case, assuming one accepts the attribution of the attack to Russia and the extensive documentation that it was part of the conflict with Ukraine.

The *Universal* ruling offers perhaps the most support for Mondelez's contention that NotPetya was not a warlike action. In that case, the Ninth Circuit highlighted the "indiscriminate nature" of the unguided missiles used by Hamas as evidence that they were trying to injure and kill civilians, conduct that the court ruled was "far closer to acts of terror" than "warlike action." NotPetya could also be viewed as an indiscriminate or unguided weapon, one that caused significant damage to civilian targets—including Mondelez. Indeed, Mondelez's distance from the Russia-Ukraine conflict could work in its favor. Just as the Second Circuit ruled that the Pan Am hijacking could not be considered a "warlike operation" because "that term does not include the inflicting of damage on the civilian property of non-belligerents by political groups far from the site of warfare," so too a court could conceivably determine that it was a stretch to deem "warlike" the inflicting of damage on the civilian property of a multinational food company headquartered in Chicago, Illinois, far from Russia and Ukraine. Of all of these cases, it's hard not to view NotPetya as far and away the least warlike. After all, the Pan Am, Holiday Inn, and Universal incidents all involved the obvious, physical alteration of property and risk to human life in ways that NotPetya absolutely, unambiguously did not.

NO CLAW BACKS

One of the more fascinating elements of Mondelez's lawsuit is its description of Zurich's behavior in the aftermath of issuing its formal coverage denial letter on June 1, 2018. According to Mondelez, soon after sending that letter, Zurich appeared to change its mind and told the firm that it would rescind the declination of coverage and resume adjustment of Mondelez's claim. On July 18, 2018, Zurich sent Mondelez an email "formally rescind[ing]" its previous coverage denial and promising to resume work on the claim. Then, in another email sent less than a week later on July 24, Zurich offered Mondelez a $10 million partial payment toward the company's insurance claim, which the insurer's head of property claims later promised would be "unconditional" and "not subject to a 'claw back' provision." However, that payment never materialized—nor did Zurich ever appear to resume work on the claim.[66]

Mondelez, in its complaint against Zurich, was quick to assert that these prevarications on Zurich's part stemmed from the insurer's fears that denying Mondelez's claim might lead to bad publicity. In particular, Mondelez hypothesized in the suit, Zurich feared the possibility of Mondelez taking legal action, as it would, indeed, ultimately go on to do. The July 2018 emails promising a $10 million advance payment and a continued claim adjustment process were aimed at convincing Mondelez "to refrain from filing immediate litigation," the company alleges in its lawsuit. If that was in fact the intention of those emails, then they seem to have worked, since Mondelez waited until October 2018 to file its lawsuit, more than four months after its initial claim was denied by Zurich. Mondelez later claimed that it "refrained to its detriment from instituting immediate litigation challenging the June 1, 2018 denial letter" because of the "explicit representations and promises from Zurich" made in the July 2018 emails from the insurer.[67]

Zurich was hoping to prevent, or at the very least delay, a lawsuit, Mondelez contended, because the insurer feared the publicity surrounding such a suit would draw attention to all the ways that Zurich policies might not actually cover cyberattacks. Mondelez goes so far as to claim in its lawsuit that Zurich feared the publicity would "adversely impact its dealings with actual and prospective policyholders who were considering the purchase or renewal of insurance coverage from Zurich." Whether or not this was actually the line of reasoning behind the mixed signals Zurich sent Mondelez in the summer of 2018, it is clear that the insurer was undecided, or at the very least uncertain, about how to handle the NotPetya claim. For one thing, it was an extraordinarily expensive cyberattack—the White House dubbed it "the most destructive and costly cyber-attack in history" in February 2018, and later reports estimated that the damages totaled roughly $10 billion.[68]

For Zurich, and other insurers, the issues raised by the Mondelez claim were much larger than just coverage for the losses borne by one company— they spoke to the question of who would bear the costs of NotPetya inflicted on hundreds of companies affected across the world. For instance, pharmaceutical firm Merck estimated that it had suffered $870 million in damages from NotPetya, ranging from its 30,000 infected laptop and desktop computers to its inability to meet demand for the Gardasil 9 vaccine used to prevent HPV. Merck, like Mondelez, had extensive insurance coverage for property damage and catastrophic risks—a total of $1.75 billion in coverage, in Merck's case, less a $150 million deductible. But most of Merck's thirty insurers and reinsurers, like Zurich, denied the pharmaceutical company's claims citing war exclusions. Merck, like Mondelez, subsequently sued those insurers—a group that included several prominent cyberinsurance providers such as Allianz and AIG—for $1.3 billion under its property insurance policies.[69] Merck's arguments for why the war exclusions did not apply to NotPetya closely mirrored Mondelez's and primarily centered on the claim that those exclusions were never intended to address cybersecurity incidents nor were they tailored to that purpose. "The 'war' and 'terrorism' exclusions do not, on their face, apply to losses caused by network interruption events such as NotPetya. . . . They do not mention cyber events, networks, computers, data, coding, or software; nor do they contain any other language suggesting an intention to exclude coverage for cyber events," Merck argued in its lawsuit.[70]

These arguments hint at some of the ways NotPetya may reshape the cyber exclusions in property policies. But the incident had perhaps even more significant impacts on the exclusions written into stand-alone cyber policies. However, to construe policies that had been specifically marketed as protecting against cyber losses so that they excluded large and damaging cyberattacks was more problematic for insurers. Understandably, they were concerned about reassuring their customers that war exclusions would not prevent them from being able to exercise such policies. Some insurers even told policyholders and brokers they would not enforce war exclusions for cyber-related claims because they didn't want to "scare off customers."[71] Kenneth Abraham and Daniel Schwarcz point out that construing war exclusions to apply broadly to cyberattacks initiated by nation states could lead to exclusion of many types of online threats that policyholders would expect to have covered by cyber-insurance policies. They note that, "unlike in traditional insurance settings, it is often difficult or impossible for cyber insurers to identify in coverage exclusions the causal mechanisms of potentially catastrophic cyber risks without eviscerating coverage for ordinary cyberattacks that policyholders demand."[72]

In order to reassure policyholders that stand-alone cyber policies would still be useful in the wake of NotPetya claim denials, insurers began to explicitly include coverage for "cyberterrorism" in stand-alone cyberinsurance policies, without ever quite clarifying how cyberterrorism differed from warlike acts. For instance, Zurich's stand-alone cyberinsurance policy template, covering first- and third-party losses related to breaches, extortion, privacy incidents, and social engineering, included a "war or civil unrest" exclusion for costs incurred by:

1. war, including undeclared or civil war;
2. warlike action by a military force, including action in hindering or defending against an actual or expected attack, by any government, sovereign, or other authority using military personnel or other agents; or
3. insurrection, rebellion, revolution, riot, usurped power, or action taken by governmental authority in hindering or defending against any of these.[73]

However, perhaps in recognition of the concerns policyholders might have about this exclusion following the Merck and Mondelez claim denials, the Zurich policy explicitly stated that its war and civil unrest exclusion did not apply to "cyberterrorism." The policy defined cyberterrorism separately as:

the use of information technology to execute attacks or threats against Your Network Security by any person or group, whether acting alone, or on behalf of, or in connection with, any individual, organization, or government, with the intention to:

1. cause harm;
2. intimidate any person or entity; or
3. cause destruction or harm to critical infrastructure or data,

in furtherance of financial, social, ideological, religious, or political objectives.[74]

In a 2020 analysis of fifty-six cyberinsurance policies, Daniel Woods and Jessica Weinkle suggest that this emerging trend for cyberinsurance to affirmatively cover cyberterrorism had "weakened" the war exclusions in such policies.[75] But it was not clear from those broad definitions which category an attack like NotPetya would fall under, so the inclusion of cyberterrorism in their coverage did little to resolve the ambiguities and uncertainty faced by policyholders.

The rewriting of insurance policy exclusions is typical of the aftermath of significant legal controversies over denied claims tied to war—Sun Life broadened its life insurance exception to apply to "war, whether declared or not" after Pearl Harbor, Aetna excluded hijackings following the explosion of Pan Am flight 093. Clearly, insurers need to do a better job of describing more clearly which computer-based threats are excluded from their coverage, but rephrasing the insurance exclusions that apply to cyber risks will be no small feat for insurers as the attempts to differentiate between cyberwar and cyberterrorism already indicate. Defining clearer exclusions for cyberattacks will be challenging both because of the broad range of threats carriers have to consider and because at the same time they are trying to exclude certain threats many of them are also aggressively developing and marketing cyberinsurance policies designed to cover other, closely related online threats. There is also still tremendous disagreement and uncertainty about what cyberterrorism actually looks like and what types of incidents would fall into that category, who the perpetrators of those attacks will be, and what kinds of damage they will cause.

One of the striking differences between the definitions of warlike actions and cyber terrorism in these cyberinsurance policies is that while the former relies primarily on attribution and being able to reliably identify whether a nation state, governmental authority, or military force is the perpetrator of an attack, the latter focuses instead on the impacts of the incident in question. Classifying cyberattacks according to the kind of damage they do to data or critical infrastructure has several advantages over trying to categorize them based on their perpetrators and broader political context. First, attribution remains a challenging and slow process for many cyberattacks, but the impacts of those incidents are often much clearer and less controversial in their immediate aftermath. So using those impacts as a means of determining whether a cyberattack is covered under an insurance policy has the potential to avoid disputes over attribution and instead focus on the less contentious fall-out of those attacks. Second, this approach could allow for the disaggregation of different victims impacted by the same malware or attack vector. Instead of considering NotPetya, as a piece of malware, to be itself a warlike act because it was created by a particular entity, the code's impacts on different victims and targets could be evaluated separately, each in its own, respective context. This would help address the challenge of narrowly targeting cyberattacks and the subsequent wide range of geographically diverse collateral damage that can result from the release of malware. Moreover, while this approach would certainly not solve the threat of correlated risks, it might reframe the risk correlation challenges that insurers face in modeling and covering cyber risks. By allowing the disentangling of different victims affected by the same piece of malware, or other attack vector, insurers might be able to reconsider how they can use the different threats that their policyholders face to allow for more diversification of their risk pools. For instance, this might allow for the risks that critical infrastructure operators face to be treated differently from those faced by other firms—even if all of those policyholders could be affected by the same piece of malicious code. It will still be the case that a single piece of malware can cause widespread and varied damages to many victims across different sectors and locations, but perhaps for insurance purposes it would make more sense to consider which of those types of damages are covered or not, rather than arguing over which types of attacks are or are not excluded from a policy.

Over time, war exclusions in insurance policies have been shaped by a series of historical events to encompass an increasingly broad range of activities carried out by a variety of different actors. As concerns that these exclusions may be overly broad when it comes to cyberattacks force insurers to start crafting explicit inclusions for cyberterrorism activity, it may be time consider whether the historical emphasis of these exclusions on being able to definitively identify the perpetrator and motive of such attacks is ill-suited to the nature and breadth of cyberattacks. Instead, there may be more value in predicating such exclusions of large-scale cyberattacks that present the possibility of significantly correlated risks on their particular victims, impacts, and scale—characteristics that are both more easily verified and allow for more granular distinctions in the cyber domain.

III

CYBER COVERAGE AND REGULATION

"THE BIG KAHUNA": STAND-ALONE CYBER COVERAGE

The legal disputes over whether cyber-related losses could be claimed under CGL, computer fraud, and property insurance led to growing restrictions on when policyholders could exercise those lines of coverage in the wake of cybersecurity incidents. Some of those restrictions stemmed directly from legal rulings that clearly sided with the carriers, such as the *Sony* decision that no liability costs tied to malicious cyber intrusions fell under CGL coverage. Other rulings, such as *American Tooling* and *Zurich*, that yielded more unfavorable or uncertain results for insurers spurred carriers either to scope more narrowly the language defining what computer-related costs their coverage included or to broaden the exclusions of cyber risks in those policies. The goal of these revisions was to squash the so-called silent cyber problem that arose from nonaffirmative risks, that is, risks that were neither explicitly included in nor explicitly excluded from an insurance policy. Addressing these silent risks would provide both carriers and their customers with greater clarity but it would also significantly shrink the potential coverage for cyber risks tied to other lines of coverage, such as property, cars, or crime. For instance, on November 13, 2019, the Lloyd's Market Association introduced new cyber exclusions, the Property D&F Cyber Endorsement, or LMA5400, and the Property Cyber and Data Exclusion, LMA5401, both of which would exclude from coverage any losses resulting from malicious cyber acts as well as nonmalicious cyber incidents resulting from errors or omissions in the operation of computer systems or any outages or malfunctions of those systems.[1] The combined effect of these legal disputes and the resulting editing of non-cyber-specific insurance was a distinct shift, driven by insurers, toward excluding cyber risks from their existing lines of coverage and instead bundling those risks together in stand-alone policies.

Stand-alone cyber risk policies covered both first- and third-party costs associated with incidents ranging from online extortion and data breaches to network outages and social engineering. In 2015, premiums for add-on cyberinsurance sold as part of package policies were almost double the premiums for stand-alone cyber risk policies in the United States. But from 2015 to 2019, premium sales for stand-alone cyberinsurance policies grew by 379 percent, nearly quintupling from $483,197,973 to $2,314,745,104, far surpassing sales of add-on cyber coverage. During that same period, premiums for package policies including some cyber coverage increased by less than 40 percent, from $932,645,734 to $1,283,180,459.[2] Stand-alone cyber risk policies took the named peril approach of enumerating the growing number of different risks and associated first- and third-party costs that they covered. However, this named peril approach was complicated by the fact that the online threat landscape was constantly changing, so policyholders had no way of knowing whether the policies they purchased would cover the cyber risks they faced in the future. Moreover, "cyber risks" did not just describe a set of threats; increasingly, policyholders were looking to protect their digital assets and infrastructure against any kind of computer-related problem or loss. In this regard, stand-alone cyberinsurance tried to encompass elements of multiple different types of coverage simultaneously. Like fire insurance, it was designed to protect policyholders from a specific type of threat, but like property insurance, it was also aiming to protect a certain class of assets from a variety of threats. It adopted a named peril approach to achieving both of these goals, leaving clear gaps in policyholders' coverage for emerging online risks, especially as those risks were being explicitly excluded from all-risk property insurance policies in much broader terms than they were being covered in stand-alone policies.

In fact, as exclusions of cyber risk grew broader over time, spurred by legal disputes over claim denials, the definitions of covered cyber risks in stand-alone policies grew narrower and more specific. This, too, was a lesson that insurers had learned from their years fighting cyber-related claims in court—that the more carefully they scoped their coverage the less likely they were to be on the line for covering new variations on cyber threats. One possible solution to the growing gap between the coverage offered by stand-alone named peril cyber policies and the broad cyber exclusions being built into other lines of coverage was for cyberinsurers to adopt an all-peril approach to cyber risk and start selling customers policies that would cover damage to their digital assets regardless of what caused that damage, so long as it wasn't caused by anything specifically excluded by the policy. Another approach might have been to incorporate different types of cyber risks into existing lines of coverage, rather than deliberately excising them, thereby leveraging the considerable expertise and history of those departments and underwriters, rather than starting from scratch with brand new cyberinsurance departments that were often isolated from the rest of a carrier's business groups. This might have enabled insurers to tailor different types of cyber risk coverage—for third-party liability costs, or for first-party crime or extortion losses, or for damage to digital infrastructure and networks—within the broader framework of the liability, named peril, or all-risk coverage area that most closely aligned with each. Instead, insurers seemed determined to carve out cyber-related risks from their existing product lines as much as possible. From a business perspective, this approach allowed carriers to shield their largest, most lucrative departments from having to deal with new risks and alter their existing models. But from a cybersecurity perspective it completely ignored one of the most fundamental characteristics of cyber risks, namely that they were not a single kind of risk but instead a wide array of ever-changing risks that interacted with nearly all of the other types of risk insurers were already covering. This effort to isolate cyber risks from other policy lines in stand-alone policies exacerbated many of the challenges carriers faced in trying to develop these products and suggested a singularly short-sighted perspective on the part of insurers about how intertwined cyber risks were becoming with other forms of risk.

Carriers were wrestling with three major challenges in developing cyberinsurance offerings: a lack of reliable, consistently collected data, the possibility of massive accumulated cyber risk, and a persistent inability to effectively assess or limit their customers' exposure to cyber risk. Each of these challenges was exacerbated, to some extent, by the approach insurers had chosen of crafting stand-alone comprehensive cyber risk policies that covered all types of online threats as well as any risks to cyber infrastructure and data. Despite the trend toward stand-alone cyber coverage, insurers were not trying to develop one new type of insurance to cover a single type of risk; rather they were trying to tackle a vast and varied set of risks related to computers and the Internet, many of which overlapped or intersected with existing forms of coverage that they already offered. At the Senate subcommittee hearing on March 19, 2015, where Senator Moran extolled cyberinsurance as a "market led approach to help businesses improve their cybersecurity" and small business owner Ola Sage testified about her inability to understand her own cyberinsurance coverage, Zurich senior vice president

Catherine Mulligan also stressed that Zurich generally tried not to use the word "cyber" in its coverage because it "erroneously may suggest that the coverage could respond to every type of damage caused by an attack on a network."[3] But cyberinsurance only gained traction as a catch-all term in the decades following the 1997 Breach on the Beach party in Honolulu, especially with the rise in stand-alone cyber risk policies. To insurers, selling those stand-alone policies was an opportunity to grow their carriers' business. As early as 2014, firms were highlighting cyberinsurance as "one of the few growth markets in the U.S. property and casualty industry"—but it also posed enormous risks and challenges to insurers.[4]

INCOMPLETE AND INCONSISTENT DATA

One of the challenges Mulligan highlighted in her 2015 testimony was the lack of "robust actuarial data" about cyber-related losses. The best data related to cybersecurity incidents was that pertaining to breaches of personal data, thanks to the rapid proliferation of data breach notification laws in the early 2000s, but even those numbers often painted a very unclear picture of how frequent and costly such breaches were. To be able to price insurance policies for these incidents, insurers needed reliable information about the expected claims activity such coverage would yield, but it was difficult for analysts to reach consensus about the costs of even an individual data breach, much less the average costs across all such incidents.

In 2015, just one month before Mulligan testified before the Senate subcommittee, the Congressional Research Service (CRS) published a report analyzing the costs of the 2013 Target data breach during which seventy million records were stolen from the retailer, including forty million payment card numbers. CRS compiled estimates of the breach's costs from several different sources, ranging from the 2013 annual Cost of a Data Breach Study conducted by Ponemon to Target's quarterly financial filings and the Congressional testimony of Visa's chief enterprise risk officer, Ellen Richey. The final report featured a table with seven different estimates of the total losses associated with the Target breach based on these sources—the total loss estimates ranged from $11 million to $4.9 billion.[5] Incidentally, Target estimated that roughly $90 million of its expenses related to the breach had been offset by insurance, and then, in 2019, filed a lawsuit against ACE American Insurance Co., for refusing to reimburse the retailer for $74 million it had paid to replace payment cards compromised in the breach—a cost the retailer insisted should have been covered under its general liability policy with ACE.[6]

The inability to pin down concrete loss figures associated with data breaches was not limited to large breaches, like Target's. Large-scale analyses of the average costs of data breaches were similarly inconsistent. In 2017, Ponemon's annual report estimated that the average cost of a breach was $3.62 million and the average cost per lost or stolen record was $141. An analysis published the previous year by research firm NetDiligence using a data set of insurance claims estimated those same numbers at $665,000 and $17,035, respectively. Two analyses published in 2015 and 2016 by researchers using different proprietary data sets of breaches also showed significant differences. One found the average cost of a breach to be $5.87 million, with a median cost of $170,000, while the other calculated those numbers at $40.53 million and $1.87 million, respectively.[7] Data breach notification laws and SEC guidance notwithstanding, no one seemed to have any solid idea of how much these incidents cost or even how frequently they occurred—and that was the type of cybersecurity incident for which insurers possessed the best data!

Insurers wanted regulators to help establish a repository of cyber risk data that would "house anonymized enterprise loss information."[8] The data would be anonymized so that companies who contributed reports to it would not receive unwanted public scrutiny or media attention, but insurers would still be able to use their information to build more accurate actuarial models. Several advocates of such a reporting system cited the model of the National Transportation Safety Board (NTSB) as an example of a similar mechanism used for airlines to report safety problems and to allow for effective government analysis of trends, accidents, and safety risks in civil aviation. The idea of an anonymized incident data repository had been raised many times before the March 2015 hearing—it had come up again and again during working group meetings convened by the Department of Homeland Security in 2013 and 2014—but little progress had been made on actually establishing such a repository or even ironing out the details of how it would work.

Ben Beeson, the vice president for cyber security and privacy at insurance brokerage Lockton Companies, emphasized in his testimony at the

2015 hearing how important he thought such a system would be to making a robust cyberinsurance market viable. "The ability to access anonymized loss data, shared between industry and government with appropriate privacy protections, would accelerate the growth of the marketplace, and crucially accelerate the ability of cyber insurance to act as a market incentive for industry to invest in cybersecurity," he told the Senate subcommittee. Mulligan was more cautious in her endorsement of the proposal, saying at the hearing, "In theory, the idea of a data repository is a good one," but adding that there were still several implementation issues that needed to be clarified, including "the question of ownership, who has access, what kind of information would be put in there, how would it be anonymized, and then how would it be made most useful to the insurance community and the non-insurance community."[9]

While the lack of reliable data about cyber risks was a serious problem for insurers, it was not an especially unusual one for a new insurance product. Nor was it new for insurers to look to the government for help in passing policies that would compel the reporting of that data or even for help collecting some data directly themselves through various relevant agencies. Data collection had been a central theme of the early initiatives focused on reforming auto and flood insurance, and in both cases government actors played a role in making sure insurers had access to the actuarial data they needed. For instance, while data collection was certainly not the primary focus of the 1932 Columbia report by the Committee to Study Compensation for Automobile Accidents, it did note that "to measure the effectiveness of safety devices and to aid in the planning of such devices it is essential that accident statistics be compiled by a central bureau in each state. When the legislatures adjourned in the spring of 1931 there were eighteen states with no provision for compiling such data and ten other states whose requirements were very meagre, being limited in most cases to the numbers of fatal injuries."[10]

The 1966 report by the Task Force on Federal Flood Control Policy framed the collection of better data about flooding as a crucial prerequisite to any sort of insurance program, charging the federal government with the task of gathering that information.[11] Decades later, insurance companies would look to the federal government to play a similar role in helping to collect data about cybersecurity risks that could aid the development of an insurance market. But beyond state data breach notification laws, most of which pre-dated any strong interest in collecting actuarial data on the part of insurers, the US government seemed hesitant to take any tangible steps toward establishing any formal data repository or collection system. While the challenge of collecting comprehensive, reliable data about cyber risks was not a new one, cyber risks did present some unique difficulties that appeared to hinder collection efforts in both the private and public sectors. The data required to track cybersecurity incidents was inherently much less straightforward for the government to access than information on car accidents or floods—events that occurred in plain view of all involved and typically required at least some intervention on the part of government authorities, from police officers to rescue workers.

Cybersecurity incidents often had no such outward-facing dimension—no obviously visible crash or damage, no need to go to the hospital or call in emergency response workers. While targeted organizations might approach law enforcement about breaches they detected, they might equally well decide that there was no point given the inability of many local law enforcement agencies to track such intrusions to their source or the likelihood of the perpe-trators operating overseas and therefore being impossible for the police to go after even if they could be identified. Unlike data on flood plains, the govern-ment would not be able to seek out cyber risk information on their own, they would have to solicit it from companies and individuals. And unlike car acci-dents, which affected individuals had little reason—and even less ability—to hide from government officials, the victims of cybersecurity breaches had very little incentive to report their misfortunes any more widely than absolutely necessary for fear of inviting lawsuits, bad press, and even regulatory penalties.

Another problem with collecting the data associated with cyber losses was that there were so many different types of losses and information to consider—with new categories cropping up all the time—and no universally agreed way to measure many of them. For instance, a 2010 cyber risk policy template by Travelers covered three types of third-party liability and seven categories of first-party losses, while a 2018 Zurich Cyber Insurance policy template offered coverage for six types of third-party liability in addition to thirteen categories of first party costs, as listed in table 6.1.[12]

The Zurich liability categories illustrate how much more complicated and sophisticated the regulatory and legal landscape around cyber risk had

Table 6.1

Comparison of coverage in 2010 and 2018 cyberinsurance template policies developed by Travelers and Zurich.

	Travelers cyber risk policy template, 2010	Zurich Cyber Insurance policy template, 2018
Third-party liability coverage	Network and information security wrongful acts (e.g., data breaches) Communications and media wrongful acts (e.g., copyright infringement or plagiarism) Regulatory defense expenses associated with security or communications and media wrongful acts	Security wrongful acts Media wrongful acts Costs of regulatory proceedings resulting from security or privacy wrongful acts Privacy wrongful acts Losses and defense costs of General Data Protection Regulation proceedings resulting from security or privacy wrongful acts Payment card industry demands resulting from security or privacy wrongful acts
First-party coverage	Crisis management event expenses Security breach remediation and notification expenses Computer program and electronic data restoration expenses Computer fraud Funds transfer fraud E-commerce extortion Business interruption due to computer system disruptions	Reputation damage (e.g., costs of terminated contracts or reduced value in brand due to a security, privacy, or media wrongful act) Breach costs Digital asset replacement expenses Social engineering theft of personal funds Social engineering funds transfer fraud Cyber extortion Lost business income due to disruptions in the policyholder's computer systems Dependent business income losses (i.e., losses due to a disruption to a service provider's computer system rather than the policyholder's computer system) System failure business income losses (i.e., losses due to a disruption caused by an accident or employee negligence) System failure dependent business income losses Social engineering theft of funds held in trust Reward payment costs (i.e., money paid for information leading to the arrest and conviction of someone committing an act of cyber extortion) Claim avoidance costs

become by 2018, with an entire dedicated coverage section for costs associated with the European GDPR, as well as a distinction between security and privacy liability that stemmed from a distinction between "security events" and "privacy events." The latter category Zurich defined as "1. the loss, theft, or unauthorized disclosure of Protected Information or Personal Information in the care, custody, or control of any Insured, someone for whom you are legally responsible, or a Service Provider; 2. a violation of any Privacy Regulation; 3. a violation of the GDPR; or 4. the unauthorized or wrongful collection, retention, or use of Personal Information."[13] In addition to coverage for the costs of general regulatory proceedings, analogous to what Travelers had offered, by 2018 Zurich included special third-party coverage for GDPR proceedings.

The categories of first-party coverage had also expanded significantly since Travelers drafted its 2010 policy. Where Travelers' older policy had covered computer fraud and funds transfer fraud, the 2018 Zurich template divided financial fraud coverage into three different categories of social engineering incidents, tying its coverage not just to the type of financial crime perpetrated but also to the specific mechanism used to carry it out. The emphasis on social engineering was not the only new element of the Zurich template. The categories of coverage in the Zurich cyberinsurance policy highlight how different types of cyber-related losses had become increasingly well defined over time along several dimensions. Where the 2010 Travelers policy had offered coverage for "business interruption," Zurich had broken that out into four different types of business interruption losses by 2018, depending on who was responsible for the interruption and how it was caused. The 2018 Zurich template included coverage for lost business income due to both malicious service disruptions and accidental system failures, including when those disruptions or failures affected one of the policyholder's service providers rather than their own systems directly. Both policies included coverage for extortion payments, but the newer Zurich specifications also included coverage for reward payments made to help arrest the perpetrators of such extortion schemes.

As their coverage categories evolved and became more specific, insurers needed more granular and detailed data about security incidents. For instance, in order to determine whether acts of fraud were caused by social engineering and were covered under those provisions, insurers and their policyholders had to be able to conduct sufficiently thorough analysis to identify the root causes of a security breach. Similarly, the 2018 Zurich policy template indicated a much more thorough understanding of the role of third parties and vendors in causing outages and security compromises, but identifying those instances also required more extensive investigation than the broader categories used in the earlier Travelers template. Investigating the root causes of cyber risk–related incidents required new types of expertise which many insurers—as well as their customers—did not necessarily have in-house, and even with expert analysis those investigations often yielded slow or uncertain results.

The challenges of collecting consistent data that identified the root causes and perpetrators of incidents were significant—but in many ways they seemed like the types of problem that might be solved given enough time. The lack of mandatory reporting regulations for security incidents other than breaches of personal information was a significant obstacle but it was mitigated in part by the implementation of GDPR, which included broader reporting requirements for security and privacy incidents. Furthermore, even if governments weren't mandating the reporting of that data or building a repository, insurers could eventually hope to build up sufficient information about the size and frequency of such incidents just by using their own claims data.

However, it was not clear that historical data on cybersecurity incidents would necessarily yield useful insights about future patterns and costs. Actuarial models for auto or life or flood insurance depend largely on the idea that it is possible to predict how severe the losses in each of these areas are likely to be by analyzing a variety of different factors ranging from environmental variables (the cost of gas, or the availability of good medical care, or the climate) to individual policyholder traits (e.g., past driving record, or blood pressure, or the height a home is built above sea level). But it was surprisingly difficult for insurers to identify either environmental or policyholder characteristics that significantly influenced the impact of cyber-related losses, and since the threats evolved over time it was unclear whether data about how those characteristics had influenced losses in the past would hold true for predicting future trends. Any time an insurer thought it had a handle on the threat landscape, there was always a possibility that attackers could shift their tactics or targets, as they had in shifting their attention from theft of payment card numbers to theft of medical and tax records and then, again, to ransomware.[14] Crime insurance also dealt with an evolving, adversarial threat—that is, people actively trying to evade safeguards and find new models for committing crime. But traditional crimes simply could not be carried out at the same scale as cybercrime, so historical data provided a more reliable prediction of how much crime was likely to be committed in the future. When it came to cybersecurity incidents, it was possible to imagine a scenario in which a single attack targeted thousands of victims simultaneously, all over the world, across every sector—an attack like NotPetya—leading to losses so severe an insurer would be unable to cover them.

INTERCONNECTED AND SYSTEMIC RISKS

The possibility of a large-scale interconnected cyber event that would cause catastrophic, accumulated losses was enough to dissuade some insurers from moving too quickly into cyberinsurance. At a July 2014 workshop hosted by the Department of Homeland Security, one underwriter referred to risk accumulation as "the big kahuna" of cyber risk exposures.[15] Years later, Warren Buffett made headlines in May 2018 when he told an audience in Omaha, Nebraska, at the Berkshire Hathaway annual meeting, "I don't think we or anybody else really knows what they're doing when writing cyber [policies]." He specifically cited the risk of an incident that could cause $400 billion or more in losses as a reason why the company should be cautious about entering the cyberinsurance market, telling his employees, "We don't want to be a pioneer on this."[16]

Several factors contribute to the interconnectedness of cyber risks and the potential for the losses associated with them to accumulate rapidly. One is simply the interconnectedness of computer systems via the Internet and other networks—malware can spread rapidly across the world, from a Ukrainian tax software firm to multinational shipping, confectionery, and energy companies, for instance, in a matter of minutes. Almost all other catastrophic or systemic risks—natural disasters, terrorism, war—are much more geographically constrained, so the odds of a group of diverse policyholders all being simultaneously affected by one of those risks are much lower. Put another way, insurers know how to diversify risk pools for other types of risk—by insuring customers in different regions or sectors, for example. Even with catastrophic risks like pandemics that had the potential to transcend boundaries, insurers had found ways to diversify their risk pools by insuring individuals of different ages with different health profiles.

When it comes to diversifying the cyber risk pool, however, insurers have few good options. Not only can malware cut across geography and industry sectors but companies increasingly rely on the same few software vendors and cloud service providers. This makes their risk profiles even more interconnected—a vulnerability in one of the very small number of popular operating systems, like Windows or MacOS, or an outage at one of the equally small number of large-scale cloud computing providers, such as Amazon Web Services and Microsoft Azure, could have far-reaching consequences.[17] In 2018, the insurance firm Lloyd's together with the risk-modeling firm AIR Worldwide estimated that an outage at a top cloud provider lasting at least three days could cause $15 billion in damages in the United States alone. "If a cyber attack occurs on a critical node of the cyber supply chain, such as a major cloud vendor, the attack could cause systemic business interruption to all associated businesses that rely on the vendor's services and systems to operate," the companies cautioned.[18]

Some of the systemic risks that could be caused by cyber threats are new and rely on the ubiquity of new technologies, like cloud computing. Others are magnified forms of existing risks that could now, potentially, be executed at much larger scale than ever before thanks to the interconnectedness and homogeneity of computer systems. James Scheuermann notes that "while extortion and financial theft historically have been 'one-off,' 'normalized' risks, cyber extortion and cyber financial theft are examples of what now may be systemic risks in some circumstances."[19] In his analysis of systemic cyber risks, Scheuermann distinguishes between which types of cyber risk are almost always systemic (for instance, attacks on critical infrastructure), which are rarely, if ever, systemic (such as the creation of defamatory media content), and which are sometimes systemic, depending on the circumstances. He concludes that "many, or most, categories of cyber risk are systemic only in certain circumstances" and that underwriters must therefore "determine the particular cyber risks that a firm may face in order to assess and manage those risks cost-effectively."[20] In this regard, cyber risks differ from other types of systemic risk, such as climate change, war, or financial crises—they span the full range from relatively small, minor events to potentially enormous, catastrophic ones and they are not constrained to any particular system. The difference between a systemic cyber risk and a relatively trivial one is largely determined by the scale of a cybersecurity incident and the system—or systems—that it affects. This means that insurers can't easily exclude systemic cyber risks from their coverage—as they would some other systemic risks—without stripping their policies of most of the provisions that customers find appealing and useful.

The possibility of systemic cyber risks led insurers offering cyber risk policies to be cautious with both their pricing and their policy limits. In 2014, following the Target breach that led to such wide-ranging estimates of the retailer's costs, the company turned out to have purchased about $100 million in cyberinsurance coverage, on top of a $10 million deductible. Target had "cobbled together" that amount from multiple different carriers because each one was only willing to offer a policy with limits too low to satisfy Target. Tower policies like these enable small insurance companies to diversify their risk across multiple policyholders and can allow for insurers to concentrate underwriting expertise in the market's lead underwriter, but they also come with significant risk to insurers, especially when they lead to highly correlated claims.[21] Even that $100 million coverage tower was less than Target had hoped to purchase—the company had reportedly tried to buy more prior to the breach but had been turned down by at least one carrier.[22] At that time, so soon after the *Sony* ruling had made clear that CGL policies would not be useful for covering breach-related legal costs, many companies in the United States, especially those that handled large volumes of customer data, were looking to invest in more breach coverage but quickly ran up against the relatively low limits set by carriers for those policies. In June 2014, just months after the decision in the dispute between Sony and its CGL carriers, the *New York Times* reported, "The most coverage a company can hope to acquire, using multiple underwriters, is about $300 million, experts say, significantly less than the billions of dollars' worth of coverage available in property insurance."[23]

Limiting coverage caps—and including substantial deductibles—helped insurers address concerns about interconnected risks in the short term by restricting how much they would have to pay out to any individual policyholder in the event of a catastrophic cyberattack. But it also limited the growth of the industry in the long term by constraining how much coverage insurers could sell. Some insurers sought out partnerships that would allow them to increase these caps—for instance, in 2016, insurance firm Beazley joined forced with reinsurer Munich Re to offer individual clients up to $100 million in coverage, as much as Target had been able to scrape together from multiple carriers just two years earlier. Previously, Beazley had capped cyberinsurance coverage for individual clients at $50 million.[24] It was a striking partnership, not just because it highlighted the importance of reinsurers in acting as a backstop for large-scale risks, but also because it indicated a significant divergence between the approach of the two largest reinsurers, Munich Re and Swiss Re. Just two months before the announcement about Munich Re and Beazley, Swiss Re's chief executive at the time, Michel Liès, had told the *Financial Times*, "It is too early for me to make a statement on whether cyber is an opportunity, a threat—or in the middle. . . . I don't think there is anybody wanting to profile themselves as a winner in this cyber risk coverage."[25] Years later, in 2021, Swiss Re CEO Christian Mumenthaler said in an interview about cybersecurity incidents, "the problem is so big it's not insurable. It's just too big. Because there are events that can happen at the same time everywhere."[26]

The idea that large-scale cyberattacks might be fundamentally uninsurable led some insurers to lobby for a government backstop. The model for this government backstop was the Terrorism Risk Insurance Act (TRIA) passed in the United States in November 2002, following the September 11 attacks, to provide a "system of shared public and private compensation for insured losses resulting from acts of terrorism." The text of the original law specified that the program had two purposes:

(1) protect consumers by addressing market disruptions and ensure the continued widespread availability and affordability of property and casualty insurance for terrorism risk; and

(2) allow for a transitional period for the private markets to stabilize, resume pricing of such insurance, and build capacity to absorb any future losses, while preserving State insurance regulation and consumer protections.[27]

The cyberinsurance market might also require a similar such government backstop that would serve these same two functions of ensuring continued widespread availability and affordability as well as providing a transitional period for stabilization, some insurers argued. Part of their justification lay in the potential for large-scale systemic cyber risks that could exhaust insurers' resources and undermine the entire market without government support. But the argument that a cyberattack could, in theory, be as expensive and damaging as the September 11 attacks proved to be largely ineffective in motivating legislation. TRIA, after all, had emerged from an actual incident, not a hypothetical one. If governments were going to provide a backstop for cyber risk insurance, it was possible that they would first want to see actual examples of cyberattacks that seemed legitimately uninsurable. In 2016, the Treasury Department did issue guidance on how TRIA might apply to cybersecurity incidents and cyberinsurance, but that guidance did little to clarify what types of cyberattacks TRIA might cover, merely asserting that "stand-alone cyber insurance policies reported under the 'Cyber Liability' line are included in the definition of 'property and casualty insurance' under TRIA and are thus subject to the disclosure requirements and other requirements in TRIA."[28] In other words, the Treasury Department seemed willing, in theory, to permit that TRIA could apply to cyberattacks but unwilling to actually specify how that would work or what criteria a cyberattack would have to meet to trigger TRIA.

MORAL HAZARD AND PREVENTIVE MEASURES

In her 2015 testimony at the Senate subcommittee hearing on cyberinsurance, Ola Sage talked about going to renew her cyberinsurance policy the previous year, after spending several months investing heavily in new security controls and rigorously implementing the National Institute of Standards and Technology Cybersecurity Framework at her tech consulting firm. Despite these changes, her insurer asked only one question about cybersecurity: Had she experienced a breach in the past year? Sage responded no. Three weeks later, Sage received her renewed policy and learned that her premium had increased by 12 percent. The additional security systems she had implemented in the previous year had not factored into the pricing at all—indeed, her insurer did not even know about them. "After a year of investing in processes and tools to strengthen our cybersecurity posture, the result was an increase in premiums. Doing the right thing didn't seem to pay, literally," Sage told the Senate subcommittee. "We went back to our broker to better understand how this could have happened and were informed that there were a variety of factors that went into the underwriting process. In our case, ironically, because our revenues grew in 2014 [versus] 2013, that appeared to be the primary contributor to the increase."[29]

Sage's experience was not unusual. In their 2019 analysis of 235 templates for property and casualty policies for the states of New York, Pennsylvania, and California collected by the National Association of Insurance Commissioners from a variety of different insurers, Sasha Romanosky, Lillian Ablon, Andreas Kuehn, and Therese Jones found that several insurers relied on other insurance products offered by their own companies to inform the premiums for their cyber policies. Others looked to the premiums set by their competitors to help determine their own prices. The majority of insurance policies that the researchers studied used a base rate pricing model, in which the policyholder's premium—like Sage's—was "assessed as a function of the insured's annual revenue or assets (or, with some niche products, number of employees or students)." For one policy they looked at, for instance, a company with annual revenue under $10 million, the annual gross base premiums totaled $1,913.91, compared to premium payments of $2,602.92 for companies with revenue between $10 million and $20 million, and $5,224.98 in premium payments for a firm generating between $50 million and $100 million in annual revenue.

Different insurers' policies also had very different pricing schemes, the researchers found, hinting at the lack of standardization in the market. For a company with $100 million in sales or assets looking to buy a policy with a $1 million limit and a $10,000 deductible, premium payments ranged from $3,300 to $7,500—and one insurer charged $42,000 for a similar such policy with a $0 deductible. The researchers conclude: "we found a surprising variation in the sophistication (or lack thereof) of the equations and metrics used to price premiums. Many policies examined used a very simple, flat rate pricing (based [on] a single calculation of expected loss), while others incorporated more parameters such as the firm's asset value (or firm revenue), or standard insurance metrics (e.g. limits, retention, coinsurance), and industry type."[30]

What is most striking in Sage's story is her description of the security-related questions her insurer asked in the process of renewing her policy—or rather, the one security-related question about whether the company had experienced a breach. Security questionnaires and assessments are a staple of cyber risk underwriting. Insurers want some sense of a would-be customer's security posture before deciding whether or not to cover their risks and how much to charge them, so just as they would ask questions about a house or a car or an event before insuring it, they typically ask questions about how firms protect their computer networks and data before pricing and issuing cyberinsurance coverage. The 2019 analysis of template policies found that more than half of the insurers who authored those policies factored a potential customer's information security controls into the pricing of their coverage. The original—and still quite common—means of assessing those controls was a security questionnaire that posed questions like the one Sage answered, and oftentimes failed to pose the other questions she was expecting.

These questionnaires can vary substantially in their comprehensiveness and focus, however, reflecting the same lack of standardization and uniformity as the cyberinsurance pricing schemes. For example, the thirty-four security questionnaires that Romanosky and his colleagues analyzed in their study ranged in length from fewer than ten questions to nearly seventy questions and, according to the researchers' analysis, covered 118 different topics across four broad themes: organizational, technical, policies and procedures, and legal and compliance. Organizational questions focused on understanding a company's risk profile, security budget, breach history, and dependencies. These questions included basic information about the company as well as some preliminary security information about whether the applicant had experienced previous security incidents, whether it outsourced any of its computer systems or security services, and what kind of data it handled.

Technical questions on these questionnaires focused more narrowly on the specific security controls that a firm employed to protect its data and networks—whether it used encryption or firewalls or multifactor authentication, for instance, or how many devices and IP addresses the company owned, or whether it segmented its network to isolate the servers that stored personal information. The researchers comment that "only a few insurers cover[ed] this aspect in their questionnaire," and further note that "when they did, only a few questions were posed." The overall result was a fairly incomplete and basic assessment of the applicant's technical security posture, the researchers conclude, writing: "Information about the technology and infrastructure landscape would clearly help a carrier understand, if only at a basic level, the overall attack surface of a potential insured and, with more information, help assess their overall information security risk posture. However, it seems that only very rudimentary information is collected."[31]

Questions in the policies and procedures category typically dealt with issues like whether the firm had an incident response plan in place, or who within the organization was responsible for data privacy and security, or whether the company had a data retention and destruction policy, as well as whether there were regularly updated security and privacy policies that had been reviewed by a lawyer. "The questions did not cover the substance of a particular policy (i.e. what should be in those policies, and how should they regulate particular issues) but rather only tested their existence," the researchers note, again indicating the superficial nature of many elements of these questionnaire-based assessments. Finally, in the legal and compliance category, questions generally covered whether the applicant was compliant with various standards and regulations such as the Payment Card Industry Data Security Standards or the Health Insurance Portability and Accountability Act.

Several things were conspicuously absent from the questionnaires. The researchers note that the NIST Cybersecurity Framework—which Sage was particularly proud of having implemented at her company—was not mentioned in any of the questionnaires they reviewed. Furthermore, only one questionnaire actually asked explicitly about a company's security budget and breakdown among prevention, detection, and response to security incidents. Overall, they conclude of the questionnaires they had evaluated, "there is little attention given to the technical and business infrastructure, and their interdependencies with environment in which the applicant is operating."[32] In an earlier study, Daniel Woods, Ioannis Agrafiotis, Jason Nurse, and Sadie Creese analyzed a set of twenty-four cyberinsurance questionnaires distributed by US and UK insurers and compared them to the widely used ISO/IEC 27002 standard and the Center for Internet Security Critical Security Controls. They identified gaps between the industry best practices laid out by these widely used documents and the security controls highlighted in the insurer questionnaires, noting that the insurance forms "predominantly focus[ed] on a small range of controls related to malware defences, managing back-ups and use of encryption."[33]

A representative from one carrier told regulators at a May 2013 cyberinsurance roundtable hosted by the Department of Homeland Security that carriers were under pressure to shorten the questionnaires they used to vet potential customers for fear of losing sales to other insurers. "My form might ask 50 questions, but another insurer might ask only ten questions," he said. "Companies won't want to fill out our 50-question application form."[34] The carriers may have been hoping that if they could sign up customers early then those policyholders would stick with their coverage for years to come and the insurers would be able to figure out the complexities of risk assessment and cybersecurity controls later on. And perhaps, with more time and more data, the standards for assessing a potential policyholder's security posture would become clearer and more codified, but there were also reasons to believe that establishing clearer standards could remain an elusive goal for insurers. In particular, the changing nature of online threats and computer security controls made it difficult for insurers to establish clear, set guidelines for what they expected from the firms they insured. Moreover, insurers found that bringing in law firms to oversee the cybersecurity incident response process for their policyholders sometimes meant they were unable to learn anything about the incidents themselves because the forensics reports detailing what had happened were often covered by attorney-client privilege and therefore were not shared with the insurers.[35] Without access to those reports, the insurers had no way to collect statistics on why and how their customers' computer systems were being breached, so they could not establish whether particular security practices or controls were especially helpful or effective for preventing or mitigating security incidents. This made it even harder for insurers to make progress toward establishing empirically grounded standards and requirements for vetting their customers' security postures.

The goal of the security questionnaires was to combat moral hazard, or insured entities not sufficiently protecting themselves from certain risks because they know that their insurer will bear some or all of the costs of those risks. Insurers have two basic techniques for addressing moral hazard so that their customers do not unnecessarily expose themselves to extra risk the moment they know they are safely insured. The first of these techniques is requiring policyholders to cover some significant portion of the costs associated with a risk themselves; in other words, charging a deductible or co-payment. The other way insurers can try to combat moral hazard is by requiring policyholders to take certain precautions that limit their risk exposure. A fire insurance policy might require that the insured entity install working smoke detectors, fire extinguishers, or sprinklers in order for it to be valid. These requirements depend on insurers being able to identify a set of effective, easy-to-assess safeguards against specific risks. For several types of risk, such as fire, theft, or car accidents, these safeguards are generally well understood and accepted, sometimes even required by law—smoke detectors and fire extinguishers, front door locks and security cameras, and seatbelts and air bags are standard safety features in many homes and cars. However, when it comes to defining the essential safeguards for cyber risk, there is much less clear consensus or empirical evidence about what cyber-security controls are most effective. This leaves insurers with comparatively fewer tools for combating moral hazard in this domain, and this lack of clear standards for protection is manifested in the relatively high-level, nontechnical questionnaires that they distribute to their customers.

Historically, in other areas of insurance, carriers have played a pivotal role in identifying and lobbying for crucial safety features that reduce risk. For instance, in their analysis of how the insurance industry has contributed to the reduction of moral hazard, Omri Ben-Shahar and Kyle Logue note:

> [T]he auto insurance industry has, for many years, funded research designed to identify ways to reduce the losses associated with automobile accidents. The industry operates an institute that tests and rates the crashworthiness of automobiles, and it organizes concerted efforts to lobby for mandatory safety devices (such as airbags). Likewise, many of the standards relating to fire pre-vention and building fire codes were developed by the insurance industry and were subsequently accepted by builders, firefighters, courts, and lawmakers as being state of the art. The homeowners' insurance industry has its own associa-tion researching and promulgating standards of safety with respect to property risks.[36]

But no such insurance industry initiatives have coalesced around cyberse-curity controls with the same degree of success or consensus around what the equivalent of airbags would be for computer networks. A government-organized data repository might play a role in helping to identify such controls, but in the past the insurers, rather than policymakers themselves, have often taken the lead in identifying the most effective safeguards for risk reduction, occasionally turning to government to help implement those tactics through regulation. Ben-Shahar and Logue cite as examples of insurers leading the way on public safety regulation the "efforts of insur-ers to upgrade and enhance the content and enforcement of state and local building codes" as well as insurers' lobbying activity in the 1980s on behalf of compulsory airbags, and more recent lobbying efforts advocating for stricter laws governing driver licensing.[37]

When it comes to cyber risks, however, insurers have been relatively slow to draw conclusions about which security controls are most essential for risk reduction, much less to lobby regulators to enforce those standards. Shauhin Talesh conducted interviews and observations of insurers, concluding that insurers act as "compliance managers" for their customers, helping policyholders figure out how to comply with privacy laws and standards in addition to providing incident response services. But even Talesh's findings suggest that much of this assistance came after a breach occurred. He writes, "the insurance company, through the risk management services it offers with cyber insurance, largely drives the company's incident response when a data loss occurs."[38] Helping customers avoid regulatory penalties or lawsuits is different from helping them figure out which preventive controls and policies will reduce their risk exposure. One reason the effectiveness of particular cybersecurity controls can be tricky to assess is the range of threats that fall under the umbrella of cyber risk. Tools like multifactor authentication may be very effective when it comes to preventing compromised accounts but offer little protection against other types of intrusions, such as the delivery of a piece of malware like NotPetya via a compromised software update, or the computer fraud incidents that rely on phishing emails to trick employees into initiating financial transfers. Similarly, strong encryption can provide considerable protection against data breaches in which perpetrators steal stored, encrypted data, but will offer minimal help if the perpetrators are able to steal credentials that can be used to decrypt that data. Insurers could condition their coverage on the implementation of multiple lines of defense, but there are so many security products and services available that it is not immediately obvious which controls should be included in such a list. Furthermore, some security controls may even counteract others in certain circumstances. For instance, the effectiveness of monitoring outbound traffic to check whether stolen data is being exfiltrated from a computer system could be undermined by strong encryption that makes it difficult for a system to determine what types of data are entering or leaving its servers.[39]

For insurers to assess the security postures of their policyholders requires considerable time and expertise, as compared to fire or auto safety assessments. "Because an insurer underwriting cyber-risk coverage possesses finite resources to monitor an insured's actions that affect the probability of loss after an insurance contract has been signed, it may be difficult to determine whether an insured has engaged in behaviors that increased the likelihood of a covered loss," Liam Bailey points out in his analysis of moral hazard in the cyberinsurance market.[40] The inability to perform effective security audits of customers can be frustrating to customers like Sage who feel their efforts and expenditures should be recognized, and it can be a major source of frustration for insurers, who feel their policyholders do not have sufficient security monitoring and protections, and are therefore subject to unnecessary and avoidable risks. To bolster their own auditing and risk monitoring abilities, insurers have increasingly partnered with security firms to conduct more effective assessments of potential customers and strengthen the technical elements of their customers' security postures. While these partnerships are often announced and advertised by insurers with much fanfare, it remains unclear—even after two decades—how much they have helped insurers refine their risk models and auditing tactics.

CYBER RISK INSURANCE PARTNERSHIPS

In July 2000, Lloyd's of London and Counterpane Internet Security announced a partnership whereby Lloyd's would offer special coverage to companies that used Counterpane's security service for cyber-related losses, such as repairing software, online extortion payments, and business lost due to denial-of-service attacks.[41] Strikingly, that announcement—like many of its successors—did not make clear what specific financial or coverage benefits would be offered to policyholders who engaged with the partner security firm over those who did not. For instance, while Lloyd's made much of the fact that a Counterpane customer would only have to pay between $12,000 and $20,000 in annual premiums for coverage totaling $1,000,000, it never clarified whether similar coverage was available to non-Counterpane customers and, if so, how much more it would cost them.[42] Nearly two decades later, in 2018, insurer Allianz announced a cyberinsurance partnership with Apple, Aon, and Cisco, in which Allianz would offer "enhanced" coverage to customers who used Apple and Cisco technology, as well as Aon's cyber resilience evaluation service. Those customers who agreed to use the Allianz partners' services and products might be eligible for policies that covered costs not included in other customers' policies, such as hardware replacement costs. But Allianz had so little confidence in its partners' ability to reduce customer risk that it declined to adjust any policyholders' premiums based on their use of those partners' technologies or the results of their resilience evaluations performed by Aon.[43]

The press release put out by the four companies in February 2018 touted the partnership as "a first in cyber risk management" but, in fact, it was only the latest in a long line of close partnerships between insurance carriers and security firms—dating back to Lloyd's and Counterpane—in which neither the carriers nor their policyholders seemed to gain any clear benefits from the addition of new partners.[44] Insurers still did not have sufficient confidence in those partners to link their pricing schemes to those companies' services or assessments, and policyholders therefore received no clear value from engaging with those partners. The only parties who clearly benefited from the proliferation of these partnerships were the outside partners themselves, who could use them as a way to expand their customer base without having to promise any concrete results to either their partner carriers or their new customers.

These partnerships were intended to help fill the gaps in insurers' knowledge about cybersecurity and to enable them to perform more robust and reliable hands-on assessments of their potential customers' security postures than would be possible through a generic questionnaire. Given the challenges of assessing all the different dimensions and elements of a particular firm's cyber risk exposure, and keeping that assessment up to date as the threat landscape evolved, it made sense that insurers would turn to companies with deep technical expertise to help them scale up and refine their assessment techniques as the market for cyberinsurance grew. Partnering with insurers could also benefit the security firms, not just by bringing them more customers but also by providing them with access to claims data about whether or not their services were effective and what types of security incidents and losses their customers experienced. By 2018, major technology companies like Apple and Cisco and leading incident response and security firms like FireEye were entering into these partnerships—as were a bevy of smaller start-ups that had entered the market more recently specifically to cater to the needs of insurers in assessing cyber risk.

These cyberinsurance partnerships fell into three general categories. The first category was partner firms that helped carriers assess potential customers' risk exposure and implement ex ante security and privacy protections intended to help prevent incidents. The Allianz partnership with Aon, Cisco, and Apple, for instance, fell into this category—all three partner firms were focused on helping policyholders reduce or assess their risk exposure prior to any actual security incident occurring. Within this set of partnerships are firms that provide strictly assessment services, such as Aon, and those that assist with security controls and network monitoring, like Cisco and Apple, as well as some that provide a combination of both services.

A second category of insurer partnerships focused on firms that assisted policyholders with incident response and damage mitigation in the aftermath of a cybersecurity incident to help reduce costs. For instance, in 2018, AIG advertised no fewer than twenty-six data breach and privacy counsel partners—law firms that they encouraged their policyholders to consult following an incident to provide legal guidance on any response to a breach and help reduce the risk of subsequent litigation. In addition to law firms, insurers sought out other incident response partners, including firms that provided forensics and incident investigation services, firms that offered customer breach notification and identity protection services, and public relations firms that could help policyholders manage the external messaging for a cybersecurity incident. The third, and less frequent, type of partnership was between insurers and reinsurers, as in the case of Beazley and Munich Re, in order to offer larger cyberinsurance policies with higher coverage limits than carriers were comfortable providing on their own.[45]

The largest cyberinsurance firms, as measured by premium sales for cyber-specific policies, took three distinct approaches to pursuing these partnerships. The most popular approach among the largest carriers was to engage many, diverse partner firms that primarily provided ex post incident response and mitigation services but also offered some ex ante assessment and protection functions. For insurers that did not want to actively pursue dozens of partners across all these different categories, a second approach was to forge partnerships with just a select few firms that provided a wide variety of different security-related services rather than partnering widely with a large number of specialized firms. For instance, Travelers, rather than establishing partnerships with dozens of companies, focused on cultivating a single full-service partnership with Symantec, spanning both pre-breach and post-breach services, as well as a security assessment partnership with NetDiligence. This approach may have allowed Travelers to standardize its approach across all of its customers and focus on a few firms it believed could best provide security support to its policyholders, also limiting the time and resources that the carrier had to spend vetting potential partners. The third approach, taken by Beazley, offered even more limited services to customers through partnerships, with the carrier instead choosing to ramp up its own in-house security services, including an internal breach response team and a dedicated cyber risk management portal. Beazley also operated a separate subsidiary, Lodestone Security LLC, to provide ex ante security guidance and assessment services, and formed outside partnerships only to raise the limit on its policies for individual customers through its arrangement with Munich Re.[46] This idea that the future of cyberinsurance lay in merging cybersecurity firms with insurance carriers gained some traction among start-ups in the tech world as well. For instance, in 2020 a San Francisco–based security company called Coalition that offered integrated security management services and cyberinsurance coverage to clients, backed by Swiss Re, raised $90 million in venture financing.[47]

The variation in these models—from forming dozens of partnerships with outside firms to cultivating only a few partnerships to focusing almost exclusively on enhancing in-house security services—highlights how much uncertainty there was around these partnerships in the cyberinsurance industry. Adding to this uncertainty was the lack of any evidence that these partner institutions really did help reduce policyholders' risk exposure or drive down insurers' costs by helping them do a better job of screening and auditing their customers' security postures. The clearest sign that insurers were skeptical about the value of these partnerships came from their unwillingness to link cyberinsurance premiums to their customers' use of partner institutions, even in the case of partnerships that were explicitly aimed at helping the carriers assess their customers' security practices and risk exposure.

Insurers themselves have mixed views about the purpose and effectiveness of these partnerships. "From a cost perspective it helps to have a pre-negotiated rate with vendors, but on the prevention side I wouldn't say that we have data to suggest that the money that we have spent or our customers have spent on prevention partners has improved the security performance," XL Catlin chief underwriting officer John Coletti said in 2018, adding, "We haven't developed the algorithm that correlates what technology they're using and what their premium should be."[48] By contrast, Chubb vice president Michael Tanenbaum said in a 2018 interview that the carrier had seen some empirical evidence that the incident response partners actually reduced the costs associated with policyholder incidents, perhaps

explaining why so many insurers had more partners in that category than in
the ex ante protection and assessment area. Chubb found that there was only
an 18 percent chance of a third-party liability action being brought against
one of its customers when one of the carrier's vetted breach response partners was involved in the aftermath, compared to an industry standard of
42 percent, according to Tanenbaum. Like Coletti, Tanenbaum also noted
that it was possible for insurers to drive down the costs associated with
breaches just by virtue of having pre-negotiated rates with their partners. In
some ways, the emphasis on ex post partners seemed to derive from cyberinsurance's origins in data breach policies. The major expenses associated with
data breaches were often tied to lawsuits and legal settlements, so it was perhaps not surprising that many insurers chose to focus more on legal partnerships rather than technical ones. Ex ante protections posed other concerns
as well. Insurers promoting a uniform set of security firms and services to
their customers may undermine the diversity of their customers' security
postures, leading to a uniform set of technical protections, hardware, and
monitoring systems across all of their policyholders. This lack of diversity in
firms' security technology could be beneficial, if insurers are able to establish
that it provides reduced risk exposure, but it could also backfire by creating a
more uniform security landscape that attackers can compromise across multiple customers simultaneously, thereby compounding the threat of interconnected cyber risk.[49]

THE FALLACY OF THE STAND-ALONE MODEL

Insofar as cyber risks are a coherent category of risks, it is only because
they all manifest through the manipulation and vulnerabilities of computers and network infrastructure. The impacts of those threats, the precise
mechanisms by which they are executed, the people and systems they target, all vary enormously and often intersect and overlap with other risks.
The shared technical infrastructure that underlies these risks is therefore
the primary—perhaps the only—reason to group them together in stand-
alone policies separate from other types of risks. The same safeguards and
security controls, such as encryption, firewalls, authentication systems,
network segmentation, and others, help organizations defend their technical infrastructure from cyber risks in all their many forms. So if grouping
cyber risks and claims data together yielded any insight into which of these

safeguards provided the most effective protection against different cyber-security threats, that would be a strong reason to look at these incidents together, separately from other, less technical incidents. But the growing popularity of stand-alone cyberinsurance policies has provided very little insight into what protection mechanisms are most effective across the broad spectrum of cyber risks, raising the question of whether this is actually a productive or useful way of organizing coverage for these diverse risks. Rather than isolating cyber risks in their own stand-alone policies, insurers and their policyholders might be better served by integrating them into the other domains of risk where they already possess some empirical data, expertise, and coverage.

Designing a comprehensive stand-alone insurance policy for cyber risks is, in some ways, significantly different from insuring auto risks or fire risks—unlike cars and fires, it is nearly impossible to enumerate all the possible ways cyber threats could cause harm. This makes it difficult to take the named peril approach to cyber underwriting that carriers have adopted without leaving significant holes in customers' coverage or uncertainty about how their coverage will apply to future risks. At the same time, stand-alone cyberinsurance is very different from the all-risk model of property insurance, where it is possible for insurers to clearly identify and assess the value of a policyholder's covered assets. It can be much more difficult to assess the cost of damage to digital assets and infrastructure, and stand-alone cyberinsurance is concerned with much more than just those losses—it also deals with third-party liability costs, financial fraud, and reputation damage.

It's hard to imagine how either a named peril or all-risk approach could effectively tackle such a wide range of threats to and from digital technologies—it would be like trying to write an electricity insurance policy or a telephone insurance policy that simultaneously protected policyholders from all the possible threats those technologies posed as well as all possible threats to those technologies. In trying to treat cyber as a risk analogous to cars, floods, fires, or property, by creating stand-alone coverage, insurers actually undercut their ability to use the wide range of different coverage formats and risk-modeling tactics at their disposal to address different facets of cyber-related risks. This conflation of all cyber risks into stand-alone policies has also exacerbated the challenges insurers face in trying to gather reliable data on these risks and diversify their risk pools through recruiting customers with different risk profiles. That inability to diversify risk has, in turn, forced insurers to grapple more immediately and directly with the threat of catastrophic, large-scale risks that could affect many of their customers simultaneously.

The current trends in cyberinsurance policies suggest that insurers are specifying more and more particular online risks and costs that they are willing to cover, for both first- and third-party losses. But listing cyber threats one by one is a tricky endeavor in the context of a rapidly changing risk environment—while covering them all under a comprehensive all-risk policy appears infeasible and unwise given concerns about risk accumulation. Ultimately, it's not clear that a set of risks as dynamic and broad as those presented by and to computers and networks will be well suited to comprehensive stand-alone policies that adopt either a named peril or an all-risk approach. Instead, different types of cyber risks, like different risks related to electricity, should be split into different types of insurance. Some of those risks may be so new or distinct that they call for separate cyber policies or riders but others could be closely tied to existing lines of coverage and belong inside policies that deal with, for instance, liability, crime, property, and cars.

Insurers are understandably wary of embedding cyber risks in their existing lines, and finding ways to do so without threatening their core business will take time—and perhaps also some assistance from policymakers. Catherine Mulligan, the Zurich senior vice president, told the Senate subcommittee at its 2015 hearing on cyberinsurance that "the scope of the [cyber] exposures is too broad to be solved by the private sector alone." Her argument that managing cyber risks requires the involvement of government stakeholders echoed similar, earlier asks by insurers who were being pressured by policymakers to offer cyber coverage that could help drive down online risks and costs. Time and time again, beginning in the early 2010s, insurers told regulators that they needed help gathering data about cybersecurity incidents and providing coverage for large-scale systemic cyber risks, but when it came to actually trying to design and implement public-private programs that might help meet these requests, carriers and policymakers in many countries found it surprisingly difficult to actually agree on what role governments could—or should—play.

"WHAT IS THE POINT OF COLLECTING DATA?":
GLOBAL GROWTH OF CYBERINSURANCE
AND THE ROLE OF POLICYMAKERS

In May 2021, a ransomware attack forced Colonial Pipeline to shut down more than 5,000 miles of its fuel pipeline that supplied gas and jet fuel to the southeastern United States. As gas prices in the areas supplied by the pipeline skyrocketed, the company consulted with its insurance carrier about what to do next. Following that consultation, Colonial paid its attackers a $4.4 million cryptocurrency ransom—and promptly filed a claim for the payment with its cyberinsurance provider. "I suspect that it will be covered," Colonial Pipeline CEO Joseph Blount later said of the claim during questioning before the House Homeland Security Committee on June 8, 2021.[1] The previous day the Department of Justice had announced that it had successfully recovered $2.3 million of Colonial Pipeline's ransom payment, raising complicated questions about the roles of government, insurers, and victims in deciding how to respond to cyberattacks and strengthen cybersecurity.[2] Had Colonial Pipeline, its insurer, and US law enforcement all coordinated this response to the ransomware attack? Whose decision had it been to pay the ransom? Who would receive the recovered funds? And would the government's success at clawing back part of the ransom encourage more victims—and their insurers—to make payments to criminals moving forward?

Policymakers cannot extract themselves from the discussions and dilemmas surrounding cyberinsurance any more than they can remove themselves from the broader challenges of cybersecurity. Policy interventions aimed at the cyberinsurance market can take a number of different forms. Daniel Woods and Andrew Simpson proposed a framework of six different types of policy measures related to cyberinsurance: policies that push for wider adoption of cyberinsurance, policies that help define the coverage cyberinsurance policies offer, policies that initiate or standardize data collection efforts, policies that promote information sharing to better inform insurers' underlying risk models, policies that clarify or impose cybersecurity best practices, and policies aimed at responding to catastrophic cyber losses.[3] Insurers have repeatedly called on governments for assistance in developing more robust cyberinsurance offerings through several of these different categories of policymaking, even as policymakers have tried to encourage the industry in hopes it will serve as a vital component of private-sector cyber risk management.

But despite repeated efforts by policymakers and insurers to work on cyberinsurance initiatives together, these discussions have ultimately accomplished very little beyond highlighting the disconnect between what insurers view as their role in the cybersecurity ecosystem and what policymakers view as the role of cyberinsurance. Policymakers have promoted cyberinsurance as a means of incentivizing security controls and best practices and driving cybersecurity investment without having to mandate those measures through more heavy-handed regulation. But insurers have been slow to push specific controls and technical measures on their policyholders, relying instead on questionnaires and more process-based and organizational assessments of their customers. Meanwhile, insurers have pushed policymakers to develop cyber incident data repositories that they can use to inform their risk models and clarify government backstop coverage for large-scale cyberattacks, but these efforts have met with little success. Insurers and policymakers seem to be working at cross-purposes in other ways, too, notably when it comes to ransomware attacks like the one directed at Colonial Pipeline. Insurers often have incentives to encourage their policyholders to pay ransoms, as Colonial did, rather than face much larger business interruption and system restoration claims. But these payments help fund the criminal groups perpetrating cyberattacks and contribute to the profitability of ransomware, leading to more such attacks, so policymakers have for years been trying to discourage organizations from caving to attackers' demands—though governments have stopped short of outright forbidding either insurers or victims from paying ransoms. The ambiguity surrounding questions like whether it's legal for insurers to cover ransom payments prompted at least one insurer, AXA, to stop covering ransom payments only for customers in France in 2021, pending further clarification by French regulators.[4] This lack of clarity about the rules and regulations for cyberinsurers has contributed to the counterproductive relationships that governments and carriers have had in several countries, as more regulators around the world have developed an active interest in cybersecurity regulation and, by extension, cyberinsurance.

THE CYBERSECURITY POLICY BOOM

For more than a decade after it was first introduced in the United States, cyberinsurance had been almost exclusively purchased by US-based companies, who were driven to buy such policies first by the rise of data breach notification laws in individual states and later by the wave of cybersecurity incident–related litigation that gained traction partly because of those regulations. By 2018, however, when Singapore's minister for finance, Heng Swee Keat, gave a speech about cyberinsurance at a conference of reinsurers in Singapore, companies in many other countries all over the world—as well as their governments—had begun thinking about whether insurance could play a role in their approach to cyber risk management. While the early cyberinsurance market was almost entirely confined to the United States, the late 2010s saw gradual increases in sales of cyberinsurance policies in other countries, including in the European Union member states, China, Brazil, India, and Singapore. In part, this growing global interest in the cyberinsurance market was due to increasing regulatory activity around data security and privacy, which had given rise to a series of significant new laws and draft regulations in many of these countries. These regulations included the Chinese Cybersecurity Law, passed in 2016; the General Data Protection Regulation implemented in the EU in May 2018; the Singaporean Cybersecurity Act, passed in 2018; the Personal Data Protection Bill, introduced by the Indian government in December 2019; and the Brazilian General Data Protection Law, or Lei Geral de Proteção de Dados (LGPD), which went into effect in August 2020. While each of these laws reflected the particular political climate of the place where it was passed, they shared some themes. The three primary components of these data regulations that affected cyberinsurers were incident reporting requirements, penalties for security and privacy failures, and security standards.

Cybersecurity incident reporting requirements, which featured in different ways in all of these data protection laws, could provide insurers with potential avenues for accessing more incident data. But the reporting requirements included in many regulations did little to address insurers' needs for better data, whether because the reported information was not shared with industry stakeholders or because it did not include the relevant range of incidents and details carriers needed in order to build better risk models. Reporting requirements also created new concerns for companies about the liability and bad publicity issues associated with having to report breaches—fears that insurers hoped might motivate companies to purchase cyberinsurance coverage. The penalties for security failures imposed by many of these laws were also a source of considerable concern for organizations and similarly drove interest in cyberinsurance. Additionally, these provisions guided insurers in offering new coverage specifically aimed at investigations and violations of different data protection laws, like the GDPR. By setting specific caps on these fines, data protection laws also offered insurers a clearer sense of the potential costs of security incidents and enabled them to adjust their policy limits and pricing accordingly. Only a few of the data regulations actually prescribed specific security standards, but those that did offered insurers at least a partial road map for how to guide their policyholders toward compliance and what security measures to require of them. Mandated security standards could also make companies feel confident that they knew exactly what was required of them in terms of data protection and how to avoid liability and penalties, however, potentially leaving them less inclined to invest in insurance coverage or rely on carriers to act as their compliance managers.

As these new regulations were passed in countries around the world, companies became increasingly aware of their own liability and responsibilities with regard to data protection and purchased more cyberinsurance policies with larger coverage caps. In some cases, companies looked to the global growth of cyberinsurance and the insurance industry more broadly to serve as a sort of global regulator for cybersecurity standards and risks across these different countries, many of which embraced very different policies and regulatory approaches to data security. Not only were companies facing a growing tide of regulatory requirements, they were also realizing that it was possible to sustain significant cyber-related losses even outside the intensely litigious environment of the United States because of the evolving nature of cyber threats. The breaches of personal information that appeared to be the most common type of cybersecurity incident in the late 1990s and early 2000s were primarily a risk to companies if their customers sued them or regulators fined them for negligence. In the United

States, where customers did regularly file class action lawsuits in the wake of large-scale data breaches, some organizations in certain sectors, such as retail, purchased insurance policies designed to cover the third-party losses associated with these civil suits. But as online threats like ransomware, denial-of-service attacks, and social engineering–enabled cyberespionage became increasingly common, and cyberinsurance policies began to cover more of the first-party costs associated with these types of incidents, interest in purchasing this type of coverage spread beyond the United States. The high potential penalties for data privacy and security missteps written into regulations like the GDPR bolstered this interest, just as the data breach notification laws in the United States had done for the US cyberinsurance market in the early 2000s.

Global interest in the cyberinsurance market outside the United States was not constrained to the private sector. Governments, too, were interested in whether they could foster stronger cybersecurity in their countries through robust cyberinsurance offerings that put in place stringent security requirements for policyholders and helped companies weather the ill effects of breaches and cyberattacks. Government efforts focused specifically on fostering cyberinsurance took three general forms: data sharing and aggregation initiatives, back-stops for claims associated with large-scale cyber risk incidents, and risk pools that provided smaller-scale funding to insurers to help launch their cyberinsurance offerings. Notably, for all the government discussions, workshops, and reports on cyberinsurance, few governments managed to get any of these actual initiatives underway. Instead, policymakers would meet with industry representatives, compile nearly identical lists of recommendations drawn from those three broad categories, sometimes get as far as actually starting to hammer out the details of a data sharing repository or possible back-stop program, and then give up on actually trying to set it up. Not just in the United States, which made the earliest such efforts, but in many other countries too, discussions over how governments could support the cyberinsurance industry were often repetitive, noncommittal, and unproductive.

The one exception to these failures was Singapore, which in 2016 launched its Cyber Risk Management Project, an initiative aimed at supporting "robust underwriting and pricing of cyber risks" and "fostering an efficient cyber risk insurance market place." The program had three components: developing a standardized taxonomy for describing cybersecurity incidents, creating a database of cybersecurity incidents and their resulting losses, and benchmarking different models of cyber-related losses to support actuarial pricing. On Monday, October 29, 2018, at the Fifteenth Singapore International Reinsurance Conference in the Sands Expo and Convention Centre, Singapore's minister for finance, Heng Swee Keat, commended the progress of the Cyber Risk Management Project and unveiled the next step in Singapore's cyberinsurance efforts. "Today, I am pleased to announce the formation of the world's first commercial cyber risk pool in Singapore," he told the conference attendees. The pool would have a capacity of up to $1 billion, he said, and would be funded by a combination of insurance firms and insurance-linked securities in order to provide "bespoke cyber coverage" to businesses in the Association of Southeast Asian Nations (ASEAN) and other countries in Asia. "The cyber risk pool reflects Singapore's standing as a specialty insurance hub, and our commitment to driving forward-looking insurance solutions to tackle new and emerging risks," Heng concluded, imploring the audience members to join the pool. "I encourage you to consider participating in this joint effort, and to work together to develop better risk models to price cyber risks appropriately. With proper pricing, more corporates will be encouraged to take-up cyber risk protection."[5]

Many countries and their governments did not broach any of the issues around cyberinsurance until several years after the Department of Homeland Security began thinking about them in the United States, so the US policy efforts, and sometimes EU efforts, shaped the trajectory of many of those debates in other countries, sometimes as a model for how to engage with private industry and, in other cases, as a counterexample: what not to do if a government wants to have any actual impact. In the EU, for instance, regulators had begun considering their role in cyberinsurance markets as early as US government agencies had, but European policymakers still fell into many of the same patterns and processes as the US government when it came time to evaluate their role in supporting the cyberinsurance industry, despite implementing a very different data protection regulatory regime. In China, the development of the cyberinsurance market intersected with two different regulatory regimes, one focused on slowing growth of the Chinese insurance market and opening it to foreign firms and another focused on data protection and localization. Both of these regulatory initiatives offered some benefits as well as some setbacks to insurers looking to sell cyber risk coverage. The regulatory frameworks put in place by the EU and China served as crucial models for Brazilian and Indian data protection laws, but regulators in those countries directed less explicit attention to the future of cyberinsurance because the markets in both countries remained so small. In Singapore, by contrast, regulators were not just intensely focused on the cyberinsurance market in particular, they were also well aware of the many failings of the US process and cited the US government recommendations and shortcomings specifically in their reports.

Strikingly, whether legislators deliberately modeled their efforts on the US process or not, and whether they drew from the GDPR, the Chinese Cybersecurity Law, or US regulations in drafting their respective data protection laws, few countries were able to actually escape the pitfalls that US regulators had encountered. Furthermore, none of them replicated the rapid growth of cyberinsurance that had been seen in the United States. For all the lessons they might have learned from the United States about how to regulate the cyberinsurance industry, most governments ended up following the same hands-off approach and relying on insurers to figure out how to use their products to improve cybersecurity on their own. And while insurers themselves often lobbied, in vague terms, for government assistance, when it came to actually working out the details and logistics of such initiatives, the carriers also often seemed to decide they would prefer a lighter regulatory touch. Ultimately, however, the failure of regulators to address the challenges faced by cyberinsurers meant that the increasingly global market for cyber coverage did not have access to international risk data or support and could not be well tailored to different countries and regulatory environments. Instead, cyberinsurance policies worldwide were based heavily on the models insurers had built using the data they had been able to gather in the United States.

CYBERINSURANCE POLICY EFFORTS IN THE UNITED STATES

On October 22, 2012, DHS convened its first formal workshop on cyberinsurance. Titled "Defining Challenges to Today's Cybersecurity Insurance Market," the 2012 workshop was a one-day event, held at the Intellectual Property Rights Center in Arlington, Virginia. The sixty attendees included government employees, representatives from insurance carriers, corporate risk managers, cybersecurity experts, researchers, and critical infrastructure owners and operators, who were the crucial link to the workshop's organizer and host: DHS's National Protection and Programs Directorate, the branch of DHS that was at the time charged with protecting critical infrastructure in the United States and was later folded into the Cybersecurity and Infrastructure Security Agency.

The NPPD had little authority to regulate private industry outside of specific critical infrastructure silos, but it had taken an interest in cyberinsurance as a possible means of pursuing one of DHS's central objectives: promoting cybersecurity in the civilian sector. Over the course of the daylong workshop, DHS identified three primary reasons that first-party cyber coverage was "expensive, rare, and largely unattractive" to buyers. The first was "a lack of actuarial data which results in high premiums for first-party policies that many can't afford," the second was "the widespread, mistaken belief that standard corporate insurance policies and/or general liability policies already cover most cyber risks," and the third obstacle insurers faced was the "fear that a so-called 'cyber hurricane' will overwhelm carriers who might otherwise enter the market before they build up sufficient reserves to cover large losses."[6] The US government concluded, in its report on the event, that "evolving the cybersecurity insurance market to one that offers more coverage to more insureds at lower prices therefore depends on two key factors: (1) the development of common cybersecurity standards and best practices; and (2) a clearer understanding of the kinds and amounts of loss that various cyber incidents can cause." As for the concern about "cyber hurricanes," participants at the workshops proposed two possible ways the government could help in that area as well. One was the creation of a "federal reinsurance entity" modeled on the TRIA approach that would "promote the development of actuarial data that carriers will need to create new insurance products." The second was the passage of a "Cyber Safety Act," modeled on the Support Anti-Terrorism by Fostering Effective Technologies Act (SAFETY Act) of 2002, that would "promote the development of (1) new cybersecurity-enhancing technologies and services; (2) insurance requirements for purchasers of those offerings; and (3) corresponding liability caps."[7] This latter set of recommendations gained little traction in DHS, perhaps in part because in 2016 the Treasury Department signaled that a sufficiently devastating cyberattack would already trigger the provisions of TRIA without requiring an additional law, though it was far from clear under what conditions, specifically, TRIA would apply to cyber incidents.[8] TRIA's definition of an "act of terrorism" required an incident to "be a violent act or an act that is dangerous to" human life, property, or infrastructure, and "to have been committed by an individual or individuals as part of an effort to coerce the civilian population of the United States or to influence the policy or affect the conduct of the United States Government by coercion." Even the most devastating and expensive cyberattacks, like NotPetya and the Colonial Pipeline ransomware attack, were not violent or coercive in quite the manner that TRIA seemed to envision.[9]

A second NPPD-hosted cybersecurity insurance roundtable meeting on May 13, 2013, focused on the need for more first-party cyber coverage, as opposed to the third-party liability coverage that carriers had been offering since the early days of cyberinsurance. Unlike the third-party losses associated with breaches of personal data, first-party costs could be caused by incidents that companies had no obligation to report, leaving insurers even more in the dark about how to build accurate risk models than they were when it came to third-party policies. There was no clear consensus among the participants about the best way for the government to help address this lack of information, however. Some attendees advocated for a shared database of cyber claims information, or a federal government-run "cyber data sharing clearinghouse," but others said they thought that sharing data with their competitors would be a nonstarter for their companies, or even a violation of antitrust law.[10] At a roundtable held the following year, on April 7, 2014, in the Eisenhower Executive Office Building in Washington, DC, carriers aired more conflicting opinions about the ideal design for a cyber incident data repository:

> Several participants . . . suggested that it might make sense to initially scope a cyber incident data repository to address only cyber incidents with potentially catastrophic consequences. A second underwriter disagreed, asserting that catastrophic cyber loss "spooks" the insurance industry, will likely not be covered in any event, and therefore should not be the focus of a repository development effort. A third underwriter added that a wide spectrum of cyber incidents that fall far short of a catastrophe exists—including cyber incidents that may cause significant physical damages. He commented that a repository therefore would be better served by bifurcating received cyber incident data in a way similar to how the property insurance market divides potential property losses into both catastrophic and non-catastrophic loss. The underwriter concluded

that repository planners should similarly identify where that line should fall in the cyber loss context. . . . A reinsurer concurred with this recommended approach, noting that more data on non-catastrophic but systemic cyber incidents would be especially useful for the reinsurance community.[11]

Not only did attendees of the insurance industry working group meeting disagree about what types of incidents should be included in a repository, they also disagreed about how best to incentivize carriers to participate—with some suggesting that reporting should be made mandatory by the government and others predicting that such a requirement would "shut this data sharing effort down."[12]

One underwriter at the April 2014 meeting proposed establishing a new working group that would "advance repository conversations to the next stage," modeled on the National Fire Protection Association, which gathers information about fire safeguards.[13] So Tom Finan, the NPPD official who had organized the first cyberinsurance workshop in 2012, formed a dedicated Cyber Incident Data and Analysis Working Group (CIDAWG) to look at the value proposition for a Cyber Incident Data and Analysis Repository (CIDAR) and consider what types of data such a repository should collect. In September 2015, the CIDAWG published a white paper listing sixteen specific categories of data that might be relevant to collect through such a repository, everything from the type and severity of an incident to its timeline, impacts, costs, and contributing causes, as well as the motivation of its perpetrators, the incident response processes used by its targets, and the security controls that failed to prevent it. Unlike most earlier government analysis of this topic, the CIDAWG white paper didn't gloss over the challenges of defining these types of data, it included templates for input fields that could be given to carriers submitting data as well as examples of different severity scales for cyber incidents. For each category of data, the CIDAWG paper laid out exactly what questions should be asked of the reporting insurer and what multiple-choice answers they should be given to choose from. For instance, to gather information about a perpetrator's motivations, insurers might be asked, "What was the attacker's apparent end-state goal? Check all that apply," and then be given a list of twelve possible answers to select from, ranging from theft or bodily injury to disruption of systems or technical advantage.[14] Compiling all of these data categories and reporting templates was a significant accomplishment—the closest anyone had ever come to actually defining a standardized reporting scheme for cybersecurity incidents that got at many of the different, relevant dimensions of these incidents for insurers. The September 2015 white paper was the rare example of a document so detailed and specific that it seemed almost possible it could actually yield real results. But shortly thereafter, work on the repository effort was all but abandoned by the US government. The cybersecurity insurance industry working group disappeared and the CIDAWG was disbanded.

Several factors contributed to this abrupt evaporation of all of the DHS efforts on cyberinsurance—Finan departed DHS in late 2015, and the November 2016 presidential election prompted even more turnover among the officials who had been working on cyberinsurance. But personnel changes were not the only factors at play in halting the cyberinsurance initiatives. Industry actors also contributed to the failed plans for a CIDAR. Despite expressing interest during the 2014 workshops in the potential role of the federal government in contributing cybercrime data to such a repository, ultimately, carriers announced that they did not want it to be run by the government. When DHS proposed that the insurers form an Information Sharing and Analysis Organization (ISAO) to coordinate a repository themselves, the carriers appeared to decide that, actually, they would prefer not to share data with their own direct competitors either. Still, the work done by the CIDAWG was not entirely wasted—some carriers adopted the data categories and templates from their white paper and used those for their own internal claims analysis and reporting processes.

Then, in March 2020, the United States Cyberspace Solarium Commission—a group established in the legislative branch to tackle cybersecurity threats and make recommendations to Congress—issued its final report, which refocused US government attention on cyberinsurance. Among many recommendations in the Solarium Commission report, there was a significant emphasis on the importance of cyberinsurance, and also on the vital role of the government in trying to assist the market's growth and development. The report recommended that the US government fund a research and development center "to work with state-level regulators to develop certifications for cybersecurity insurance products." It also proposed that the government help the insurance industry "create more accurate risk models" and explore the possibility of "placing a cap, via standards or certifications of insurance products, on insurance payouts for incidents that involve unpatched systems."[15]

The commission devoted four full pages of its report to discussing how the government could enable the cyberinsurance industry to function better. "A robust and functioning market for insurance products can have the same positive effect on the risk management behavior of firms as do regulatory interventions," the report noted, emphasizing that insurance could serve as a form of regulation, potentially relieving government entities of the responsibility for setting mandatory security standards. The report continued, "the US government is well placed to play the same role it has taken with other emerging insurance industries throughout history, facilitating collaboration to develop mature and effective risk assessment models and expertise."[16]

Because insurance regulation happens primarily at the state level, the Solarium Commission was wary of advising the federal government to overstep its bounds in influencing the cyberinsurance market, but it did recommend that Congress allocate funds for DHS to start a Federally Funded Research and Development Center (FFRDC) that would "work with insurers, state regulators, and experts in cybersecurity risk management to develop curricula and training courses for cyber insurance underwriters" as well as cyber claims adjusters. In addition, the Solarium Commission recommended that the FFRDC work with state regulators to set minimum standards for cyberinsurance policies and "develop cybersecurity product certifications based on a common lexicon and security standards." The report also recommended reviving the defunct CIDAWG group and establishing a new "public-private working group at DHS to convene insurance companies and cyber risk modeling companies to collaborate in pooling and leveraging available statistics and data that can inform innovations in cyber risk modeling" and "identify common areas of interest for pooling anonymized data from which to derive better, more accurate risk models."[17]

The 2020 Solarium Commission report didn't stop at recommending the revitalizing of the DHS cyberinsurance efforts, it also recommended that the US government "explore the need for a government reinsurance program to cover catastrophic cyber events" modeled on TRIA. Specifically, the report charged the Government Accountability Office (GAO) with studying "the existing scoping of the TRIA to assess whether it is sufficiently broad to cover cyber events perpetrated by nation-states, which most general property and casualty insurance policies currently exclude or attempt to exclude," as well as whether "the triggering threshold for the TRIA—a loss of $200 million, as of the 2020 reauthorization—is the appropriate size to trigger a similar backstop for catastrophic cyber events." The report highlighted the need for the government to provide greater clarity about what types of cybersecurity incidents qualify as "certified acts of terrorism" and "whether this provides a sufficient backstop for insurers, as many major cyber events—particularly those perpetrated by nation-states—may not fit squarely under" such a definition. The commission also recognized the complicated international elements of cyberattacks and raised the question of whether a government backstop for insurers like TRIA, which was designed for terrorism, might require further consideration "given that terror attacks generally take place in and affect a confined area, while some cyber incidents are not bounded by geography." For instance, the report proposed, the GAO analysis of TRIA "should address whether a cyber-attack on an American company affecting only assets in another jurisdiction would qualify."[18]

The Solarium Commission report explored roles for policymakers in the cyberinsurance market in much more detailed and specific ways than any previous US government initiative. The ideas of providing assistance to insurers for collecting data or certifications for their products or a government backstop for catastrophic cyber risk were all old ones that dated back at least to the first 2012 workshop hosted by DHS, but just as the CIDAWG report on data categories had provided a concrete template of what a reporting scheme for an aggregate incident data repository might look like, so too the Solarium Commission report provided concrete recommendations for what different US government actors could do to help clarify, stabilize, and standardize the cyberinsurance market that provided a much clearer roadmap than any of the earlier workshops had done. In July 2020, the commission went even further and released a set of legislative proposals for Congress to implement its recommendations, including a draft bill to establish its proposed FFRDC.[19]

In the summer of 2020, Congress was certainly not rushing to pass that bill—or indeed any of the others contained in the commission's lengthy set of legislative proposals. But still, it seemed like a significant milestone that discussions about cyberinsurance were regaining momentum in the US government, that those discussions were happening with increasingly vivid detail and specificity, and that the legislative branch was taking a renewed interest in its role, and even starting to draw up regulatory language that could be used to implement some of the ideas that had been circulating in the government for almost a decade. By 2020, the United States was far from the only government to have taken an interest in cyberinsurance markets and related regulatory efforts—if anything, it had started to fall behind some other countries that had used the time since the CIDAWG disbanded to embark on ambitious data protection regulatory schemes and partnerships with insurers—but the Solarium Commission recommendations suggested that the United States might still have an opportunity to make up for lost time and demonstrate that as the nation with far and away the largest market for cyberinsurance in the world, it was still proactively tackling the challenges that buyers and sellers in that market faced. Even if Congress failed to act on the Solarium Commission recommendations, the parallel processes in other regulatory bodies across the world illustrated just how influential the early US efforts had been in setting the terms of government debates about the role of policymakers in the cyberinsurance market and the complicated balance of trying to use insurance to replace regulations while leveraging regulations to enable insurance.

CYBERINSURANCE IN THE EUROPEAN UNION

In 2018, the same year that the GDPR went into effect, raising the specter of much larger fines for data security and privacy incidents than ever before across the EU, the European Insurance and Occupational Pensions Authority (EIOPA), an EU financial regulatory body, published the results of a cyberinsurance survey it had conducted with thirteen insurers and reinsurers based in Switzerland, France, Italy, Germany and the United Kingdom. At the time, EIOPA estimated that roughly 90 percent of the stand-alone cyberinsurance market was based in the United States, with between 5 and 9 percent—or between $150 million and $400 million in premiums—based in Europe. But by 2018 that seemed poised to change. Growing awareness about cybersecurity incidents and cyberinsurance products might have contributed to European organizations' interest in coverage for cyber losses regardless of the regulatory environment, but the GDPR made clear just how high the stakes could be for a security or privacy failure.[20]

Under the GDPR, companies could be fined up to 4 percent of their annual, global revenue for certain types of security and privacy violations, creating a significant financial risk for European organizations even in the absence of civil litigation. But unlike the legal fees and settlements associated with class action lawsuits in the United States, it was not clear at the outset whether or not insurers would be permitted to cover the costs of GDPR fines and penalties, or whether regulators would end up deciding that coverage of that sort invalidated the whole point of fining companies in the first place. The GDPR was not the only new piece of data protection policy that European companies were grappling with. The EU Network and Information Security (NIS) Directive, adopted in 2016 with a deadline for individual EU member states to implement it in national legislation by May 9, 2018, also created new obligations and risk exposure for European organizations, particularly those that provided critical infrastructure. In particular, the NIS Directive called for mandatory reporting by telecom providers and e-trust services of all cybersecurity incidents "with significant impact," not just breaches of personal information, which companies were required to report under the GDPR. Those reports included data on the incidents' root causes, including hardware failure, faulty software updates, or malware, as well as the specific technical assets affected by the incident, such as certification authority platforms, hardware, switches and routers, or underground cables, and whether the incidents were caused by human error, malicious actors, or system failures. These were precisely the types of data that insurers were looking to collect—especially in Europe, where the relatively small number of cyber-insurance customers meant that carriers had even less historical information to use for building predictive risk models.

In March 2018, Insurance Europe, the industry organization of European insurers and reinsurers, even developed a "template for data breach notifications" that they hoped regulators would use for developing reporting requirements under the GDPR.[21] The reporting template was divided into three sections. The first contained identifying information about the reporting organization that could be easily removed before sharing data with third parties.[22] The second part asked for details about the data breach that could be gathered within seventy-two hours of discovering a breach— the time limit for reporting data privacy and security breaches under the GDPR. These short-term questions included information about the target organization's sector and size as well as the type of data stolen, nature of the attack, and measures taken to mitigate adverse effects of the breach.[23] Finally, the third section of the template included details that could be completed within four weeks of discovering a breach, after the seventy-two-hour reporting window had elapsed and the breached organization was able to "gain more in-depth knowledge of the nature of the breach." This portion of the reporting template included questions about the estimated financial losses due to the breach, the measures taken to prevent a similar attack from being executed in the future, the motivation behind the attack, and the type of exploit or malware used to cause the attack (e.g., cross-site scripting, session hijacking, denial-of-service attack, credential reuse, man-in-the-middle attack, SQL injection attack).[24]

GDPR and the NIS Directive offered cyberinsurers two significant opportunities to break into the European market: the looming threat of major repercussions for cybersecurity and data privacy missteps, and the potential to partner with regulators to gather more detailed and extensive information about these missteps, what caused them, and what impacts they had. Indeed, all thirteen of the carriers that EIOPA surveyed in 2018 reported seeing a recent "substantial increase in the demand for cyberinsurance," particularly among European customers. One insurer told the agency that it had observed a more than 50 percent increase in premium sales for its cyberinsurance products in 2017, another said that in the year prior to the survey the number of stand-alone cyberinsurance policies it sold had increased by a factor of seven. One firm reported to EIOPA that in 2003 the average time between its offering a customer a quote for cyberinsurance coverage and actually selling that policy was three years; by 2018, the conversion time of successful sales had dropped to between one and six months.[25] The carriers noted that much of the growth came from companies looking to purchase business interruption policies, rather than tradition privacy liability coverage, perhaps due to the high-profile ransomware attacks the previous year that had so dramatically interrupted operations of several European firms. In 2017, in addition to the massive disruptions caused by NotPetya, the WannaCry ransomware infected hundreds of thousands of computers across 150 countries by exploiting a vulnerability in the Windows operating system dubbed EternalBlue that had been stolen from the National Security Agency. North Korea is believed to have been behind the WannaCry campaign, which significantly disrupted the operations of the UK's National Health Service, as well as Renault, Nissan, and FedEx, among others.

By then, European regulators had already been predicting for years that the implementation of the GDPR and the NIS Directive would drive greater adoption of cyberinsurance in the EU. Interestingly, part of the basis for those predictions seemed to derive from the relatively larger size of the cyberinsurance market in the United States, even though US data protection regulations were relatively lax in most regards and, on the whole, quite different from those being implemented in Europe. Still, a 2016 report authored by the European Union Agency for Cybersecurity (ENISA) noted that "the adoption of the EU NIS Directive and GDPR may have an effect similar to the one that relevant law-making had on the US cyber insurance market."[26] But the GDPR and the NIS Directive, given their emphasis on regulatory fines, user rights, critical infrastructure, and incident reporting, were unlikely to engender either the litigious environment surrounding data breaches that the US state notification laws had enabled or the culture of corporate financial disclosures related to potential cyber losses encouraged by the SEC guidelines. Still, the insurers EIOPA spoke with in 2018 were cautiously optimistic that the GDPR would help drive greater sales of cyberinsurance, though they did not anticipate that the market would grow anywhere near as rapidly as it had in the United States, partly because it was unclear whether GDPR fines and fees would be insurable.[27] In September 2019, EIOPA released another, larger survey of forty-one major European cyberinsurers and reinsurers across twelve European countries. Based on the responses, EIOPA estimated that European cyberinsurance premiums had increased by 72 percent in 2018, but that growth only brought the total premiums to 295 million euros for 2018 (up from 172 million euros in 2017).[28]

European regulators had been interested in cyberinsurance even before the passage of the GDPR. ENISA had commissioned a report on security economics that touched briefly on issues of cyberinsurance as early as 2008,[29] and in 2012 it published a report specifically focused on cyberinsurance policy.[30] In October 2017, ENISA even hosted a cyberinsurance workshop aimed at proposing "recommendations to support the uptake of cyber insurance and the growth of the cyber insurance market in the EU."[31] By then, individual countries within the EU had also begun looking at these issues; in March 2015, for instance, the UK Cabinet Office had issued a report together with Marsh intended to "set out joint initiatives between government and the insurance sector to tackle UK cyber security risk," including a new Cyber Essentials accreditation risk assessment process for which Marsh agreed to cover the costs for small and medium-sized enterprises.[32] But while individual countries like the UK were sometimes able to extract promises like these from insurers, especially when regulators at the highest levels of government got involved, much less progress was made at the EU level where the lead agencies like ENISA and EIOPA appeared to have little authority or power to influence any concrete outcomes, in much the same way that DHS seemed to struggle to affect any real change within the US government.

On April 1, 2019, EIOPA hosted a daylong Cyber Insurance Workshop in Frankfurt. In many regards, the event echoed the workshop hosted almost seven years earlier in Arlington, Virginia, by DHS—it was intended to bring together insurers, reinsurers, corporate risk management officers, researchers, and government regulators to have a discussion about the state of the cyberinsurance market in Europe, the challenges that insurers and policyholders faced, and the potential role of government in trying to mitigate those challenges. Unsurprisingly, the summary report of the workshop highlighted almost exactly the same findings as the readout report from the 2012 workshop in the United States. European insurers and reinsurers who attended the workshop wanted regulators to consider "a government back-stop for systemic cyber events and cyber warfare," as well as "a 'Cyber' database with anonymized data on cyber incidents, based on common definitions to facilitate data collection and data sharing."[33] The process and a set of recommendations that were emerging in Frankfurt were almost identical to those the United States government had initiated seven years earlier. Even after more than a decade of EU agencies and regulators discussing cyberinsurance, it seemed that almost no progress had been made toward facilitating better incident data aggregation or defining clearer policy measures for addressing systemic cyber risks since these issues had been raised years earlier by ENISA and DHS. Possibly, this state of affairs and the inability of either ENISA or DHS to make real progress on cyberinsurance simply reflected how peripheral these two departments were within the larger European and US government ecosystems. As compared to the ability of the UK cabinet to elicit concrete commitments from Marsh, or the US Treasury Department's ability to clarify the terms of TRIA, neither ENISA nor DHS seemed able to make much headway, despite a much longer history working on these issues and much greater engagement with outside stakeholders.

The European Union and the United States were also, ostensibly, working together on these efforts, through the EU-US Insurance Dialogue Project. This initiative launched in 2012 with representatives from EIOPA and the European Commission on the European side and participants from the US Federal Insurance Office in the Department of Treasury and the National Association of Insurance Commissioners in the United States. It included a Cyber Insurance Working Group which, in February 2020, published a report calling out the NAIC Cyber Supplement that insurers used to report their claims, premiums, and direct losses, as well as the TRIA as two models that the EU could learn from, despite the fact that US insurers had expressed significant dissatisfaction about the state of data collection and government risk backstops.[34] In many regards, the EU was poised to offer much stronger support to the cyberinsurance industry than the US government ever had been, thanks to the more stringent and standardized reporting requirements of the GDPR and the NIS Directive. But instead of following through on this—as their own industry associations, like Insurance Europe, were urging them to do—European regulators instead turned to their US counterparts for guidance. Rather than trying to tailor a cyberinsurance model that suited their own regulations, European policymakers kept looking to the United States to figure out how to stabilize and grow their cyberinsurance market to little avail.

CYBERINSURANCE IN CHINA

If adoption of cyberinsurance was gradual in Europe, it was slower still in China. In 2017, insurers had made much of the idea that the Chinese cyberinsurance market was about to expand dramatically, thanks to a combination of the May 2017 WannaCry ransomware attacks that had affected computers at nearly 30,000 institutions in China and the Chinese Cybersecurity Law implemented in June 2017. In August 2017, AIG told Reuters that it had seen an 87 percent increase in inquiries for cyberinsurance policies in China and Hong Kong following the WannaCry attacks.[35] A November 2017 report by Frank Wang, the head of property and casualty products in the Shanghai office of reinsurer Gen Re, also predicted that the WannaCry ransomware and the new Chinese cybersecurity law would "prompt more businesses in China to explore insurance protection."[36]

But cyberinsurance remained significantly less common in China than in the United States and lagged behind European uptake as well.[37] In 2018, when industry estimates suggested that roughly two-thirds of US companies had purchased some form of cyberinsurance, whether through stand-alone policies or package policies, fewer than 20 percent of companies in Asia had cyber coverage.[38] A May 2019 report published by Swiss Re deemed China's cyberinsurance market "under-developed compared with economies at a similar level of digitalisation," attributing the low demand for cyber coverage in the country to "over-confidence in existing data security and low awareness of availability of cyber insurance."[39]

The global rise of cyberinsurance also coincided with a particularly fraught moment in Chinese insurance regulation. In April 2017, just one month before WannaCry and two months before China's Cybersecurity Law came into force, the chairman of the China Insurance Regulatory Commission (CIRC), Xiang Junbo, was dismissed from his office, which he had held since October 2011. During that time, Xiang had overseen enormous growth in the Chinese insurance industry and had passed reforms that eased licensing requirements. During Xiang's tenure, premium income for Chinese insurance companies doubled and their assets tripled.[40] Following Xiang's departure from CIRC, the Chinese government set a goal of much slower growth for its insurance industry, aiming for only a 6.5 percent increase in premiums in 2018. At the same time, CIRC refocused its attention on reducing financial risk in the industry and creating greater openness to foreign investment in the Chinese insurance sector. China's deliberate slow-down in rising insurance sales instituted in 2017, right at the moment when companies like AIG and Gen Re were predicting a sharp increase in cyberinsurance sales in the country, was a blow to cyberinsurers hoping to capitalize on the rapid growth in the Chinese insurance market. However, the simultaneous opening of that market to foreign investment also created new opportunities for foreign insurance companies and brokerages, including those who offered cyber coverage, to enter the Chinese market. In 2018, China started rolling back a requirement that foreign insurance companies establish a representative office in China for two years prior to their being able to even apply to establish a foreign-invested insurance company. That same year, China also began lifting some of the restrictions on foreign insurance brokers, including revising the policy that stated "wholly foreign-owned brokers could only broker large-scale commercial, international maritime, aviation, and transportation insurance and reinsurance."[41] Under the new rules, foreign brokers would be able to draft insurance plans and help customers apply for policies, as well as assist with claims, and provide consultation services related to risk assessment and risk management. These changes were announced on April 27, 2018, and less than a month later, Willis Towers Watson—a broker with a growing cyber risk management practice that had, the previous year, hired Tom Finan, who previously led DHS's cyberinsurance efforts to head up its cyber risk division—became the first foreign broker to receive a license allowing it to conduct all brokerage business in China.[42] By 2019, the Chinese cyberinsurance market was dominated by four foreign carriers: AIG, Allianz, Chubb, and Zurich.[43]

Opening the Chinese insurance industry to foreign insurers and brokers, many of whom had significant experience with cyber policies by 2018, should have helped grow the cyberinsurance offerings in China. But even as the relaxation of old rules allowed foreign insurers to enter the Chinese market, the country's Cybersecurity Law created some new obstacles. China passed its Cybersecurity Law on November 6, 2016, and it took effect on June 1, 2017, just weeks after the WannaCry attacks. Several of the law's provisions seemed to benefit insurers by creating clearer security guidelines and expectations for private industry. For instance, under Article 15 of the law, the Chinese government committed to establishing "national and industry standards for cybersecurity management, as well as for the security of network products, services, and operations." Clear standards of this nature would not just be useful to organizations but would also provide clearer guidance to insurers about what safeguards to look for when assessing potential customers' security postures. Similarly, Article 21 laid out a list of five "security protection duties" for network operators, including determining the people within an organization who are responsible for cybersecurity, adopting technical measures to prevent malware and monitor intrusions, storing at least six months of network logs, implementing encryption, and backing up important data. Article 25 also required those network operators to "formulate emergency response plans for cybersecurity incidents" and mandated that "when cybersecurity incidents occur, network operators should immediately initiate an emergency response plan, adopt corresponding remedial measures, and report to the relevant competent departments in accordance with relevant provisions." Critical information infrastructure operators were also required to submit annual cybersecurity reports to the government following an "inspection and assessment of their networks' security and risks that might exist."[44]

While the list of security controls set out in the law was not particularly new or unusual, requiring these safeguards at the national level was a new—and important—development for driving down organizations' risk exposure. That, all by itself, could have aided insurers in their efforts to combat moral hazard and gauge customers' risk profiles. Beyond just forcing companies to secure their data and networks more effectively, though, China's willingness to set out a prescribed list of security expectations also had the potential to help carriers understand what their policyholders needed to do to reduce the risk of regulatory penalties and liability, if not necessarily actual cyberattacks. In this regard, the Chinese Cybersecurity Law went much further than either US or European regulations in defining which security controls companies were required to implement. But the law's potential to drive cyberinsurance sales was limited by the fact that it applied only to network operators and critical information infrastructure operators, so unlike in Europe, there was still "no uniform personal data protection law that applie[d] exclusively to all information controllers."[45] Moreover, insurers worried that the provisions of the law might apply to them in ways that would make it difficult to enter China's rapidly growing insurance market. For instance, the Cybersecurity Law's requirements for foreign firms operating in China seemed poised to create a significant burden for the foreign carriers and brokers who dominated the Chinese cyberinsurance market. Even businesses that were not considered critical information infrastructure operators were "encouraged" under the law to "voluntarily participate in the critical information infrastructure protection system."[46] In 2018, law firm Winston & Strawn published its annual review of the Chinese insurance market, predicting that the Cybersecurity Law— and in particular the stipulations limiting overseas transfer of data—would be "onerous" for foreign insurers, who "typically collect insureds' personal information in high volumes and store such information on computer networks (that may or may not be physically located in the PRC)."[47] Since foreign carriers were the primary providers of cyberinsurance coverage in China and they desperately needed more data to build their evolving risk models, this limitation on overseas data transfers and storage created a particular setback for the growth of cyber coverage in the country.

The Chinese cyberinsurance market was hindered by many of the same obstacles insurers faced in other countries—a lack of historical data on the frequency and costs of cybersecurity incidents, and unclear regulatory regimes, even after the passage of the Cybersecurity Law, which established "basic rules for protecting personal information."[48] But beyond these standard challenges, the rise of cyberinsurance in China was further complicated by its intersection with evolving cybersecurity and insurance regulations that simultaneously aimed to slow the growth of insurance sales, ramp up private-sector cybersecurity efforts, introduce more foreign insurers and brokers into the Chinese market, and significantly restrict how those foreign firms handled data about Chinese clients. These conflicting goals and the changing policy landscape contributed to the uncertainty surrounding the cyberinsurance market in China and the gradual, rather than sudden, increase in both buyers and sellers, as carriers and Chinese companies took tentative steps toward figuring out how best to comply with both cybersecurity and insurance regulations in flux.

EMERGING CYBERINSURANCE MARKETS: BRAZIL, INDIA, AND SINGAPORE

Insurers with experience in the US cyberinsurance market have occasionally made efforts to offer their products in other countries. In 2017, for instance, Beazley announced a partnership with carrier Generali to offer cyber liability and data breach coverage to Brazilian companies.[49] In a November 2018 report, the Brazilian insurance regulator Superintendencia de Seguros Privados (SUSEP) also told the International Monetary Fund that it had "carried out a monitoring study on cyber insurance" and had "a plan to set up a dedicated team" to evaluate cyber policies.[50] Two years later, in 2019, when SUSEP began compiling data on premiums for cyberinsurance policies within the country, it found that they remained extremely low, totaling approximately $3.66 million. Furthermore, only nine insurers had registered with SUSEP in 2019 to offer cyberinsurance products, and of those only six had recorded receiving any premium payments for such policies: AIG Seguros, Allianz Seguros, Chubb Seguros Brasil, Tokio Marine, XL Seguros, and Zurich Minas Brasil.[51] Although Brazil requires firms to purchase insurance from locally licensed carriers in the country, most of those insurers already had successful US-based cyberinsurance divisions they could draw on for data.

Unlike the Chinese Cybersecurity Law, the LGPD did not lay out security requirements for companies. Instead, the LGPD echoed the structure of the GDPR in many ways. Like the GDPR, the Brazilian law set out a list of rights belonging to "data subjects" whose information was collected by companies, as well as a list of lawful bases for data processing, or conditions under which companies could legally process their customers' data. Article 48 of the LGPD also required that companies report "to the national authority and to the data subject the occurrence of a security incident that may create risk or relevant damage to the data subjects." The law also specified that those reports contain not just a "description of the nature of the affected personal data" and "information on the data subjects involved" but also "an indication of the technical and security measures used to protect the data," as well as "the measures that were or will be adopted to reverse or mitigate the effects of the damage."[52]

These stipulations could potentially provide insurers with valuable data on the effectiveness of security controls if regulators were willing to share the collected data, but it would take time for that information to accumulate and for government officials to figure out how, if at all, they would pass it on to carriers. The maximum penalties set out in the LGPD for data protection and privacy violations were also significantly smaller than those in the GDPR. The LGPD authorized fines totaling as much as 2 percent of a company's annual revenue in Brazil up to a maximum of 50 million reals, or just under $10 million—much larger than the Chinese penalties, though still half the size of the maximum fines permitted under the GDPR. Those sums might be sufficient to drive smaller organizations to purchase insurance policies that could help cover such penalties, but it was unclear whether they would be significant enough to draw cyberinsurance coverage to the attention of larger customers.

As the LGPD neared its implementation in the summer of 2020, India was also in the midst of a lengthy process of drafting a data protection and privacy law dubbed the Personal Data Protection Bill. Like the LGPD, India's Personal Data Protection Bill was based heavily on the framework of the GDPR and listed rights of data principals as well as specific grounds for lawful processing of personal data without those principals' consent. The process of drafting the Indian bill dated back to a landmark case in the country's Supreme Court, *K. S. Puttaswamy v. Union of India*, which was decided in August 2017. In that ruling, the Supreme Court of India held that privacy was a fundamental right in the Constitution of India, spurring the Indian government to begin crafting a data protection bill that would codify digital privacy protections. In December 2019, that bill was introduced into the Parliament of India.

The Indian draft bill designated companies that held and processed personal data as "data fiduciaries" and, among other responsibilities, it tasked them with reporting breaches of their customers' personal data. Article 25 of the draft required that "every data fiduciary shall by notice inform the [Indian data protection] Authority about the breach of any personal data processed by the data fiduciary where such breach is likely to cause harm to any data principal." According to the bill, those reports had to include details about what type of data had been stolen, the number of people affected by the breach, and its possible consequences, as well as the actions taken by the breached firm to mitigate or remedy the incident—information that would, potentially, be valuable to insurers. However, like the Chinese Cybersecurity Law, the Indian Personal Data Protection Bill also placed some restrictions on where data about Indian citizens could be stored. Specifically, it required that certain types of undefined "critical personal data" be stored and processed exclusively on servers within India—a measure that could potentially make it harder for foreign insurers to enter the Indian market and thereby slow the spread of cyberinsurance in the country.[53]

Still, all of these potential outcomes of the Indian bill—both the benefits and the obstacles they might create for insurers—were purely hypothetical prior to its passage, and by mid-2020 the bill was still being reviewed by a joint parliamentary committee. So it was no surprise that the cyberinsurance industry in India remained almost nonexistent. In a 2019 report, the Data Security Council of India (DSCI), an industry coalition, reported that approximately 350 cyberinsurance policies had been sold in India in 2018, up from about 250 policies the year before. The premium payments for all cyberinsurance customers across the entire country totaled between $11 million and $14 million in 2018, and individual policies ranged in coverage from $1 million caps for small companies to $200 million in coverage for large IT service providers.

The main providers of those policies were Tata AIG, ICICI Lombard General Insurance Company, Bajaj Allianz, the New India Assurance Company Limited, and HDFC Ergo, again indicating the significant influence of insurers with global operations who were able to draw on experience and data from other countries.[54] Soon after the DSCI report was released, Lloyd's India announced its intention to ramp up cyberinsurance sales in the country, saying it would focus on first-party coverage for business interruption and ransomware attacks. Coverage of the initiative noted that in order to model the online risk environment in India, Lloyd's India "extrapolates its global experience for the Indian region after extensive consultations with brokers, insurance companies and risk managers."[55]

The idea that insurers could build on their experience in countries like the United States that had a relatively robust cyberinsurance market by 2020 to extrapolate models and policies for firms in other countries made a certain amount of sense. After all, the interconnectedness of cyber risks across industry sectors and geography meant that the threats and attack models firms in China, Brazil, and India faced were not necessarily so different from those being dealt with in the United States and Europe. At the same time, the shifting regulatory landscape in each of these countries presented challenges for insurers trying to figure out what kind of penalties they might need to cover and what compliance requirements they had to be certain their policyholders met.

While several countries crafted data protection regulations that impacted the cyberinsurance landscape, perhaps no country approached the challenge of growing its cyberinsurance market more directly or determinedly as a goal in itself than Singapore, which in April 2016 launched its Cyber Risk Management (CyRiM) project aimed at "fostering an efficient cyber risk insurance market place" and "promoting both the demand and the supply of insurance coverage." The project was led by the Insurance Risk and Finance Research Centre at the Nanyang Technological University in Singapore but included a heavy government presence and the Project Oversight Board included representatives from both the Monetary Authority of Singapore and the Cyber Security Agency of Singapore.[56]

Following the same general model as the United States and the European Union, but operating on a much faster timeline, CyRiM hosted three roundtable meetings in August, September, and November 2017, and then issued a report in March 2018, the month after Singapore's Cybersecurity Act was passed and six months before Heng announced the $1 billion Singaporean cyber risk pool. CyRiM participants clearly drew both inspiration and a strong sense of potential pitfalls of their work from observing the earlier efforts in the United States. In the summary report from the first roundtable, held in August 2017, participants drew a direct comparison between their own process and that undertaken by DHS. The report notes, "The United States Department of Homeland Security (DHS) held a similar exercise over a period of three years with insurance companies (these workshop findings were provided to the group in advance of the roundtable). However, this process hit a roadblock and does not seem to have progressed any further . . . this is a reminder of how much can be achieved in Singapore, perhaps even achieving more than the United States has been able to so far."[57]

Armed with the findings of the DHS workshops and motivated to outperform the United States, the CyRiM project tackled the question of whether regulation was needed to help stabilize and encourage the cyberinsurance industry. Perhaps inevitably, it came up against many of the same questions that DHS had posed years earlier, including how best to deal with the lack of historical incident data and whether Singapore needed a broader mandatory breach notification regime that extended beyond just critical information infrastructure providers. For instance, the first CyRiM roundtable report hypothesized that breach notification "should drive better cyber hygiene and there will then be a need for more cyber risk assessments which will provide data, and more purchase of cyber insurance. . . . [T]here could be a role for the regulator to create those databases from which data could be obtained."[58]

While the Cybersecurity Act that was passed the following year dealt with some of these issues, including establishing a framework for sharing cybersecurity information, it did not mandate incident reporting for anyone other than critical information infrastructure (CII) operators in defined CII sectors that included energy, banking and finance, healthcare, and government. During the second CyRiM roundtable, participants in the project expressed some skepticism about the value of a broader mandatory reporting, turning again to the example of the United States. The report from the September 28, 2017, meeting noted, "Mandatory reporting requirements in the United States has meant an increase in insurance purchase and demand since organisations do not want a breach to occur without cover. However, the data from this reporting has not necessarily led to insurers being able to develop good products since it is not very helpful data. Therefore, what is the point of collecting data?"[59]

At its third roundtable session on November 21, 2017, CyRiM was still wrestling with the question of what role, if any, the Singaporean government could or should play in creating an efficient cyberinsurance market. After watching what had transpired in the United States, the CyRiM participants were dubious about the ability of the private sector to move forward without government intervention. "If the insurance industry could be used as a tool to enhance cybersecurity for all industries and to incentivise entities, this would be a good way forward. However, a key issue is whether this is in fact possible," CyRiM's first session report had noted. "Instead, government regulation may be needed that would make such cybersecurity standards mandatory rather than waiting for the insurance industry to develop them."[60] At the third roundtable, three months later, participants hypothesized that some regulation might be needed just to get the industry going. "In the United States, while legislation kick-started the purchase of cyber insurance, it is becoming increasingly market-driven. For example, SMEs [small and medium-sized enterprises] may require insurance in order to obtain contracts," the report from the third session stated.[61]

Here, again, Singapore seemed to be strongly influenced by what it had observed in the United States cyberinsurance market—at once admiring of how quickly the market had grown and scornful of how unhelpful the regulations to which it attributed that growth had been at actually providing insurers with useful data or effective security standards. The lesson Singapore appeared to derive from the United States' efforts to stimulate the cyberinsurance sector was that government involvement could be helpful in initially spurring growth, but that none of the US regulations had actually been helpful to insurers beyond scaring firms into buying policies. So CyRiM came up with its own recommendation—a cyberinsurance pool of money drawn from both the public and private sectors that could be used to help cover claims and mitigate the risk that insurers took on while the industry matured.

POLICY APPROACHES TO CYBERINSURANCE

Government interest in cyberinsurance coincided with growing regulatory attention to cybersecurity in the early twenty-first century, as well as a trend across the insurance industry, beginning in the late twentieth century, of increased government involvement in coverage for international risks. Virginia Haufler traces this trend throughout the development of the market for cross-border insurance, beginning in 1870 all the way through 1989. Haufler identifies a growing role for the public sector in propping up private insurance coverage that applies to international risks, as well as several benefits to such government involvement. She writes:

> The power of a sovereign government to recover losses in foreign countries clearly exceeds that of the private sector. Moreover, backing a guarantee program with the full faith and credit of the government reduces the amount of financial reserves that must be held, an option not available to private insurers. Government agencies also have access to superior information sources on political events abroad, and may be better able to calculate political risk probabilities. Finally, the private insurers do not always step in to respond to all demands for protection, especially when they involve large-scale and long-term projects in developing countries. In general, the public agencies insure risks that the commercial insurers themselves find too risky or simply beyond their financial capacity.[62]

The role of government programs in supporting cross-border coverage for property focused primarily on filling gaps left by private sector policies—a role not dissimilar to the one some insurers have asked regulators to consider taking on in the cyberinsurance context.

While the policy initiatives that governments have actually pursued, however half-heartedly, have fallen into three main categories—data repositories, government backstops, and risk pools—there is actually a significantly wider range of policy options available to regulators. Because these policy proposals have typically emerged from working groups and meetings with insurers, they have focused primarily on helping carriers. But government interventions in the cyberinsurance market need not focus solely on helping insurance providers, they can also aim to help insurance customers or raise the level of overall cybersecurity while driving down the incentives for cyberattacks. Each of these three goals leads to different types of policymaking. Regulators may aim to protect carriers from insolvency by helping improve their risk models and providing a backstop for catastrophic or accumulated risks. They can try to protect policyholders by requiring carriers to clarify and codify the terms of cyberinsurance coverage so that buyers better understand what their policies do and don't cover, as well as by providing coverage for those risks that private companies refuse to cover. Policymakers may also aim, more broadly, to diminish the profitability of cybercrime, and bolster and strengthen cybersecurity practices. This last may involve helping cyberinsurance carriers identify and promote awareness about which security controls are most effective in reducing risk exposure or restricting extortion payments made by insurers to criminal organizations, or preventing negligent companies from dodging the full cost of regulatory fines and class action settlements through insurance coverage.

A variety of proposals in all of these categories have been floated by insurers, regulators, and researchers, ranging from the very modest—such as voluntary participation in data sharing initiatives—to the much more extreme, such as calls to mandate cyberinsurance coverage for all companies nationwide.[63] But the cyberinsurance market is too divided for the former to have any impact and not nearly evolved enough for national mandates to be remotely feasible, much less effective. The most important role policymakers can play in trying to strengthen cybersecurity through encouraging adoption of cyberinsurance is helping insurers and their customers disentangle the many different types of risks to and from digital technologies that have been increasingly packaged together in stand-alone named peril policies that fail to recognize the deep ties these risks have to other, existing lines of coverage. This goal of integrating relevant cyber risks into existing lines of coverage that recognize and reflect the diversity of online threats and cyber infrastructure could serve the interests of both insurers and policyholders if it provided greater clarity about how different types of cyber risks are covered and enabled that coverage to be better tailored to each type. This is a significant undertaking that goes against the current prevailing trend toward stand-alone cyber policies and will require regulatory interventions aimed at helping both carriers and their customers, as well as interventions that neither group will appreciate but which are nevertheless needed to disincentivize cybercrime more broadly.

First, regulators must consider how they can help carriers struggling to navigate the changing landscape of online threats and infrastructure. Policymakers can benefit in this endeavor from their years of consultation with carriers, who have been clear about what they most want: help covering the costs of large-scale catastrophic cyber risks and access to better data. To achieve the former goal, policymakers should first clarify the role of existing government reinsurance programs, such as TRIA, in relation to cyber threats. After defining how their existing insurance backstops apply to cyber risks, if at all, legislators should also consider whether there are other types of catastrophic cyber risks for which carriers should be eligible to receive government assistance. As the disputes over coverage for NotPetya make clear, drawing these boundaries between warlike acts, terrorism, and everyday attacks in cyberspace is far from straightforward. Just as policyholders like Mondelez and Merck have been taken by surprise that they cannot count on their insurers to provide coverage for certain types of cyberattacks, regulators should not expect insurers to trust that they will receive the assistance they need from their governments under existing programs like TRIA without further clarification. Importantly, clarifying which types of cyber risk could trigger government backstop support would also enable regulators to help cyberinsurance customers through a corresponding requirement that threats or attacks that do not meet this threshold may not be exempted from cyberinsurance coverage as acts of war or terrorism. This combination of policy measures would help bolster insurers' confidence in their ability to handle large-scale attacks while also clarifying for customers that they will not be denied coverage merely because they suffer a sophisticated or state-sponsored attack that affects many victims.

To support insurers in their efforts to develop better risk models with more reliable data, policymakers could consider requiring insurers to report to regulatory authorities aggregate, anonymized claims data on the correlations between different cybersecurity products, frameworks, and guidelines and claims data. This would help businesses, governments, and researchers learn from the collected experience of insurers in trying to assess the effectiveness of different cybersecurity techniques, tools, and services. It might also allow insurers to aggregate more data across their customer bases and develop stronger data sets to determine the cybersecurity best practices that actually yield better outcomes. While it would help smaller insurers, who have access to less data, more than it would be likely to help larger carriers, it would still serve an important societal purpose in providing greater access to information about the overall effectiveness of different security controls and cybersecurity mitigation measures. Since private industry has shown little appetite for taking on this endeavor itself through establishing an ISAO, government actors might reasonably conclude that the only way for this information to be collected and analyzed, and eventually become publicly available is for them to mandate its reporting and aggregation.

For cyberinsurance customers, regulators could help clarify and standardize the policies available to them and then work toward filling any crucial gaps in that coverage. Regulators should require insurers to use standardized templates and wording, developed in partnership with insurance industry organizations like the Insurance Services Office, for designating which cyber risks are and are not covered under their policies. This could help clarify for customers what risks they are purchasing protection from and enable clearer comparisons across insurance policies for brokers and policyholders. Additionally, regulatory requirements that certain lines of insurance provide some well-defined baseline coverage of cyber risks would contribute to standardization across the market and possibly also help fill any notable gaps in coverage.

Finally, regulators must not neglect cyberinsurance regulations that serve the purpose of strengthening overall cybersecurity, even at the cost of limiting the cyberinsurance market and upsetting both carriers and policyholders. A prohibition on insurers paying online extortion demands, including ransoms to recover files and infected systems, might be unpopular but it would serve an important social goal of decreasing cybercrime. It would prevent businesses from using cyberinsurance policies to insulate themselves from the direct costs of ransomware and other forms of online extortion, but more importantly it would reduce the profits reaped by the criminals perpetrating these schemes. Such a prohibition would also affect the role of public-sector entities as purchasers of cyberinsurance policies, since local governments have themselves exercised cyberinsurance policies to pay significant online ransom demands. For instance, in 2019, Riviera Beach, Florida, paid a $592,000 ransom demand through its insurance policy, and Lake City, Florida, authorized a $460,000 ransom payment, of which it was responsible for paying only $10,000 thanks to its generous insurance coverage. At the time, coverage of those payments highlighted the fact that cities such as Atlanta and Baltimore that had chosen not to cave to ransomware demands had ended up spending much larger sums remediating the attacks than it would have cost them to simply pay the ransoms. But even if a victim pays a ransom it still must bear the costs of securing computer systems against future attacks. More importantly, the line of reasoning that weighs the cost of a ransom against the amount of money needed to restore a computer system without giving in to the ransomer's demands neglects to take into account the costs of future such attacks that the perpetrators will commit supported by the funds they received from their victims—much less the future such attacks that others will undertake when they see what a lucrative line of business ransomware is for its perpetrators. Government entities, arguably even more than other victims of ransomware attacks, have some responsibility to disincentivize cybercrime and resist the normalization of making online extortion payments through institutionalized insurance policies.[64] By adopting a blanket policy against such payments, policymakers might slow their own recovery from such attacks, but they would also be contributing to the larger effort of making cyber extortion less profitable and therefore less likely to be actively pursued by criminals in the future.

Such a prohibition would contradict policies governing kidnapping and ransom insurance, through which insurers are permitted to make ransom payments for kidnapped individuals, but that contradiction might be warranted given two key differences between kidnapping and cyber extortion. The first is that the stakes of ransomware are often—though not always—lower than in cases of kidnapping, where individuals' lives are presumably at stake. The second is that kidnapping cannot feasibly be scaled up to the same frequency as online extortion, so each individual ransom payment is unlikely to drive significant increases in the overall rate of kidnappings. Though, it is worth noting, that when the frequency of kidnappings has increased dramatically—as in Italy in the 1970s and 1980s—governments have sometimes been willing to forbid ransom payments even for those events.[65] Anja Shortland argues that the small number of tightly networked professionals selling kidnapping and ransom insurance and negotiating claims are able to prevent overpayment by carefully monitoring each other's behavior and withdrawing work from poor negotiators.[66] But given the number of ransomware attacks and resulting claims, the cyberinsurance industry could not conceivably rely on a similarly small, tight network of insurers and negotiators to police each other, adding to the motivations for policymakers to take a strong, clear stand against this type of coverage.

Finally, in a related vein, policymakers may consider limiting how much insurance money can be put toward paying government fines by companies who experience cybersecurity breaches and are found to be negligent in their security practices. This has been the source of considerable uncertainty around regulations like the GDPR, where there is no clear policy on whether or not fines can be covered by insurers. Forbidding insurers from covering regulatory penalties would add force to data protection regulations and potentially make firms more directly face the financial consequences of their security decisions, ultimately allowing regulatory investigations to serve as more effective deterrents of poor security practices.

Haufler describes how in the 1980s "the role of public authorities was to sanction the legal and institutional structures put in place by the commercial underwriters and then make a decision on whether or not the government should provide the 'missing' insurance. Officials creating government programs relied heavily on the private sector for assistance in the design and execution of public insurance and appropriated many of the common practices of the industry."[67] This is one potential role for policymakers in the evolving market for cyberinsurance—identifying and providing "missing" coverage—but it is far from the only one that private-sector actors and public agencies have considered. Across stakeholders and national borders, there seems to be broad consensus with Catherine Mulligan's contention at the 2015 Senate subcommittee meeting that, when it comes to cyberinsurance, "the scope of the challenge is too broad to be solved by the private sector alone."[68] But the question of what exactly the roles and responsibilities of the public sector should be remains so uncertain and contentious that few governments have done more than just discuss such issues at workshops and roundtables, in commissions and working groups, always circling back to the same conclusion that it would be good for government to do *something*, but finding it difficult to figure out what, exactly, that should be. The reluctance of governments to make any hasty decisions in the face of a still new and rapidly evolving market is understandable but also potentially counterproductive. If policymakers are waiting for cyberinsurance to become more widespread, standardized, stable, and effective at strengthening private-sector cybersecurity before acting to regulate it, they must also face the possibility that insurers may not be able to achieve those goals without the assistance, support, and restraints of government regulation.

CONCLUSION: IS CYBER RISK DIFFERENT?

Viewed alongside the emergence of other types of insurance, the development of the cyberinsurance market over the past three decades has been both disarmingly rapid and surprisingly slow. The rapidity has been demonstrated most vividly in the vast array of different policies and products that insurers have begun offering linked to cyber risks in the span of just a few decades. Unlike car, flood, or fire insurance, cyberinsurance does not cover a single, coherent type of threat, and unlike CGL or property and casualty insurance it does not cover a particular, coherent set of damages. Instead, cyber risk insurance, in its various forms from stand-alone policies to add-on products, tries to tackle a range of different threats, from cybercrime and data breaches to network outages, user errors, and online extortion—and across that wide range of threats it also aims to encompass an astonishing number of different types of damage, from first-party costs, such as lost business, breach notifications, and ransom payments, to third-party costs tied to lawsuits and liability.

Trying to describe the cyberinsurance industry makes clear the extent to which cyberinsurance is fundamentally not a single thing but rather a range of different products that deal with computer-, data-, and network-related risks that intersect with any number of different threats and types of losses. This would make the entire endeavor of studying cyberinsurance as a topic seem almost foolish were it not for the fact that insurers have increasingly tried to establish it as a single, coherent market with dedicated policies and coverage specifically for cyber risk. To this end, they have also excluded cyber-related losses from their other coverage, steering customers toward stand-alone cyber policies instead. Even in their internal structure and organization, many insurers have set up dedicated cyber risk groups to develop these policies, in many cases leaving the cyberinsurance team siloed apart from the groups working on modeling and pricing other, related risks in different departments.

The cyberinsurance market has grown slower than many carriers anticipated, even in the aftermath of a series of high-profile cybersecurity incidents and data protection regulations which insurers had predicted would significantly boost sales. For instance, a 2015 PricewaterhouseCoopers report titled "Insurance 2020 & beyond: Reaping the Dividends of Cyber Resilience" projected that the cyberinsurance industry would triple between 2015 and 2020, reaching annual premiums of roughly $7.5 billion by 2020.[1] Instead, in 2020, the NAIC estimated that the US market for cyberinsurance was still under $4 billion in premiums, and that the take-up rate for cyber policies remained "relatively low" at 33 percent.[2] A slew of ransomware attacks and other cybersecurity incidents beginning in 2019 also reduced the sizeable profit margins that carriers had previously enjoyed on cyber risk policies. In 2019, Aon estimated that the loss ratio for US cyberinsurance policies increased by 10 percent, to approximately 45 percent, compared to 35 percent in 2018.[3] That meant that in the span of one year, carriers went from paying out roughly 35 cents in claims for each dollar of premiums collected to paying out 45 cents per dollar of premium payments—a significant change, particularly given the reputation cyberinsurance had acquired by then for being "more profitable for insurers than other lines of insurance," as one 2019 *ProPublica* article put it, comparing the 35 percent loss ratio for cyberinsurance in 2018 to the 62 percent loss ratio for property and casualty insurance coverage.[4]

But these changes have not deterred insurers from developing and marketing new policies and new partnerships to address cyber risks. This drive to sell cyberinsurance may stem in part from carriers' desire to land customers while the market is still relatively new and businesses have not yet committed to a carrier, with carriers counting on their own ability to refine the risk models and pricing later, as they collect more data and learn more about the nature of cyber risk and the best methods for reducing exposure. But that assumption—that with time and data it will be possible to tame cyber risk using the same tools and techniques that have been applied with such success to so many other kinds of risk—relies on the idea that cyber risks are fundamentally no different from robberies or floods or car accidents or kidnappings in that they can be modeled and priced in their own comprehensive, stand-alone policies. This is not the case.

What differentiates cyber risk from other types of risk is not simply its scale, or how quickly it has evolved, or the complexity of computer networks, or the presence of determined and intelligent adversaries, or the uncertainty about how to mitigate these risks most effectively—though all of those characteristics undoubtedly do add to the considerable challenges of trying to craft cyberinsurance coverage. What makes cyber risk different is that it is not a single type of risk, that it extends to and interconnects nearly every other type of risk—from crime to liability to property and casualty losses—in ways so unpredictable and unprecedented that it is hard to imagine these actuarial complexities being captured simply by the collection of more data or the use of more sophisticated modeling tools. These challenges of scale and interconnection echo, to some extent, the complexities that insurers have faced in covering growing environmental risks. Daunted by the potentially massive consequences of these risks for all forms of natural disaster and property coverage, insurers have at various times tried to limit their environmental liability by refusing coverage, raising rates for coverage, and even engaging with policymakers on initiatives such as signing an accord with the United Nations to address climate change. Not all of these approaches were necessarily constructive for actually preventing climate change. As Haufler points out, "the unavailability or high costs of insurance may simply mean that a lot of business will be uninsured; when accidents occur, someone else will have to pay for the cleanup, which often comes down to public money."[5]

At least for the time being, there appears to be no shortage of insurers willing to sell cyberinsurance policies at rapidly rising prices for businesses of all sizes. It's not necessarily clear, however, that those policies actually cover the range of risks that policyholders believe or expect them to. Those unmet expectations are partly a function of the lack of standardized policy templates or clarity around exceptions, but they are also tied to the fact that, unlike environmental risks that correspond to a fairly clear and well-understood set of natural disasters, neither carriers nor policyholders are necessarily able to anticipate the kinds of cyber risks that will emerge even one or two years into the future. From a policyholder's perspective, that would seem to make cyber risks a good candidate for a broad all-risk policy, in the style of property and casualty insurance, that promises to cover any type of risk other than those explicitly excluded by the carrier, relieving the policyholder of anticipating all the possible risks they may require coverage for in the future. But, for exactly the same reasons, insurers have been reluctant to offer overly broad all-risk cyber policies, and have chosen instead to tailor narrow add-on products to existing coverage types and craft stand-alone named peril cyber policies that cover only a specific set of types of losses and liability. Over time, that set of losses has grown significantly larger as insurers have added more types of coverage to their stand-alone policies, particularly for first-party losses. That expansion of stand-alone cyber policies has been paralleled by a growing tide of resistance to policyholders claiming cyber-related losses under other types of coverage, even when that coverage includes riders and other add-on products specifically designed to cover computer-related losses.

The legal disputes over denied CGL, crime, and property and casualty insurance claims for cyber-related losses have helped clarify some of the ambiguities about what different types of insurance do and do not cover and have also, at times, reinforced the idea that there are many different, competing interpretations of what constitutes a cyber risk. For instance, while there is clear consensus that CGL policies do not apply to data breach litigation in most cases, there is much more uncertainty around whether incidents involving phishing emails are acts of computer fraud or not, or what constitutes a warlike act in cyberspace. In some ways, that uncertainty has been productive, driving carriers to clarify the language in their policies and exceptions. At the same time, however, it may also dissuade would-be customers from purchasing pricy coverage that they fear might not actually apply in the event of a significant cybersecurity incident. This, then, can lead to an outcome similar to the one Haufler observed for environmental risk insurance—companies choosing not to purchase coverage so that the costs of cyberattacks end up being borne by the public sector or individual victims.

Reliance on public funding to pay for cybersecurity incidents is not necessarily a terrible outcome—in fact, it is precisely what some insurers are lobbying for when they talk about extending TRIA to cyberattacks—but it does leave insurers in a less powerful position to enforce security standards and controls across a large customer base. For cyberinsurance to serve as an effective form of cybersecurity governance, insurers must be able to identify and incentivize policyholders to implement preventive measures that actually reduce the private sector's exposure to cyber risks, rather than just functioning as a form of compensation and risk pooling for victims of security incidents. It is striking that the insurance industry has, thus far, demonstrated so little progress on that front. Despite all the partnerships with security firms and the years of collected claims data, insurers seem to have no greater insight into how to reduce a policyholder's risk exposure or prevent cybersecurity incidents than they did when the market emerged in the late 1990s. Policyholders are still vetted in largely cursory ways, according to brief questionnaires that typically yield little insight into an organization's technical defenses and have even less impact on their premiums.

Government interest in cyberinsurance has been predicated in large part on the notion that insurers will be able to reduce policyholders' exposure to cyber risk. As early as 2011, the United States Department of Commerce Internet Policy Task Force referred to cybersecurity insurance as a potentially "effective, market-driven way of increasing cybersecurity."[6] The following year, the DHS speculated it could "help reduce the number of successful cyber attacks by promoting widespread adoption of preventative measures, encouraging the implementation of best practices by basing premiums on an insured's level of self-protection, and limiting the level of losses that companies face following a cyber attack."[7] Nearly a decade later, the only one of those goals that insurers seem even close to being able to achieve is that last one: limiting third-party losses, post-breach, by providing policyholders with immediate incident response resources and legal counsel. But while reducing the amount of data breach–related litigation may significantly decrease the costs associated with those breaches for the companies in question and, by extension, their insurers, it's not clear that this actually increases cybersecurity for anyone, much less reduces the number of successful cyberattacks.

Reducing risk exposure is not the sole purpose of insurance. In some cases, it's not even the primary purpose, particularly when—as in the case of cyberinsurance—carriers find themselves unable to assess the risks faced by policyholders. Kenneth Abraham traces the development of workers' compensation programs designed to guarantee that employees would receive compensation for harm that befell them from accidents at work. The proposals for these programs focused more on ensuring compensation for victims than on accident prevention, Abraham argues. Carriers offering employers' liability policies in the early twentieth century struggled to even figure out what safeguards companies provided to limit accidents in the workplace and whether their customers complied with safety standards. "Travelers' own company history recounted the difficulties it encountered in getting policyholders to make safety changes," Abraham writes, citing an early Travelers liability insurance inspector who said of his experience in the company's

official history, "We enjoyed little cooperation and much downright antago-
nism. The boss had no interest in the elimination of the danger, and the
workers themselves had become so used to conditions that they resisted
change."[8] Similarly, New York's influential 1910 Wainwright Commission Report on workers' compensation made a "passing reference . . . to
the potential of a workers' compensation system to reduce the incidence of
accidents" but, Abraham points out, "the Report noted at the outset that
the Commission had not yet been able to address the causes and prevention
of accidents, promising to address these issues in a subsequent Report." He
concludes: "A Report that recommends the enactment of workers' compensation before it has had the chance to address the causes and prevention of
accidents must be understood to be concerned primarily with other issues."[9]

Much like the Wainwright Commission and the Travelers' insurance
inspectors one hundred years before them, today's policymakers and carriers
have not yet really been able to address the causes and prevention of cybersecurity incidents. For all the published frameworks, catalogs of security controls, and lists of best practices, there is no strong empirical evidence of what
defenses are most effective at reducing cyber risk or even clear consensus on
how to measure the impact of different security controls. Nothing has made
that clearer than the unwillingness of insurers to make significant adjust-
ments to premium prices based on their customers' security postures. And
yet, unlike the Wainwright Commission, policymakers working on cyberinsurance have repeatedly lauded it as a means of helping prevent cybersecurity
losses. Indeed, many government discussions appear to assume that the best
way to address the lack of empirical evidence for the effectiveness of different cybersecurity measures is by building a robust cyberinsurance market
that can collect and analyze the needed data. If that turns out not to be the
case, then the cyberinsurance market may continue to function primarily as
a means of sharing losses rather than preventing them, serving to pool premiums from a wide array of companies and using that money to compensate
the victims of breaches, outages, and other computer compromises. That, in
itself, could be a worthwhile goal, but the concern is that cyberinsurance, if
it doesn't succeed in bolstering security standards, could actually lead to the
deterioration of policyholders' security practices due to moral hazard. Even
worse, if cyberinsurance means that extortion payments become a widely
accepted and routinized part of doing business, then this type of coverage
will contribute to the growth of the cybercrime market by underwriting

extortion payments that both indirectly encourage and directly fund further criminal activity.

Nearly every challenge that insurers currently face in trying to model and price cyberinsurance reflects a problem they have encountered—and in many cases, solved—before, in the history of insurance. Selling car insurance required carriers to collect data about the evolving risks of a new and changing technology. To offer crime insurance, insurers had to take into consideration the actions of an intelligent adversary who can adapt to preventive countermeasures. Developing kidnapping and ransom policies meant dealing with the potential unintended consequences of making direct payments to criminals and thereby encouraging copycats. Designing terrorism coverage forced insurers to face the possibility of catastrophic, accumulated risk. What those types of insurance have in common—and do not share with cyberinsurance—is that they cover a coherent and relatively stable set of risks.

Car accidents, crimes, ransom, terrorism—none of those risks has changed dramatically in nature in the past several decades except for their computer-based components. The task that falls to insurers in developing cyberinsurance, then, is not just to model and understand a new class of risk but also to remodel and rethink nearly every other existing class of risk they cover. No wonder they have gone to such lengths to try to exclude many cyber-related claims from their customers' existing insurance and tried to shift as much cyber-related risk coverage as possible into isolated stand-alone cyber policies. That is the approach the insurance industry has taken with nearly every new set of risks it has expanded to cover. It allows carriers to continue to rely on their core business and products while exploring a new area, but at the same time it leaves them further entrenched in the idea that each of these classes of risk is distinct and distinguishable.

Looking ahead, cyber risks will only become increasingly intertwined with the existing classes of risks insurers cover. Autonomous vehicles will require carriers to rethink auto insurance, buildings furnished with Internet-connected heating and cooling systems, fire sprinklers, and security cameras will change property insurance. Devices that can constantly monitor users' heart rates, activity levels, and other health indicators may similarly transform the field of health insurance. In some cases, these new technologies may enable insurers to monitor their policyholders more closely and require or recommend more stringent, high-tech safeguards against risks like car accidents, robberies, or heart attacks. But, inevitably, even as technologies like self-driving cars, security cameras with facial recognition capabilities, or health trackers may help reduce our exposure to some of these threats, they will also create new risks and introduce new avenues of attack via the complicated systems they connect to our cars, homes, and bodies.

Designing car insurance for autonomous vehicles won't just require adjusting the existing models and policies, it will require radically reimagining them for a set of risks we know very little about, such as computer vision errors and vulnerabilities in car software systems. Beyond just trying to collect enough data to understand how frequently these types of risks occur and what their financial impacts are, insurers and policymakers will also have to rethink questions related to liability: who is responsible for car accidents that occur because of malicious software compromises or faulty machine learning algorithms? The introduction of computers and computer networks to existing systems doesn't just create new risks for those systems, it also introduces a new set of stakeholders and intermediaries who are involved in designing the relevant software and hardware, connecting those legacy systems to a larger network of computers, and then monitoring those connections to restrict malicious activity. All of these stakeholders, in addition to those who were already involved—the car manufacturer and the drivers, for instance—play a role in mitigating risks that are in some way connected to computers and are therefore important for thinking about effective and comprehensive liability regimes.

Insurers will probably look to the courts, and perhaps also to regulators, to help decide how these complicated liability issues will be resolved. This has been true in the past, as insurers have taken their cues about what types of liability coverage to offer and to whom from civil lawsuits and the resulting rulings. Reflecting on the history of liability insurance, Abraham argues that "tort law continually seeks an available source of recovery, creating or expanding the liability of individuals and businesses that are likely to be covered by or have access to liability insurance. And liability insurance has usually responded, by creating new forms of insurance to meet the new liabilities when such insurance was not already available."[10] But for there to be civil lawsuits about who is liable for autonomous vehicle accidents there first have to be enough such accidents for someone to sue, and it's not clear that people will begin driving—or even selling—autonomous vehicles in any significant numbers until there is adequate insurance in place to protect them from liability. In other words, the typical cycle of insurers waiting for courts to dictate new liability regimes and then crafting policies to fit those regimes may not work for certain types of cyber risks associated with activities like driving where insurance is expected, if not required. If insurers are unable to get a handle on coverage for cyber risks of all varieties, that could significantly slow, or even prevent, the process of people and business beginning to adopt new technologies available to them.

Another concern is the possibility that emerging cyber risks will lead to a narrowing of insurance coverage rather than an expansion. Already, cyber-related losses are being explicitly excluded from many types of insurance but, for the most part, those exclusions are balanced by the development of new cyber risk policies that cover much of what is excluded from carriers' other coverage. However, as they encounter new types of risk, insurers may decide there are some kinds of cyber risks they simply do not see themselves being able to cover. Abraham points out that while insurers often respond to court rulings that create or expand liability in new areas by expanding their coverage offerings, this is not always the case. "Sometimes insurers cannot, or will not, provide insurance against a new liability," he writes.

As an example, Abraham points to the expansion of pollution cleanup liability in the 1980s, following the passage of the Comprehensive Environmental Response, Compensation and Liability Act (CERCLA). In this case, instead of leading to broader insurance coverage for pollution cleanup, the new, stricter liability regime "led to the virtual disappearance of pollution liability insurance rather than to its expansion. Expansive judicial interpretations of insurance policies that had seemed to insurers to provide only limited pollution liability insurance to their policyholders eventually caused the insurance industry to insert an 'absolute' pollution exclusion into subsequently issued policies."[11] It is not hard to imagine similar exclusions for certain types of cyber risks emerging in the wake of expansive judicial interpretations of insurance policies that insurers thought offered only limited cyber coverage. For instance, if the courts rule that the property policies held by Mondelez and Merck actually do cover the damages caused by NotPetya, the CERCLA example suggests that insurers might decide to reduce the scope of their cyber coverage for certain types of risks rather than expanding it.

If insurers do continue to expand their coverage of cyber risks, there is no shortage of looming threats and problems on the horizon from which businesses—and perhaps even, eventually, individuals—will be eager to protect themselves. Insurance has only barely begun to grapple with the risks presented by the Internet of Things and the proliferation of artificial intelligence (AI) and the use of machine learning algorithms for decision making. The risks associated with Internet of Things devices are likely to be entangled with existing insurance products, including auto insurance and property insurance, while the risks associated with AI may present more opportunities for entirely new forms of coverage. In an article titled "The Case for AI Insurance," Ram Shankar Siva Kumar and Frank Nagle point out that "AI failures resulting in business interruption and breach of private information are most likely covered by existing cyber insurance, but AI failures resulting in brand damage, bodily harm, and property damage will not likely be covered by existing cyber insurance."

Kumar and Nagle propose that companies should be taking stock of the safety and security of their AI systems and talking to their insurers about potential coverage for both intentional and unintentional failures of those systems. "We believe that AI insurance will first be available via major insurance carriers as bespoke insurers may not have sufficient safety nets to invest in new areas," they predict. "From a pricing perspective, using the past cyber insurance market as a template, businesses can expect stringent requirements when AI insurance is introduced to limit the insurance provider's liability with rates cooling off as the AI insurance market matures."[12] In fact, the short history of the past cyberinsurance market suggests a more complicated trajectory than just falling rates and less stringent liability limitations over time. Historical parallels might predict a gradual shuffling of different cyber risks from add-on products to stand-alone policies, accompanied by an expanding set of exclusions and no clear decrease in premium payments.

It's not surprising that insurers would look to excise cyber risks from non-cyber-specific policies and isolate them in stand-alone cyberinsurance policies in order to protect their existing core products from the uncertainty and unpredictability of cyber risk. But that isolation can also be counter-productive, for both carriers and their customers, when it gives credence to the idea that computer networks and data pose a distinct, definable set of risks that can be separated from the other categories of risk that insurers cover and policyholders face. Some cyber risks, like data breaches, AI algorithm errors, and online extortion, may in fact be so new and so unrelated to other, existing coverage that it makes sense for them to be covered in stand-alone policies, but as computer networks are increasingly embedded in existing physical infrastructure and systems, many—perhaps most—of the risks they present will belong under the same policies that already protect those domains.

This is what is most fundamentally new and different about cyber risk as compared to other types of risks that insurers have addressed in the past—not just that it can, at times, be more unpredictable or more catastrophic or more difficult to mitigate, but that it requires remodeling so many other categories of risks, in addition to creating a new class of insurance products for risks to entirely new kinds of infrastructure and operations. Insurers look to data collection to help shape their policies, but this is not a challenge that will diminish with time, as more data is collected and analyzed. Rather, it is a challenge that will only grow as computing technology continues to extend into new areas and applications. Moreover, part of the challenge of rethinking existing risk categories will involve acknowledging the increasing interconnectedness among them and the potential for a single attack to have significant impacts related to property damage, car accidents, liability, business interruption, data breaches, crime, and terrorism, simultaneously. In this regard, cyber risks may, in fact, render existing insurance risk categories more unpredictable, more catastrophic, and more difficult to mitigate than ever before.

Cybersecurity, like climate change, will require the involvement of regulators and policymakers to make an insurance market viable in the long term, and that involvement will probably not be limited to just serving as a data aggregator or financial backstop for the insurers. It may well require regulators to take an active role in requiring certain cybersecurity standards and controls—as the EU has already begun to do for critical infrastructure operators through the NIS Directive—rather than waiting for insurers to identify those safeguards themselves and screen policyholders for them. It may also require regulators to take a hardline stance on the coverage and payment of online extortion demands which benefit certain stakeholders, including both carriers and cyberinsurance policyholders, in the short term but inflict significant harm, long term, by funding criminal enterprises and driving increased cybercrime.

The idea that cybersecurity can be handled solely, or even primarily, through a market-driven approach led by insurers is fundamentally flawed—something that insurers themselves, to their credit, have been pointing out to policymakers for years. Policymakers, too, have shown greater willingness to regulate data protection, particularly where it involves individuals' personal information, and especially outside the United States, where cyberinsurance remains relatively uncommon. Some elements of those regulations, particularly incident reporting requirements and cybersecurity certifications, seem aimed, at least in part, at helping insurers develop better cyberinsurance policies. Other components, such as data localization measures, may instead serve to enervate the global cyberinsurance industry. Whether or not the wave of data protection regulations around the world in the late 2010s will actually drive greater adoption of cyberinsurance in those countries remains to be seen, but at the very least such regulations suggest that a growing number of governments are abandoning the notion that cybersecurity is something that can be solved by the private sector alone.

That should not diminish what the cyberinsurance industry has accomplished in developing a wide array of offerings for first- and third-party coverage for cyber risks all in the span of less than three decades, however. In the early 2000s, carriers significantly expanded available coverage for cyber-related losses to include insurance for network outages, restoration of encrypted systems, cryptocurrency-based crimes, and social engineering. That progress comes despite the ambiguity of some of those policies and the contentious legal disputes over what they do and don't apply to, and despite insurers' apparent inability to identify effective security controls and unwillingness to share claims data with their competitors. This expansion has been driven by demand from policyholders, but insurers have met this demand at considerable long-term financial risk to themselves since very little is known about how these threats will evolve over time or how courts will interpret the coverage and exclusions in these policies in light of future incidents.

As insurers continue to expand their cybersecurity coverage, they should also consider expanding the boundaries of how they define and conceptualize cyber risk within their organizational structures and underwriting categories. This means acknowledging the complicated and extensive connections between cyber risk and other coverage areas and crafting policies that recognize and reflect those connections. In the past, when a significant new type of risk has emerged, whether in the form of a novel type of legal liability or an innovative technology, the insurance sector has developed new products to cover those risks. When it comes to tackling cyber risk, however, the most important thing insurers can do is reinvent their old policies, rather than write new ones. Not all risks are cyber risks, but, increasingly, all types of risk have cyber components that insurers and their policyholders ignore or isolate at their peril.

NOTES

CHAPTER 1

1. Adam Satariano and Nicole Perlroth, "Big Companies Thought Insurance Covered a Cyberattack. They May Be Wrong," *New York Times*, April 15, 2019, https://www.nytimes.com/2019/04/15/technology/cyberinsurance-notpetya-attack.html.

2. Andy Greenberg, "The Untold Story of NotPetya, the Most Devastating Cyberattack in History," *Wired*, September 2018, https://www.wired.com/story/notpetya-cyberattack-ukraine-russia-code-crashed-the-world/.

3. Greenberg, "Untold Story of NotPetya."

4. Mondelez International Inc. v. Zurich American Insurance Company, No. 2018L011008 (Circuit Court of Cook County, Ill., October 10, 2018).

5. Mondelez International Inc. v. Zurich American Insurance Company.

6. Denise Matthews, "Report on the Cybersecurity Insurance and Identity Theft Coverage Supplement," National Association of Insurance Commissioners, December 4, 2020, https://content.naic.org/sites/default/files/inline-files/Cyber_Supplement_2019_Report_Final_1.pdf.

7. AM Best, "Cyber Insurers Are Profitable Today, but Wary of Tomorrow's Risks," Best's Market Segment Report, June 17, 2019, https://reaction.ambest.com/reaction/emsdocuments/Special%20Reports/2019/2019.06_Cyber_Insurance_Report.pdf

8. Josephine Wolff, "Cyberinsurance Tackles the Wildly Unpredictable World of Hacks," *Wired*, April 6, 2018, https://www.wired.com/story/cyberinsurance-tackles-the-wildly-unpredictable-world-of-hacks/.

9. Nick Economidis, interview with Josephine Wolff, February 8, 2018.

10. Mondelez International Inc. v. Zurich American Insurance Company.

11. Greenberg, "Untold Story of NotPetya."

12. Ulrich Beck and Mark Ritter, *Risk Society: Towards a New Modernity* (London: Sage, 1992), 22.

13. Beck and Ritter, *Risk Society*, 22.

14. Gregory Falco et al., "Cyber Risk Research Impeded by Disciplinary Barriers," *Science* 366, no. 6469 (2019): 1066–1069, https://doi.org/10.1126/science .aaz4795.

15. Ortwin Renn et al., "Things Are Different Today: The Challenge of Global Systemic Risks," *Journal of Risk Research* 22, no. 4 (2017): 401–415, https://doi.org /10.1080/13669877.2017.1409252.

16. Renn et al., "Things Are Different Today," 403.

17. Ian Goldin and Mike Mariathasan, *The Butterfly Defect: How Globalization Creates Systemic Risks, and What to Do about It* (Princeton, NJ: Princeton University Press, 2014), 8.

18. Richard V. Ericson, Aaron Doyle, and Dean Barry, *Insurance as Governance* (Toronto: University of Toronto Press, 2003), 14, https://doi.org/10.3138/9781 442676220.

19. Ericson, Doyle, and Barry, *Insurance as Governance*, 14.

20. Virginia Haufler, *Dangerous Commerce: Insurance and the Management of International Risk* (Ithaca, NY: Cornell University Press, 1997).

21. Haufler, *Dangerous Commerce*, 125.

22. Kenneth S. Abraham, *The Liability Century: Insurance and Tort Law from the Progressive Era to 9/11* (Cambridge, MA: Harvard University Press, 2008).

23. Abraham, *Liability Century*, 220–21.

24. Kenneth J. Meier, *The Political Economy of Regulation: The Case of Insurance* (Albany: State University of New York Press, 1988), 167.

25. Meier, *Political Economy of Regulation*, 167.

26. Patricia Mazzei, "Hit by Ransomware Attack, Florida City Agrees to Pay Hackers $600,000," *New York Times*, June 19, 2019, https://www.nytimes.com /2019/06/19/us/florida-riviera-beach-hacking-ransom.html.

27. Patricia Mazzei, "Another Hacked Florida City Pays a Ransom, This Time for $460,000," *New York Times*, June 27, 2019, https://www.nytimes.com/2019/06 /27/us/lake-city-florida-ransom-cyberattack.html.

28. Mazzei, "Another Hacked Florida City Pays a Ransom."

29. Brian D. Brown, "The Ever-Evolving Nature of Cyber Coverage," Insurance Journal, September 22, 2014, https://www.insurancejournal.com/magazines/mag -features/2014/09/22/340633.htm.

30. Trey Herr, "Cyber Insurance and Private Governance: The Enforcement Power of Markets," *Regulation and Governance* 15 (2021): 98–114.

31. Herr, "Cyber Insurance and Private Governance."

32. Herr, "Cyber Insurance and Private Governance."

33. National Protection and Programs Directorate (NPPD), *Insurance Industry Working Session Readout Report: Insurance for Cyber-Related Critical Infrastructure Loss: Key Issues* (Washington, DC: US Department of Homeland Security, July 2014).

34. United States Department of Homeland Security, *The National Strategy to Secure Cyberspace,* (Washington, DC: White House, February 2003), https://georgewbush-whitehouse.archives.gov/pcipb/.

35. Josephine Wolff, *You'll See This Message When It Is Too Late: The Legal and Economic Aftermath of Cybersecurity Breaches* (Cambridge, MA: MIT Press, 2018).

36. Herr, "Cyber Insurance and Private Governance."

37. Herr, "Cyber Insurance and Private Governance."

38. Meier, *Political Economy of Regulation,* 172.

39. Rainer Böhme and Gaurav Kataria, "Models and Measures for Correlation in Cyber-Insurance," working paper, Workshop on the Economics of Information Security, Cambridge, UK, June 2006, https://econinfosec.org/archive/weis2006/docs/16.pdf.

40. Rainer Böhme, "Cyber-Insurance Revisited," paper presented at the Workshop on the Economics of Information Security, Kennedy School of Government, Cambridge, MA, 2005, http://infosecon.net/workshop/pdf/15.pdf.

41. Rainer Böhme and Galina Schwartz, "Modeling Cyber-Insurance: Towards a Unifying Framework," working paper, Workshop on the Economics of Information Security, Cambridge, MA, 2010, https://informationsecurity.uibk.ac.at/pdfs/BS2010_Modeling_Cyber-Insurance_WEIS.pdf.

42. Aron Laszka and Jens Grossklags, "Should Cyber-Insurance Providers Invest in Software Security?," in *Proceedings, Part I, of the 20th European Symposium on Computer Security—ESORICS 2015—Volume 9326* (Berlin: Springer Verlag, 2015), 483–502, https://doi.org/10.1007/978-3-319-24174-6_25.

43. Daniel Woods, Ioannis Agrafiotis, Jason R. C. Nurse, and Sadie Creese, "Mapping the Coverage of Security Controls in Cyber Insurance Proposal Forms," *Journal of Internet Services and Applications* 8 (2017).

44. Sasha Romanosky et al., "Content Analysis of Cyber Insurance Policies: How Do Carriers Price Cyber Risk?," *Journal of Cybersecurity* 5, no. 1 (January 1, 2019), https://doi.org/10.1093/cybsec/tyz002.

45. Robert Morgus, "Cyber Insurance: A Market-Based Approach to Information Assurance," in *Cyber Insecurity: Navigating the Perils of the Next Information Age,* ed. Richard M. Harrison and Trey Here (Lanham, MD: Rowman and Littlefield, 2016), 155–170.

46. Shauhin A. Talesh, "Data Breach, Privacy, and Cyber Insurance: How Insurance Companies Act as 'Compliance Managers' for Businesses," *Law and Social Inquiry* 43, no. 2 (2018): 417–440, https://doi.org/10.1111/lsi.12303.

CHAPTER 2

1. Joshua Macht, "Safe Haase," Inc., September 15, 1997, https://www.inc.com /magazine/19970915/1427.html.

2. Macht, "Safe Haase."

3. Lynn Margherio et al., *The Emerging Digital Economy* (Washington, DC: US Department of Commerce, April 1998), https://www.commerce.gov/sites/default /files/migrated/reports/emergingdig_0.pdf.

4. Macht, "Safe Haase."

5. AM Best, "Cyber Insurers Are Profitable Today."

6. Harvey Rosenfield, "Auto Insurance: Crisis and Reform," *University of Memphis Law Review* 29, no. 1 (1998): 72.

7. Robert I. Mehr and Emerson Cammack, *Principles of Insurance*, 3rd ed. (Homewood, IL: Richard D. Irwin, 1961), 304.

8. Mehr and Cammack, *Principles of Insurance*, 843.

9. Abraham, *Liability Century*, 73.

10. US General Accounting Office, *Auto Insurance: State Regulation Affects Cost and Availability* (Washington, DC: United States General Accounting Office, August 1986).

11. James M. Anderson, Paul Heaton, and Stephen J. Carroll, *The U.S. Experience with No-Fault Automobile Insurance: A Retrospective* (Santa Monica, CA: RAND Corporation, 2010, MG-860-ICJ).

12. Mehr and Cammack, *Principles of Insurance*, 843.

13. Mehr and Cammack, *Principles of Insurance*, 842.

14. Rosenfield, "Auto Insurance," 72–73.

15. National Protection and Programs Directorate (NPPD), *Cybersecurity Insurance Workshop Readout Report* (Washington, DC: US Department of Homeland Security, November 2012), 7.

16. Anderson, Heaton, and Carroll, *U.S. Experience with No-Fault Automobile Insurance*, 24.

17. *Report by the Committee to Study Compensation for Auto Accidents to the Columbia University Council for Research in the Social Sciences* (Philadelphia, 1932) (hereafter, *Columbia Committee Report*).

18. *Columbia Committee Report*, 45.

19. *Columbia Committee Report*, 139.

20. Meier, *Political Economy of Regulation*, 118.

21. Rosenfield, "Auto Insurance," 73.

22. *Columbia Committee Report*, 134.

23. Wolff, *You'll See This Message When It Is Too Late*.

24. *Columbia Committee Report*, 212.

25. Eric Nordman, "The History of No-Fault Auto Insurance," *Journal of Insurance Regulation* 16, no. 4 (1998): 460.

26. Anderson, Heaton, and Carroll, *U.S. Experience with No-Fault Automobile Insurance*, 40.

27. Meier, *Political Economy of Regulation*, 119–120.

28. Ives v. South Buffalo Railway Co., 201 N.Y. 271, 94 N.E. 431 (N.Y. App. Div. 1911).

29. Anderson, Heaton, and Carroll, *U.S. Experience with No-Fault Automobile Insurance*, 22.

30. *Columbia Committee Report*, 20.

31. *Columbia Committee Report*, 137.

32. Meier, *Political Economy of Regulation*, 114.

33. Scott Gabriel Knowles and Howard C. Kunreuther, "Troubled Waters: The National Flood Insurance Program in Historical Perspective," *Journal of Policy History* 26, no. 3 (2014): 332.

34. Knowles and Kunreuther, "Troubled Waters," 332.

35. *A Unified National Program for Managing Flood Losses: A Report by the Task Force on Federal Flood Control Policy*, S. Rep. No. 89-465, at 23 (August 1966).

36. S. Rep. No. 89-465, at 19 (August 1966).

37. S. Rep. No. 89-465, at 39 (August 1966).

38. S. Rep. No. 89-465, at 14 (August 1966).

39. Knowles and Kunreuther, "Troubled Waters," 334.

40. Knowles and Kunreuther, "Troubled Waters," 335.

41. Knowles and Kunreuther, "Troubled Waters," 336.

42. Knowles and Kunreuther, "Troubled Waters," 337.

43. Knowles and Kunreuther, "Troubled Waters," 344.

44. Subcommittee on Oversight and Investigation, *Failed Promises: Insurance Company Insolvencies* (Washington, DC: US House of Representatives Committee on Energy and Commerce, February 1990).

45. Subcommittee on Oversight and Investigation, *Failed Promises*.

46. Baird Webel and Carolyn Cobb, "Insurance Regulation: History, Background, and Recent Congressional Oversight," Congressional Research Service, February 11, 2005, https://www.everycrsreport.com/files/20050211_RL31982_1d5eff403 f858929157d365c96ccc029206575a7.pdf.

47. Paul v. Virginia, 75 U.S. 168 (1869).

48. United States v. South-Eastern Underwriters Association et al., 322 U.S. 533 (1944).

49. Webel and Cobb, "Insurance Regulation," 8.

50. Webel and Cobb, "Insurance Regulation," 9.

51. Subcommittee on Oversight and Investigation, *Failed Promises, 3*.

52. Subcommittee on Oversight and Investigation, *Failed Promises, 3*.

53. Steven Haase, interview with the author, August 1, 2019.

54. Haase interview.

55. Haase interview.

56. Jason Roberson, "Time to Sign Up for Cyber Insurance?," *Orlando Business Journal* 17, no. 51 (2001).

57. Roberson, "Time to Sign Up for Cyber Insurance?"

58. J. Figg, "Cyber Insurance to Cover E-Business," *Internal Auditor*, August 1, 2000.

59. Susan Breidenbach, "The Policy for Protection," *Network World*, October 23, 2000.

60. Ulrik Franke, "The Cyber Insurance Market in Sweden," *Computers and Security* 68 (July 2017): 130–144.

61. Breidenbach, "Policy for Protection."

62. Breidenbach, "Policy for Protection."

63. Breidenbach, "Policy for Protection."

64. Deb Radcliff, "Got Cyber Insurance?," Computerworld, August 21, 2000, https://www.computerworld.com/article/2596915/got-cyber-insurance-.html.

65. Ann Harrison, "Counterpane Offers Internet Security Insurance," Computerworld, July 12, 2000, https://www.computerworld.com/article/2595733/counterpane-offers-internet-security-insurance.html.

66. Harrison, "Counterpane Offers Internet Security Insurance."

67. Breidenbach, "Policy for Protection."

68. Breidenbach, "Policy for Protection."

69. Daniel W. Woods, Tyler Moore, and Andrew C. Simpson, "The County Fair Cyber Loss Distribution: Drawing Inferences from Insurance Prices," paper presented at Workshop on the Economics of Information Security (WEIS), Harvard University, Cambridge, MA, 2019, https://informationsecurity.uibk.ac.at/pdfs/DW2019_CountyFair_WEIS.pdf.

70. Andy Giegerich, "E-Commerce Risks Work for Tripwire," *Portland Business Journal* 17, no. 33 (2000): 14.

71. Giegerich, "E-Commerce Risks Work for Tripwire."

72. Giegerich, "E-Commerce Risks Work for Tripwire."

73. Chana Schoenberger, "Payout: Times of Terror Are Good Times for Hacker Insurance," *Forbes*, December 24, 2001.

74. Ben Dyson, "Learning to Fly," *Reactions* 25, no. 4 (2005): 22–25.

75. Schoenberger, "Payout."

76. Schoenberger, "Payout."

77. Shelly Strom, "Egghead Favors Security over Cyber Insurance," *Portland Business Journal* 18, no. 1 (2001), https://www.bizjournals.com/portland/stories/2001/03/05 /focus2.html.

78. Strom, "Egghead Favors Security over Cyber Insurance."

79. Michael Conroy, "Cyber Insurance for Viruses, Hackers Is Gaining Speed," *Long Island Business News*, July 6, 2001.

80. Keith Ricken, "The Missing Piece: Buyer Interest," *Risk & Insurance*, December 1, 2001.

81. Ricken, "Missing Piece."

82. Ricken, "Missing Piece."

83. William Overend, "Cyber Crime Fighters Escape Funding Cut," *Los Angeles Times*, November 10, 2002, https://www.latimes.com/archives/la-xpm-2002-nov -10-me-cyber10-story.html.

84. Jaikumar Vijayan, "Recent Breaches Raise Specter of Liability Risks," Computerworld, June 3, 2002, https://www.computerworld.com/article/2576023/recent -breaches-raise--specter-of-liability-risks.html.

85. Saskia Kim, S.B. 1386 Senate Bill: Bill Analysis, Committee on Judiciary, 107th Cong. (2002), http://www.leginfo.ca.gov/pub/01-02/bill/sen/sb_1351-1400 /sb_1386_cfa_20020617_141710_asm_comm.html, 4.

86. Vijayan, "Recent Breaches Raise Specter of Liability Risks."

87. Kim, S.B. 1386 Senate Bill: Bill Analysis, 3.

88. Kim, S.B. 1386 Senate Bill: Bill Analysis, 3–4.

89. Kim, S.B. 1386 Senate Bill: Bill Analysis, 4.

90. Kim, S.B. 1386 Senate Bill: Bill Analysis, 5.

91. Bob Sullivan, "ID Theft Rampant; Options Limited," *MSNBC*, May 29, 2002.

92. Dyson, "Learning to Fly."

93. Dyson, "Learning to Fly."

94. Dyson, "Learning to Fly."

95. Jaclyn Jaeger, "More Companies Turning to Data Breach Insurance," *Compliance Week*, August 1, 2011, https://www.complianceweek.com/more-companies-turning-to-data-breach-insurance/4512.article.

96. Chuck Nicol, S.B. 1386 Senate Bill: Bill Analysis, Committee on Appropriations 107th Cong. (2002), http://www.leginfo.ca.gov/pub/01-02/bill/sen/sb_1351-1400/sb_1386_cfa_20020813_145811_asm_comm.html, 2–3.

97. Vijayan, "Recent Breaches Raise Specter of Liability Risks."

98. Andrew Pearce, "Brokers Told to Wake up to Cyber Liability," *Insurance Age*, September 10, 2012.

99. Abraham, *Liability Century*, 1.

100. Knowles and Kunreuther, "Troubled Waters."

101. US Securities and Exchange Commission (SEC), "CF Disclosure Guidance: Topic No. 2," Division of Corporate Finance, October 13, 2011, https://www.sec.gov/divisions/corpfin/guidance/cfguidance-topic2.htm.

102. SEC, "CF Disclosure Guidance."

103. SEC, "CF Disclosure Guidance."

104. Herr, "Cyber Insurance and Private Governance."

105. SEC, "CF Disclosure Guidance."

106. US Securities and Exchange Commission (SEC), "Form 10-K: Yahoo! Inc.: Annual Report Pursuant to Section 13 or 15(d) of the Securities Exchange Act of 1934 for the Fiscal Year Ended December 31, 2011," February 29, 2012, http://edgar.secdatabase.com/1700/119312512086972/filing-main.htm.

107. SEC, "Form 10-K: Yahoo! Inc."

108. *Examining the Evolving Cyber Insurance Marketplace: Hearings before the Subcommittee on Consumer Protection, Product Safety, Insurance, and Data Security of the Committee on Commerce, Science and Transportation*, 114 Cong. 171 (March 19, 2015).

109. *Examining the Evolving Cyber Insurance Marketplace.*

CHAPTER 3

1. Anthony J. Battaglia, "Order Granting in Part and Denying in Part Defendants' Motion to Dismiss Plaintiffs' Consolidated Class Action Complaint In re: Sony Gaming Networks and Customer Data Security Breach Litigation," No. 3:11-cv-02119-AJB-MDD (S.D. Cal. October 11, 2012).

2. Kyle Orland, "Sony to Pay up to $17.75 Million in 2011 PSN Hacking Settlement," Ars Technica, July 24, 2014, https://arstechnica.com/gaming/2014/07/sony-to-pay-up-to-17-75-million-in-2011-psn-hacking-settlement/.

3. E. W. Sawyer, *Comprehensive Liability Insurance* (New York: Underwriter, 1943), 21.

4. Conroy, "Cyber Insurance for Viruses."

5. Schoenberger, "Payout."

6. Wolff, *You'll See This Message When It Is Too Late*.

7. First Amended Consolidated Class Action Complaint In re: Sony Gaming Networks and Customer Data Security Breach Litigation, No. 3:11-md-02258-AJB-MDD (S.D. Cal. December 10, 2012).

8. First Amended Consolidated Class Action Complaint.

9. Defendants' Reply to Plaintiffs' Opposition to the Motion to Dismiss Consolidated Class Action Complaint In re Sony Gaming Networks and Customer Data Security Breach Litigation, No. 11-md-2258 AJB (S.D. Cal. August 12, 2012).

10. Zurich American Insurance Co. v. Sony Corporation of America, 2014 WL 8382554 (N.Y. Sup. Ct. February 21, 2014).

11. All the following quotations are from the court transcript Zurich American Insurance Co. v. Sony Corporation of America.

12. Wolff, *You'll See This Message When It Is Too Late*.

13. *Columbia Committee Report*.

14. Bohannan v. Innovak International, 318 F.R.D. 525 (M.D. Ala. 2015).

15. Bohannan v. Innovak International, 318 F.R.D. 525 (M.D. Ala. 2015).

16. Innovak International Inc. v. Hanover Insurance Co., 280 F. Supp. 3d 1340 (M.D. Fla. 2017).

17. All the following quotations are from the court transcript Innovak International Inc. v. Hanover Insurance Co.

18. Hartford Casualty Insurance Co. v. Corcino & Associates et al., No. 2:13-cv-03728-GAF-JC (C.D. Cal. October 7, 2013).

19. Innovak International Inc. v. Hanover Insurance Co.

20. Innovak International Inc. v. Hanover Insurance Co.

21. Zurich American Insurance Co. v. Sony Corporation of America.

22. St. Paul Fire & Marine Insurance Co. v. Rosen Millennium Inc. Complaint, No. 6:17-cv-540-ORL-41-GJK (M.D. Fla. March 24, 2017).

23. St. Paul Fire & Marine Insurance Co. v. Rosen Millennium Inc. Complaint.

24. St. Paul Fire & Marine Insurance Co. v. Rosen Millennium Inc. Complaint.

25. St. Paul Fire & Marine Ins. Co. v. Rosen Millennium Inc., 337 F. Supp. 3d 1176 (M.D. Fla. 2018).

26. St. Paul Fire & Marine Insurance Co. v. Rosen Millennium Inc. Complaint.

27. St. Paul Fire & Marine Insurance Co. v. Rosen Millennium Inc., 337 F. Supp. 3d 1176.

28. St. Paul Fire & Marine Insurance Co. v. Rosen Millennium Inc., 337 F. Supp. 3d 1176.

29. American Economy Insurance Co. v. Aspen Way Enterprises, No. 1:14-cv-00009, 2015 U.S. Dist. LEXIS 129274 (D. Mont. September 25, 2015).

30. American Economy Insurance Co. v. Aspen Way Enterprises.

CHAPTER 4

1. Methodist Health System Foundation v. Hartford Fire Insurance Co., 834 F. Supp. 2d 493 (E.D. La. 2011).

2. Methodist Health System Foundation v. Hartford Fire Insurance Co.

3. Brightpoint Inc. v. Zurich Am. Ins. Co., No. 1:04-cv-2085-SEB-JPG, 2006 U.S. Dist. LEXIS 26018 (S.D. Ind. March 10, 2006).

4. All the following quotations are from Brightpoint Inc. v. Zurich American Insurance Co.

5. Pestmaster Services v. Travelers Casualty and Surety Company of America, No. 2:13-cv-5039-JFW, 2014 U.S. Dist. LEXIS 108416 (C.D. Cal. July 17, 2014).

6. Pestmaster Services v. Travelers Casualty and Surety Company of America.

7. Pestmaster Services v. Travelers Casualty and Surety Company of America, 656 Fed. Appx. 332 (9th Cir. 2016).

8. American Tooling Center Inc. v. Travelers Casualty and Surety Company of America, 895 F.3d 455 (6th Cir. 2018).

9. American Tooling Center Inc. v. Travelers Casualty and Surety Company of America.

10. American Tooling Center Inc. v. Travelers Casualty and Surety Company of America.

11. Apache Corp. v. Great American Insurance Co., No. 4:14-cv-237, 2015 U.S. Dist. LEXIS 161683 (S.D. Tex. 2015).

12. Apache Corp. v. Great American Insurance Co., 662 Fed. Appx. 252 (5th Cir. 2016).

13. American Tooling Center Inc. v. Travelers Casualty and Surety Company of America, No. 5:16-cv-12108 (E.D. Mich. August 1, 2017).

14. American Tooling Center Inc. v. Travelers Casualty and Surety Company of America.

15. Pestmaster Services v. Travelers Casualty and Surety Company of America, No. 2:13-cv-5039-JFW, 2014 U.S. Dist. LEXIS 108416 (C.D. Cal. July 17, 2014).

16. Apache Corp. v. Great American Insurance Co., 662 Fed. Appx. 252 (5th Cir. 2016).

17. Interactive Communications International Inc. v. Great American Insurance Co., 731 Fed. Appx. 929 (11th Cir. 2018).

18. Interactive Communications International Inc. v. Great American Insurance Co.

19. American Tooling Center Inc. v. Travelers Casualty and Surety Company of America, 895 F.3d 455 (6th Cir. 2018).

20. American Tooling Center Inc. v. Travelers Casualty and Surety Company of America.

21. American Tooling Center Inc. v. Travelers Casualty and Surety Company of America.

22. Medidata Solutions Inc. v. Federal Insurance Co.

23. Medidata Solutions Inc. v. Federal Insurance Co.

24. Medidata Solutions Inc. v. Federal Insurance Co.

25. Medidata Solutions Inc. v. Federal Insurance Co., 729 Fed. Appx. 117 (2d Cir. 2018).

26. National Bank of Blacksburg v. Everest National Insurance Co., No. 7:18-cv-310 (W.D. Va. June 28, 2018).

27. All the following quotations are from National Bank of Blacksburg v. Everest National Insurance Co.

28. Jeff Sturgeon, "National Bank of Blacksburg Settles with Insurer over Losses from Suspected Russian Hacking," *Roanoke Times*, January 29, 2019, https://roanoke.com/business/national-bank-of-blacksburg-settles-with-insurer-over-losses-from-suspected-russian-hacking/article_acc2cff5-9ad1-57aa-bb20-d4c1f6d524b6.html.

CHAPTER 5

1. Mondelez International Inc. v. Zurich American Insurance Co., No. 2018-L-011008 (Ill. Cir. Ct. October 10, 2018).

2. William Reynolds Vance, *Handbook of the Law of Insurance* (St. Paul, MN: West, 1904), 10.

3. Vance, *Handbook of the Law of Insurance*, 12.

4. Vance, *Handbook of the Law of Insurance*, 12.

5. Vance, *Handbook of the Law of Insurance*, 14.

6. John P. Gorman, "All Risks of Loss v. All Loss: An Examination of Broad Form Insurance Coverages," *Notre Dame Law Review* 34, no. 3 (1959): 348.

7. Kenneth S. Abraham, "Peril and Fortuity in Property and Liability Insurance," *Tort and Insurance Law Journal* 36, no. 3 (2001): 783.

8. Abraham, "Peril and Fortuity in Property and Liability Insurance," 784.

9. Abraham, "Peril and Fortuity in Property and Liability Insurance," 787.

10. Abraham, "Peril and Fortuity in Property and Liability Insurance," 797.

11. Joanne Wojcik, "Y2K Bug Is Still Biting," Business Insurance, July 16, 2000, https://www.businessinsurance.com/article/20000716/STORY/10002453#.

12. GTE Corp. v. Allendale Mutual Insurance Co., 372 F.3d 598 (3d Cir. 2004).

13. GTE Corp. v. Allendale Mutual Insurance Co.

14. GTE Corp. v. Allendale Mutual Insurance Co.

15. Port of Seattle v. Lexington Insurance Co., 48 P.3d 334 (111 Wash. Ct. App. 2002).

16. Lloyd's Underwriters' Non-Marine Association Ltd., "Electronic Data Endorsement B," January 25, 2001, https://www.commund.com/Forms/cargo_rater/NMA 2915.pdf.

17. Michael Rossi, "The End of Computer Virus Coverage as We Know It?," International Risk Management Institute, May 2002, https://www.irmi.com/articles /expert-commentary/the-end-of-computer-virus-coverage-as-we-know-it.

18. NPPD, *Insurance Industry Working Session Readout Report*.

19. Rosenau v. Idaho Mutual Benefit Association, 65 Idaho 408, 145 p.2d 227 (Idaho 1944).

20. All the following quotations are from Rosenau v. Idaho Mutual Benefit Association.

21. Stankus v. New York Life Insurance Co. 312 Mass. 366. (Mass. October 29, 1942).

22. Stankus v. New York Life Insurance Co.

23. Stankus v. New York Life Insurance Co.

24. Ching Pang v. Sun Life Assurance Company of Canada, 37 Haw. 208 (Haw. 1945).

25. New York Life Insurance Co. v. Bennion, 158 F.2d 260 (10th Cir. 1946).

26. New York Life Insurance Co. v. Bennion.

27. Stankus v. New York Life Insurance Co.

28. Stankus v. New York Life Insurance Co.

29. Ching Pang v. Sun Life Assurance Company of Canada.

30. Mondelez International Inc. v. Zurich American Insurance Co.

31. Bas v. Tingy, 4 U.S. 4 Dall. 37 (1800).

32. Vanderbilt v. Travelers' Insurance Co., 112 Misc. 248 (N.Y. Sup. Ct. 1920).

33. New York Life Ins. Co. v. Bennion, 158 F.2d 260.

34. Pan American World Airways Inc. v. Aetna Casualty & Surety Co., 368 F. Supp. 1098 (S.D.N.Y. 1973).

35. Pan American World Airways Inc. v. Aetna Casualty & Surety Co., 505 F.2d 989 (2d Cir. 1974).

36. Pan American World Airways Inc. v. Aetna Casualty & Surety Co., 505 F.2d 989.

37. Pan American World Airways Inc. v. Aetna Casualty & Surety Co., 505 F.2d 989.

38. Pan American World Airways Inc. v. Aetna Casualty & Surety Co., 368 F. Supp. 1098.

39. Pan American World Airways Inc. v. Aetna Casualty & Surety Co., 368 F. Supp. 1098.

40. Pan American World Airways Inc. v. Aetna Casualty & Surety Co., 368 F. Supp. 1098.

41. Pan American World Airways Inc. v. Aetna Casualty & Surety Co., 505 F.2d 989.

42. Pan American World Airways Inc. v. Aetna Casualty & Surety Co., 505 F.2d 989.

43. Holiday Inns Inc. v. Aetna Insurance Co., 571 F. Supp. 1460 (S.D.N.Y. 1983).

44. Holiday Inns Inc. v. Aetna Insurance Co.

45. Holiday Inns Inc. v. Aetna Insurance Co.

46. Universal Cable Products LLC v. Atlantic Specialty Insurance Co., 929 F.3d 1143 (9th Cir. 2019).

47. Sean Sullivan, "Obama: North Korea Hack 'Cyber-Vandalism,' Not 'Act of War,'" *Washington Post*, December 21, 2014.

48. Mondelez International Inc. v. Zurich American Insurance Co.

49. Andy Greenberg, "Petya Ransomware Hides State-Sponsored Attacks, Say Ukrainian Analysts," *Wired*, June 28, 2017, https://www.wired.com/story/petya -ransomware-ukraine/.

50. Sam Jones, "Finger Points at Russian State over Petya Hack Attack," *Financial Times*, June 30, 2017.

51. United States, Office of the Press Secretary, "Statement from the Press Secretary," February 15, 2018, https://trumpwhitehouse.archives.gov/briefings-statements /statement-press-secretary-25/.

52. Stilgherrian, "Blaming Russia for NotPetya Was Coordinated Diplomatic Action," ZDNet, April 12, 2018, https://www.zdnet.com/article/blaming-russia -for-notpetya-was-coordinated-diplomatic-action/.

53. Denis Pinchuk, "Russia Denies British Allegations that Moscow Was behind Cyber-Attack," Reuters, February 15, 2018, https://www.reuters.com/article/us -britain-russia-cyber-kremlin/russia-denies-british-allegations-that-moscow-was -behind-cyber-attack-idUSKCN1FZ102.

54. Jones, "Finger Points at Russian State over Petya Hack Attack."

55. Jones, "Finger Points at Russian State over Petya Hack Attack."

56. Joshua P. Mulford, "Non-State Actors in the Russo-Ukrainian War," *Connections: The Quarterly Journal* 15, no. 2 (2016): 89–107, http://dx.doi.org/10.11610/Connections.15.2.07.

57. Universal Cable Products LLC v. Atlantic Specialty Insurance Co.

58. Mondelez International Inc. v. Zurich American Insurance Co.

59. Andrea Shalal, "Massive Cyber Attack Could Trigger NATO Response: Stoltenberg," Reuters, June 15, 2016, https://www.reuters.com/article/us-cyber-nato-idUSKCN0Z12NE.

60. Olga Oliker, "Russian Influence and Unconventional Warfare Operations in the 'Grey Zone:' Lessons from Ukraine," Statement before the Senate Armed Services Committee Subcommittee on Emerging Threats and Capabilities, March 29, 2017, https://www.armed-services.senate.gov/imo/media/doc/Oliker_03-29-17.pdf.

61. Greenberg, "Untold Story of NotPetya."

62. Holiday Inns Inc. v. Aetna Insurance Co.

63. Matthew McCabe, "NotPetya Was Not Cyber 'War,'" Marsh McLennan, August 2018.

64. McCabe, "NotPetya Was Not Cyber 'War.'".

65. Mondelez International Inc. v. Zurich American Insurance Co.

66. Mondelez International Inc. v. Zurich American Insurance Co.

67. Mondelez International Inc. v. Zurich American Insurance Co.

68. Greenberg, "Untold Story of NotPetya."

69. David Voreacos, Katherine Chiglinsky, and Riley Griffin, "Merck Cyberattack's $1.3 Billion Question: Was It an Act of War?," Bloomberg, December 3, 2019, https://www.bloomberg.com/news/features/2019-12-03/merck-cyberattack-s-1-3-billion-question-was-it-an-act-of-war.

70. Voreacos, Chiglinsky, and Griffin, "Merck Cyberattack's $1.3 Billion Question."

71. Jon Bateman, "Does Your Cyber Insurance Cover a State-Sponsored Attack?," *Harvard Business Review*, October 30, 2020, https://hbr.org/2020/10/does-your-cyber-insurance-cover-a-state-sponsored-attack.

72. Kenneth S. Abraham and Daniel Schwarcz, "Courting Disaster: The Underappreciated Risk of a Cyber-Insurance Catastrophe," Virginia Public Law and Legal Theory Research Paper No. 2021-15, February 2021, 35, https://papers.ssrn.com/sol3/papers.cfm?abstract_id=3792882.

73. "Zurich Cyber Insurance Policy U-SPR-300-A CW," September 2018.

74. "Zurich Cyber Insurance Policy U-SPR-300-A CW."

75. Daniel W. Woods and Jessica Weinkle, "Insurance Definitions of Cyber War," *Geneva Papers on Risk and Insurance—Issues and Practice* 45, no. 4 (2020): 639–656.

CHAPTER 6

1. Andrew Hill, "Cyber Risk Poses Ongoing Challenge for First-Party Property Damage Lines of Business," Willis Towers Watson, January 28, 2020, https://www .willistowerswatson.com/en-US/Insights/2020/01/cyber-risk-poses-ongoing -challenge-for-first-party-property-damage-lines-of-business.

2. Matthews, "Report on the Cybersecurity Insurance and Identity Theft Coverage Supplement."

3. *Examining the Evolving Cyber Insurance Marketplace*, 114 Cong. 171 (March 19, 2015).

4. *Examining the Evolving Cyber Insurance Marketplace*.

5. N. Eric Weiss and Rena S. Miller, "The Target and Other Financial Data Breaches: Frequently Asked Questions," Congressional Research Service, February 4, 2015, https://fas.org/sgp/crs/misc/R43496.pdf.

6. Kavita Kumar, "Target Sues Insurer for up to $74 Million in 2013 Data Breach Costs," *Star Tribune*, November 19, 2019, https://www.startribune.com/target -sues-insurer-for-at-least-74-million-in-2013-data-breach-costs/565169292/.

7. Josephine Wolff and William Lehr, "Degrees of Ignorance about the Costs of Data Breaches: What Policymakers Can and Can't Do about the Lack of Good Empirical Data," Paper presented at the 45th Research Conference on Communications, Information and Internet Policy (TPRC), Washington, DC, September 9, 2017.

8. *Examining the Evolving Cyber Insurance Marketplace*.

9. *Examining the Evolving Cyber Insurance Marketplace*.

10. *Columbia Committee Report*.

11. *A Unified National Program for Managing Flood Losses: A Report by the Task Force on Federal Flood Control Policy* H.R. Rep. No. 89-465 (August 1966).

12. The Travelers Indemnity Company, "Travelers CyberRisk Policy Template (CYB-3001)," July 2010, https://www.travelers.com/iw-documents/apps-forms /cyberrisk/cyb-3001.pdf.

13. "Zurich Cyber Insurance Policy U-SPR-300-A CW."

14. Wolff, *You'll See This Message When It Is Too Late*.

15. NPPD, *Insurance Industry Working Session Readout Report*.

16. Katherine Chiglinsky and Sonali Basak, "Buffett Cautious on Cyber Insurance Because No One Knows Risks," Bloomberg, May 5, 2018, https://www .bloomberg.com/news/articles/2018-05-05/buffett-cautious-on-cyberinsurance -because-no-one-knows-risks.

17. Rainer Böhme and Gaurav Kataria, "On the Limits of Cyber-Insurance," in *Trust and Privacy in Digital Business*, ed. Simone Fischer-Hübner, Stevel Furnell, and

Costas Lambrinoudakis (Berlin: Springer, 2006), 31–40, https://doi.org/10.1007
/11824633_4.

18. Lloyd's and AIR Worldwide, "Cloud Down: Impacts on the US Economy,"
2018, https://www.lloyds.com/~/media/files/news-and-insight/risk-insight/2018
/cloud-down/aircyberlloydspublic2018final.pdf.

19. James E. Scheuermann, "Cyber Risks, Systemic Risks, and Cyber Insurance
Symposium," *Penn State Law Review* 122, no. 3 (2018): 637–638.

20. Scheuermann, "Cyber Risks, Systemic Risks, and Cyber Insurance Symposium," 634.

21. Adam Raphael, *Ultimate Risk: The Inside Story of the Lloyd's Catastrophe* (New
York: Four Walls Eight Windows, 1995).

22. Nicole Perlroth and Elizabeth A. Harris, "Cyberattack Insurance a Challenge
for Business," *New York Times*, June 8, 2014, sec. Business, https://www.nytimes
.com/2014/06/09/business/cyberattack-insurance-a-challenge-for-business.html.

23. Perlroth and Harris, "Cyberattack Insurance a Challenge for Business."

24. Oliver Ralph, "Beazley and Munich Re Join up in Cyber Insurance Push,"
Financial Times, April 10, 2016.

25. Ralph Atkins, "Swiss Re Chief Cautions on Cyber Security Risks," *Financial
Times*, February 23, 2016.

26. Matt Sheehan, "Pipeline Cyber Attack Not Surprising, Says Swiss Re's
Mumenthaler," Reinsurance News, May 13, 2021, https://www.reinsurancene.ws
/pipeline-cyber-attack-not-surprising-says-swiss-res-mumenthaler/.

27. Terrorism Risk Insurance Act of 2002, Pub. L. No. 107–297 116 Stat. 2322
(2002).

28. US Department of the Treasury, "Guidance Concerning Stand-Alone Cyber
Liability Insurance Policies Under the Terrorism Risk Insurance Program," *Federal Register* 81, no. 248 (2016), https://www.federalregister.gov/documents/2016
/12/27/2016-31244/guidance-concerning-stand-alone-cyber-liability-insurance
-policies-under-the-terrorism-risk.

29. *Examining the Evolving Cyber Insurance Marketplace.*

30. Romanosky et al., "Content Analysis of Cyber Insurance Policies."

31. Romanosky et al., "Content Analysis of Cyber Insurance Policies."

32. Romanosky et al., "Content Analysis of Cyber Insurance Policies," 12.

33. Woods et al., "Mapping the coverage of security controls in cyber insurance
proposal forms," 11.

34. National Protection and Programs Directorate (NPPD), *Cyber Risk Culture Roundtable Readout Report* (Washington, DC: US Department of Homeland Security, May
2013), 32.

35. Daniel Woods and Rainer Böhme, "How Cyber Insurance Shapes Incident Response: A Mixed Methods Study," *Workshop on the Economics of Information Security*, June 7, 2021, https://informationsecurity.uibk.ac.at/pdfs/DW2021_HowInsuranceShapes_WEIS.pdf.

36. Omri Ben-Shahar and Kyle D. Logue, "Outsourcing Regulation: How Insurance Reduces Moral Hazard," *Michigan Law Review* 111, no. 2 (2012): 212.

37. Ben-Shahar and Logue, "Outsourcing Regulation," 213.

38. Talesh, "Data Breach, Privacy, and Cyber Insurance."

39. Josephine Wolff, "Perverse Effects in Defense of Computer Systems: When More Is Less," *Journal of Management Information Systems* 33, no. 2 (2016): 597–620, https://doi.org/10.1080/07421222.2016.1205934.

40. Liam Bailey, "Mitigating Moral Hazard in Cyber-Risk Insurance," *Journal of Law and Cyber Warfare* 3, no. 1 (2014): 1–42.

41. Harrison, "Counterpane Offers Internet Security Insurance."

42. Harrison, "Counterpane Offers Internet Security Insurance."

43. Josephine Wolff, "Cyberinsurance Tries to Tackle the Unpredictable World of Hacks," *Wired*, April 6, 2018, https://www.wired.com/story/cyberinsurance-tackles-the-wildly-unpredictable-world-of-hacks/.

44. "Cisco, Apple, Aon, Allianz Introduce a First in Cyber Risk Management," Apple Newsroom, February 5, 2018, https://www.apple.com/newsroom/2018/02/cisco-apple-aon-allianz-introduce-a-first-in-cyber-risk-management/.

45. Josephine Wolff and William Lehr, "Roles for Policy-Makers in Emerging Cyber Insurance Industry Partnerships," in *TPRC 46: The 46th Research Conference on Communication, Information and Internet Policy 2018* (Washington, DC: Social Science Research Network, 2018), https://papers.ssrn.com/abstract=3141409.

46. Wolff and Lehr, "Roles for Policymakers in Emerging Cyber Insurance Industry Partnerships."

47. "Coalition Launches Cyber Insurance and Security Coverage in Canada," *Insurance Journal*, May 22, 2020, https://www.insurancejournal.com/news/international/2020/05/22/569706.htm.

48. Wolff, "Cyberinsurance Tries to Tackle the Unpredictable World of Hacks."

49. Wolff and Lehr, "Roles for Policymakers in Emerging Cyber Insurance Industry Partnerships."

CHAPTER 7

1. Joseph Blount, "House Homeland Security Committee Hearing on the Colonial Pipeline Cyber Attack," C-Span video, June 9, 2021, https://www.c-span

.org/video/?512332-1/colonial-pipeline-ceo-joseph-blount-testifies-house-homeland-security-committee.

2. Josephine Wolff, "As Ransomware Demands Boom, Insurance Companies Keep Paying Out," *Wired*, June 12, 2021, https://www.wired.com/story/ransomware-insurance-payments/.

3. Daniel W. Woods and Andrew C. Simpson, "Policy Measures and Cyber Insurance: A Framework," *Journal of Cyber Policy* 2, no. 2 (2017): 209–226.

4. Wolff, "As Ransomware Demands Boom, Insurance Companies Keep Paying Out."

5. Heng Swee Keat, "Speech by Minister for Finance Heng Swee Keat at the 15th Singapore International Reinsurance Conference," October 29, 2018, https://www.mof.gov.sg/news-publications/speeches/speech-by-minister-for-finance-heng-swee-keat-at-the-15th-singapore-international-reinsurance-conference.

6. NPPD, *Cybersecurity Insurance Workshop Readout Report*.

7. NPPD, *Cybersecurity Insurance Workshop Readout Report*.

8. US Department of the Treasury, "Guidance Concerning Stand-Alone Cyber Liability Insurance Policies Under the Terrorism Risk Insurance Program."

9. Terrorism Risk Insurance Act of 2002.

10. NPPD, *Cyber Risk Culture Roundtable Readout Report*.

11. NPPD, *Insurance Industry Working Session Readout Report*, 15.

12. NPPD, *Insurance Industry Working Session Readout Report*, 16.

13. NPPD, *Insurance Industry Working Session Readout Report, 18.*

14. US Department of Homeland Security, "Enhancing Resilience through Cyber Incident Data Sharing and Analysis: Establishing Community-Relevant Data Categories in Support of a Cyber Incident Data Repository," Cyber Incident Data and Analysis Working Group (CIDAWG) White Paper, September 2015, https://www.hsdl.org/?view&did=788825.

15. United States Cyberspace Solarium Commission (CSC), "Final Report," March 2020, 77, https://www.solarium.gov/report.

16. CSC, "Final Report," 81.

17. CSC, "Final Report," 80.

18. CSC, "Final Report," 82.

19. United States Cyberspace Solarium Commission (CSC), "Legislative Proposals," July 2020, https://www.solarium.gov/report.

20. European Insurance and Occupational Pensions Authority (EIOPA), "Understanding Cyber Insurance: A Structured Dialogue with Insurance Companies," August 2, 2018.

21. Insurance Europe, "Template for Data Breach Notifications: Press Release," March 19, 2018, https://www.insuranceeurope.eu/news/297/gdpr-data-breach-reporting-templates-developed-by-insurance-industry/.

22. Insurance Europe, "Template for Data Breach Notifications, Part I: Identification of Data Controller," March 19, 2018, https://www.insuranceeurope.eu/downloads/2289/Template+for+data+breach+notifications+-+Section+1.pdf.

23. Insurance Europe, "Template for Data Breach Notifications, Part II: Principal Information on Data Breach," March 19, 2018, https://www.insuranceeurope.eu/downloads/2290/Template+for+data+breach+notifications+-+Section+2.pdf.

24. Insurance Europe, "Template for Data Breach Notifications, Part III: Complementary Information," March 19, 2018, https://www.insuranceeurope.eu/downloads/2291/Template+for+data+breach+notifications+-+Section+3.pdf.

25. EIOPA, "Understanding Cyber Insurance."

26. European Union Agency for Network and Information Security (ENISA), "Cyber Insurance: Recent Advances, Good Practices and Challenges," November 2016, https://www.enisa.europa.eu/publications/cyber-insurance-recent-advances-good-practices-and-challenges.

27. EIOPA, "Understanding Cyber Insurance," 12.

28. European Insurance and Occupational Pensions Authority (EIOPA), *Cyber Risk for Insurers: Challenges and Opportunities* (Luxembourg: Office of the European Union, 2019).

29. Ross Anderson et al., "Security Economics and the Internal Market," European Union Agency for Cybersecurity, January 31, 2008, https://www.enisa.europa.eu/publications/archive/economics-sec/.

30. European Union Agency for Cybersecurity (ENISA), "Incentives and Barriers of the Cyber Insurance Market in Europe," June 2012, https://www.enisa.europa.eu/publications/incentives-and-barriers-of-the-cyber-insurance-market-in-europe.

31. European Union Agency for Cybersecurity (ENISA), "ENISA Validation Workshop: Recommendations on Cyber Insurance," October 6, 2017, https://www.enisa.europa.eu/events/enisa-validation-workshop-on-cyber-insurance.

32. HM Government, "UK Cyber Security: The Role of Insurance in Managing and Mitigating the Risk," UK Cabinet Office, March 2015, https://www.gov.uk/government/publications/uk-cyber-security-the-role-of-insurance.

33. European Insurance and Occupational Pensions Authority (EIOPA), "Summary of the Workshop on Cyber Insurance Organised by the European Insurance and Occupational Pensions Authority (EIOPA)," Frankfurt, Germany, April 1, 2019.

34. EU-US Insurance Dialogue Project, "The Cyber Insurance Market Working Group: February 2020 Summary Report," February 2020, https://www.eiopa.europa.eu/sites/default/files/publications/eu-us-cyber-insurance-wg-feb-2020.pdf.

35. Julie Zhu, "Greater China Cyber Insurance Demand to Soar after WannaCry Attack: AIG," Reuters, August 9, 2018, https://www.reuters.com/article/us-aig-china-cyber/greater-china-cyber-insurance-demand-to-soar-after-wannacry-attack-aig-idUSKBN1AP12E.

36. Frank Wang, "Cyber Insurance Ready for Take-Off in China," Gen Re, November 2017, https://media.genre.com/documents/cmchina1710-en.pdf.

37. Wang, "Cyber Insurance Ready for Take-Off in China."

38. Alice Shen, "Asian Companies See Little Need for Insurance against Cyber Attack, with Less than 20pc Insured," *South China Morning Post*, April 22, 2018.

39. Rui Yang, "China Liability Insurance Market Trend Report," Swiss Re, May 2019, https://www.swissre.com/dam/jcr:64625acc-dd25-4719-bf2b-935b65727ed5/China%20Liability%20Insurance%20Market%20Trend%20Report%20-%20updated.pdf.

40. Winston & Strawn LLP, "2017 Insurance Review," February 2018, https://www.winston.com/images/content/1/3/v2/135129/2017-China-Insurance-Review-MAR2018.pdf.

41. Winston & Strawn LLP, "2018 China Insurance Review," April 8, 2019, https://www.winston.com/images/content/2/2/v2/227694/Corp-2018-Insurance-Review-A4-Brochure-APR2019.pdf.

42. Winston & Strawn LLP, "2018 China Insurance Review."

43. Tracy Li, "Cyber Insurance Market Set to Grow Significantly: Zurich," Shine, January 2, 2019, https://www.shine.cn/biz/company/1901027546/.

44. Rogier Creemers, Paul Triolo, and Graham Webster, "Translation: Cybersecurity Law of the People's Republic of China (Effective June 1, 2017)," *New America* (blog), June 29, 2018, https://www.newamerica.org/cybersecurity-initiative/digichina/blog/translation-cybersecurity-law-peoples-republic-china/.

45. Wang, "Cyber Insurance Ready for Take-Off in China," 3.

46. Creemers, Triolo, and Webster, "Translation."

47. Winston & Strawn LLP, "2017 Insurance Review."

48. Wang, "Cyber Insurance Ready for Take-Off in China," 3.

49. Beazley, "Beazley's Data Breach Expertise to Back New Generali Cyber Product in Brazil," press release, September 27, 2017, https://www.beazley.com/news/2017/beazleys_data_breach_expertise_to_back_new_generali_cyber_product_in_brazil.html.

50. International Monetary Fund (IMF), *Brazil Financial Sector Assessment Program: Technical Note on Insurance Sector Regulation and Supervision* (Washington, DC: International Monetary Fund, November 2018).

51. "Why Brazil's Data Law Will Boost Cybersecurity Insurance," BNamericas, October 24, 2019, https://www.bnamericas.com/en/features/why-brazils-data-law-will-boost-cybersecurity-insurance.

52. Ronaldo Lemos et al., trans., "Brazilian Data Protection Law (LGPD, English Translation)," October 28, 2020, https://iapp.org/media/pdf/resource_center/Brazilian_General_Data_Protection_Law.pdf.

53. Personal Data Protection Act of 2019, Bill No. 373 (2019).

54. Data Security Council of India, "Cyber Insurance in India: Mitigating Risks amid Changing Regulations & Uncertainties," April 26, 2019, https://www.dsci.in/content/cyber-insurance-in-india.

55. V. Bhatia, "Cyber Insurance: How Lloyd's India Is Closing the Gaps," *Money Control News*, January 6, 2020.

56. "Cyber Risk Management Project (CyRiM) Project Brief," Nanyang Technological University Singapore, http://irfrc.ntu.edu.sg/Research/cyrim/Pages/Project-Brief.aspx.

57. Caitriona Heinl, "NTU Cyber Risk Management Project (CyRiM): Roundtable Series on Optimal Governance and Regulatory Structures to Enhance Resilience. Roundtable One Session Report." (Singapore: Nanyang Technological University, September 7, 2017), 3.

58. Heinl, 7–8.

59. Caitriona Heinl, "NTU Cyber Risk Management Project (CyRiM): Roundtable Series on Optimal Governance and Regulatory Structures to Enhance Resilience. Roundtable Two Session Report: National Market and Regulatory Structures in Singapore," Nanyang Technological University, Singapore, September 28, 2017, 3, https://www.ntu.edu.sg/docs/default-source/academic-services/download-session-report2d9320a8-3677-4117-a76e-e29b63a20826.pdf?sfvrsn=45250cdf_3.

60. Caitriona Heinl, "NTU Cyber Risk Management Project (CyRiM): Roundtable Series on Optimal Governance and Regulatory Structures to Enhance Resilience. Roundtable One Session Report," Nanyang Technological University, Singapore, September 28, 2017, 7, https://www.ntu.edu.sg/docs/default-source/academic-services/download-session-report132e0472-978d-457b-9974-691b0774ac67.pdf?sfvrsn=b4daca63_3.

61. Caitriona Heinl, "NTU Cyber Risk Management Project (CyRiM): Roundtable Series on Optimal Governance and Regulatory Structures to Enhance Resilience. Roundtable Three Session Report: Good Practices and Sector Case Studies," Nanyang Technological University, Singapore, November 21, 2017, 9, https://www.ntu.edu.sg/docs/default-source/academic-services/cyrim_roundtable_report30d27659f-a2c0-410b-b2fe-68d0e4d35054.pdf?sfvrsn=b789f1e4_3.

62. Haufler, *Dangerous Commerce*, 129.

63. Lauren Miller, "Cyber Insurance: An Incentive Alignment Solution to Corporate Cyber-Insecurity," *Journal of Law and Cyber Warfare* 7, no. 2 (2019): 147–182.

64. Asaf Lubin, "Public Policy and the Insurability of Cyber Risk," *Journal of Law and Technology at Texas* 6, (forthcoming 2021), https://papers.ssrn.com/sol3/papers.cfm?abstract_id=3452833.

65. Claudio Detotto, Bryan C. McCannon, and Marco Vannini, "Understanding Ransom Kidnappings and Their Duration," *B.E. Journal of Economic Analysis and Policy* 14, no. 3 (2014): 849–871, https://doi.org/10.1515/bejeap-2013-0079.

66. Anja Shortland, *Kidnap: Inside the Ransom Business* (Oxford: Oxford University Press, 2019).

67. Haufler, *Dangerous Commerce*, 128.

68. *Examining the Evolving Cyber Insurance Marketplace*, 114 Cong. 171 (March 19, 2015).

CHAPTER 8

1. PricewaterhouseCoopers, "Insurance 2020 & beyond: Reaping the Dividends of Cyber Resilience," 2015, https://www.pwc.com/gx/en/insurance/publications/assets/reaping-dividends-cyber-resilience.pdf.

2. Matthews, "Report on the Cybersecurity Insurance and Identity Theft Coverage Supplement."

3. Luke Gallin, "US Cyber Insurance Market's Loss Ratio up 10% on Claims Frequency: Aon," Reinsurance News, June 17, 2020, https://www.reinsurancene.ws/us-cyberinsurance-markets-loss-ratio-up-10-on-claims-frequency-aon/.

4. Renee Dudley, "The Extortion Economy: How Insurance Companies Are Fueling a Rise in Ransomware Attacks," ProPublica, August 27, 2019, https://www.propublica.org/article/the-extortion-economy-how-insurance-companies-are-fueling-a-rise-in-ransomware-attacks.

5. Haufler, *Dangerous Commerce*, 135–136.

6. Department of Commerce Internet Policy Task Force, "Cybersecurity, Innovation and the Internet Economy," June 2011, 24, https://www.nist.gov/system/files/documents/itl/Cybersecurity_Green-Paper_FinalVersion.pdf.

7. NPPD, *Cybersecurity Insurance Workshop Readout Report*, 1.

8. Abraham, *Liability Century*, 49.

9. Abraham, *Liability Century*, 49–50.

10. Abraham, *Liability Century*, 220.

11. Abraham, *Liability Century*, 223.

12. Ram Shankar Siva Kumar and Frank Nagle, "The Case for AI Insurance," *Harvard Business Review*, April 29, 2020, https://hbr.org/2020/04/the-case-for-ai-insurance.

REFERENCES

Abraham, Kenneth S. *The Liability Century: Insurance and Tort Law from the Progressive Era to 9/11*. Cambridge, MA: Harvard University Press, 2008.

Abraham, Kenneth S. "Peril and Fortuity in Property and Liability Insurance." *Tort and Insurance Law Journal* 36, no. 3 (2001): 777–802.

Abraham, Kenneth S., and Daniel Schwarcz. "Courting Disaster: The Underappreciated Risk of a Cyber-Insurance Catastrophe." Virginia Public Law and Legal Theory Research Paper No. 2021-15. https://papers.ssrn.com/sol3/papers.cfm?abstract_id=3792882.

AM Best. "Cyber Insurers Are Profitable Today, but Wary of Tomorrow's Risks." Best's Market Segment Report, June 17, 2019. https://s3.amazonaws.com/external_clips/3138950/Cyber.2019report.pdf?1564432814.

American Economy Insurance Co. v. Aspen Way Enterprises. No. 1:14-cv-00009, 2015 U.S. Dist. LEXIS 129274. United States District Court for the District of Montana, Billings Division September 25, 2015.

American Tooling Center Inc. v. Travelers Casualty and Surety Company of America. No. 5:16-cv-12108. United States District Court for the Eastern District of Michigan, Southern Division August 1, 2017.

American Tooling Center Inc. v. Travelers Casualty and Surety Company of America. 895 F.3d 455. United States Court of Appeals for the Sixth Circuit 2018.

Anderson, James M., Paul Heaton, and Stephen J. Carroll. *The U.S. Experience with No-Fault Automobile Insurance: A Retrospective*. Santa Monica, CA: RAND Corporation, 2010, MG-860-ICJ.

Anderson, Ross, Rainer Böhme, Richard Clayton, and Tyler Moore. "Security Economics and the Internal Market." European Union Agency for Cybersecurity, January 31, 2008. https://www.enisa.europa.eu/publications/archive/economics-sec/.

Apache Corp. v. Great American Insurance Co. 662 Fed. Appx. 252. United States Court of Appeals for the Fifth Circuit 2016.

Apache Corp. v. Great American Insurance Co. No. 4:14-cv-237, 2015 U.S. Dist. LEXIS 161683. United States District Court for the Southern District of Texas, Houston Division 2015.

Atkins, Ralph. "Swiss Re Chief Cautions on Cyber Security Risks." *Financial Times*, February 23, 2016.

Bailey, Liam. "Mitigating Moral Hazard in Cyber-Risk Insurance." *Journal of Law and Cyber Warfare* 3, no. 1 (2014): 1–42.

Bas v. Tingy. 4 U.S. 4 Dall. 37. United States Supreme Court 1800.

Bateman, Jon. "Does Your Cyber Insurance Cover a State-Sponsored Attack?" *Harvard Business Review*, October 30, 2020. https://hbr.org/2020/10/does-your-cyber-insurance-cover-a-state-sponsored-attack.

Battaglia, Anthony J. "Order Granting in Part and Denying in Part Defendants' Motion to Dismiss Plaintiffs' Consolidated Class Action Complaint In re: Sony Gaming Networks and Customer Data Security Breach Litigation." No. 3:11-cv-02119-AJB-MDD. United States District Court of the Southern District of California October 11, 2012. https://www.steptoe.com/images/content/2/7/v1/2710/4467.pdf.

Beazley. "Beazley's Data Breach Expertise to Back New Generali Cyber Product in Brazil." Press release, September 27, 2017. https://www.beazley.com/news/2017/beazleys_data_breach_expertise_to_back_new_generali_cyber_product_in_brazil.html.

Beck, Ulrich, and Mark Ritter. *Risk Society: Towards a New Modernity*. London: Sage, 1992.

Ben-Shahar, Omri, and Kyle D. Logue. "Outsourcing Regulation: How Insurance Reduces Moral Hazard." *Michigan Law Review* 111, no. 2 (2012): 197–248.

Bhatia, V. "Cyber Insurance: How Lloyd's India Is Closing the Gaps." *Money Control News*, January 6, 2020.

Blount, Joseph. "House Homeland Security Committee Hearing on the Colonial Pipeline Cyber Attack." C-Span video, June 9, 2021. https://www.c-span.org/video/?512332-1/colonial-pipeline-ceo-joseph-blount-testifies-house-homeland-security-committee.

Bohannan v. Innovak International, 318 F.R.D. 525. United States District Court for the Middle District of Alabama, Southern Division 2015.

Böhme, Rainer. "Cyber-Insurance Revisited." Paper presented at the Workshop on the Economics of Information Security, Kennedy School of Government, Cambridge, MA, 2005. http://infosecon.net/workshop/pdf/15.pdf.

Böhme, Rainer, and Gaurav Kataria. "Models and Measures for Correlation in Cyber-Insurance." Working paper, Workshop on the Economics of Information Security, Cambridge, UK, 2006. https://econinfosec.org/archive/weis2006/docs/16.pdf.

Böhme, Rainer, and Gaurav Kataria. "On the Limits of Cyber-Insurance." In *Trust and Privacy in Digital Business*, edited by Simone Fischer-Hübner, Stevel Furnell, and Costas Lambrinoudakis, 31–40. Berlin: Springer, 2006. https://doi.org/10.1007/11824633_4.

Böhme, Rainer, and Galina Schwartz. "Modeling Cyber-Insurance: Towards a Unifying Framework." Working paper, Workshop on the Economics of Information Security, Cambridge, MA, 2010. https://econinfosec.org/archive/weis2010/papers/session5/weis2010_boehme.pdf.

Breidenbach, Susan. "The Policy for Protection." *Network World*, October 23, 2000.

Brightpoint Inc. v. Zurich American Insurance Co. No. 1:04-cv-2085-SEB-JPG, 2006 U.S. Dist. LEXIS 26018. United States District Court for the Southern District of Indiana, Indianapolis Division March 10, 2006.

Brown, Brian D. "The Ever-Evolving Nature of Cyber Coverage." *Insurance Journal*, September 22, 2014. https://www.insurancejournal.com/magazines/mag-features/2014/09/22/340633.htm.

Chiglinsky, Katherine, and Sonali Basak. "Buffett Cautious on Cyber Insurance Because No One Knows Risks." Bloomberg, May 5, 2018. https://www.bloomberg.com/news/articles/2018-05-05/buffett-cautious-on-cyber-insurance-because-no-one-knows-risks.

Ching Pang v. Sun Life Assurance Company of Canada. 37 Haw. 208. Supreme Court of Hawaii 1945.

"Cisco, Apple, Aon, Allianz Introduce a First in Cyber Risk Management." Apple Newsroom, February 5, 2018. https://www.apple.com/newsroom/2018/02/cisco-apple-aon-allianz-introduce-a-first-in-cyber-risk-management/.

"Coalition Launches Cyber Insurance and Security Coverage in Canada." *Insurance Journal*, May 22, 2020. https://www.insurancejournal.com/news/international/2020/05/22/569706.htm.

Conroy, Michael. "Cyber Insurance for Viruses, Hackers Is Gaining Speed." *Long Island Business News*, July 6, 2001.

Creemers, Rogier, Paul Triolo, and Graham Webster. "Translation: Cybersecurity Law of the People's Republic of China (Effective June 1, 2017)." *New America* (blog), June 29, 2018. https://www.newamerica.org/cybersecurity-initiative/digichina/blog/translation-cybersecurity-law-peoples-republic-china/.

"Cyber Risk Management Project (CyRiM) Project Brief." Nanyang Technological University Singapore. http://irfrc.ntu.edu.sg/Research/cyrim/Pages/Project-Brief.aspx.

Data Security Council of India. "Cyber Insurance in India: Mitigating Risks amid Changing Regulations & Uncertainties." April 26, 2019. https://www.dsci.in/content/cyber-insurance-in-india.

Defendants' Reply to Plaintiffs' Opposition to the Motion to Dismiss Consolidated Class Action Complaint In re Sony Gaming Networks and Customer Data

Security Breach Litigation. No. 11-md-2258 AJB. United States District Court, Southern District of California August 12, 2012.

Department of Commerce Internet Policy Task Force. "Cybersecurity, Innovation and the Internet Economy." June 2011. https://www.nist.gov/system/files /documents/itl/Cybersecurity_Green-Paper_FinalVersion.pdf.

Detotto, Claudio, Bryan C. McCannon, and Marco Vannini. "Understanding Ransom Kidnappings and Their Duration." *B.E. Journal of Economic Analysis and Policy* 14, no. 3 (2014): 849–871. https://doi.org/10.1515/bejeap-2013-0079.

Dudley, Renee. "The Extortion Economy: How Insurance Companies Are Fueling a Rise in Ransomware Attacks." ProPublica, August 27, 2019. https://www .propublica.org/article/the-extortion-economy-how-insurance-companies-are -fueling-a-rise-in-ransomware-attacks.

Dyson, Ben. "Learning to Fly." *Reactions* 25, no. 4 (2005): 22–25.

Ericson, Richard V., Aaron Doyle, and Dean Barry. *Insurance as Governance*. Toronto: University of Toronto Press, 2003. https://doi.org/10.3138/9781442676220.

European Insurance and Occupational Pensions Authority (EIOPA). *Cyber Risk for Insurers: Challenges and Opportunities*. Luxembourg: Office of the European Union, 2019.

European Insurance and Occupational Pensions Authority (EIOPA). "EIOPA Strategy on Cyber Underwriting." February 2020. https://www.eiopa.europa.eu /sites/default/files/publications/cyber-underwriting-in-brief.pdf.

European Insurance and Occupational Pensions Authority (EIOPA). "Summary of the Workshop on Cyber Insurance Organised by the European Insurance and Occupational Pensions Authority (EIOPA)." Frankfurt, Germany, April 1, 2019.

European Insurance and Occupational Pensions Authority (EIOPA). "Understanding Cyber Insurance: A Structured Dialogue with Insurance Companies." August 2, 2018.

European Union Agency for for Cybersecurity (ENISA). "Cyber Insurance: Recent Advances, Good Practices and Challenges." November 2016. https://www .enisa.europa.eu/publications/cyber-insurance-recent-advances-good-practices-and -challenges.

European Union Agency for Cybersecurity (ENISA). "ENISA Validation Workshop: Recommendations on Cyber Insurance." October 6, 2017. https://www .enisa.europa.eu/events/enisa-validation-workshop-on-cyber-insurance.

European Union Agency for Cybersecurity (ENISA). "Incentives and Barriers of the Cyber Insurance Market in Europe." June 28, 2012. https://www.enisa .europa.eu/publications/incentives-and-barriers-of-the-cyber-insurance-market-in -europe.

EU-US Insurance Dialogue Project. "The Cyber Insurance Market Working Group: February 2020 Summary Report." February 2020. https://www.eiopa.europa.eu /sites/default/files/publications/eu-us-cyber-insurance-wg-feb-2020.pdf.

Examining the Evolving Cyber Insurance Marketplace: Hearings before the Subcommittee on Consumer Protection, Product Safety, Insurance, and Data Security of the Committee on Commerce, Science, and Transportation. 114 Cong. 171 (March 19, 2015).

Falco, Gregory, Martin Eling, Danielle Jablanski, Matthias Weber, Virginia Miller, Lawrence A. Gordon, Shaun Shuxun Wang, et al. "Cyber Risk Research Impeded by Disciplinary Barriers." *Science* 366, no. 6469 (2019): 1066–1069. https://doi.org /10.1126/science.aaz4795.

Figg, J. "Cyber Insurance to Cover E-Business." *Internal Auditor*, August 1, 2000.

First Amended Consolidated Class Action Complaint In re: Sony Gaming Networks and Customer Data Security Breach Litigation. No. 3:11-md-02258-AJB-MDD. United States District Court, Southern District of California December 10, 2012.

Franke, Ulrik. "The Cyber Insurance Market in Sweden." *Computers and Security* 68 (July 2017): 130–144.

Gallin, Luke. "US Cyber Insurance Market's Loss Ratio up 10% on Claims Frequency: Aon." Reinsurance News, June 17, 2020. https://www.reinsurancene.ws /us-cyber-insurance-markets-loss-ratio-up-10-on-claims-frequency-aon/.

Giegerich, Andy. "E-Commerce Risks Work for Tripwire." *Portland Business Journal* 17, no. 33 (2000): 14.

Goldin, Ian, and Mike Mariathasan. *The Butterfly Defect: How Globalization Creates Systemic Risks, and What to Do about It*. Princeton, NJ: Princeton University Press, 2014.

Gorman, John P. "All Risks of Loss v. All Loss: An Examination of Broad Form Insurance Coverages." *Notre Dame Law Review* 34, no. 3 (1959): 346–357.

Greenberg, Andy. "Petya Ransomware Hides State-Sponsored Attacks, Say Ukrainian Analysts." *Wired*, June 28, 2017. https://www.wired.com/story/petya-ransomware -ukraine/.

Greenberg, Andy. "The Untold Story of NotPetya, the Most Devastating Cyberattack in History." *Wired*, September 2018. https://www.wired.com/story /notpetya-cyberattack-ukraine-russia-code-crashed-the-world/.

GTE Corp. v. Allendale Mutual Insurance Co. 372 F.3d 598. United States Court of Appeals for the Third Circuit 2004.

Gumuchian, Marie-Louise, Ben Wedeman, and Ian Lee. "Ukraine Mobilizes Troops after Russia's 'Declaration of War.'" CNN, March 3, 2014. https://www .cnn.com/2014/03/02/world/europe/ukraine-politics/index.html.

Harrison, Ann. "Counterpane Offers Internet Security Insurance." Computerworld, July 12, 2000. https://www.computerworld.com/article/2595733/counterpane-off ers-internet-security-insurance.html.

Hartford Casualty Insurance Co. v. Corcino & Associates et al. No. 2:13-cv-03728-GAF-JC. United States District Court for the Central District of California October 7, 2013.

Haufler, Virginia. *Dangerous Commerce: Insurance and the Management of International Risk*. Ithaca, NY: Cornell University Press, 1997.

Heinl, Caitriona. "NTU Cyber Risk Management Project (CyRiM): Roundtable Series on Optimal Governance and Regulatory Structures to Enhance Resilience. Roundtable One Session Report." Nanyang Technological University, Singapore, September 7, 2017. https://www.ntu.edu.sg/docs/default-source/academic -services/download-session-report132e0472-978d-457b-9974-691b0774ac67.pdf ?sfvrsn=b4daca63_3.

Heinl, Caitriona. "NTU Cyber Risk Management Project (CyRiM): Roundtable Series on Optimal Governance and Regulatory Structures to Enhance Resilience. Roundtable Three Session Report: Good Practices and Sector Case Studies." Nanyang Technological University, Singapore, November 21, 2017. https://www.ntu.edu.sg /docs/default-source/academic-services/cyrim_roundtable_report30d27659f-a2c0 -410b-b2fe-68d0e4d35054.pdf?sfvrsn=b789f1e4_3.

Heinl, Caitriona. "NTU Cyber Risk Management Project (CyRiM): Roundtable Series on Optimal Governance and Regulatory Structures to Enhance Resilience. Roundtable Two Session Report: National Market and Regulatory Structures in Singapore." Nanyang Technological University, Singapore, September 28, 2017. https://www.ntu.edu.sg/docs/default-source/academic-services/download-session -report2d9320a8-3677-4117-a76e-e29b63a20826.pdf?sfvrsn=45250cdf_3.

Herr, Trey. "Cyber Insurance and Private Governance: The Enforcement Power of Markets." *Regulation and Governance*, 15 (2021): 98–114.

Hill, Andrew. "Cyber Risk Poses Ongoing Challenge for First-Party Property Damage Lines of Business." Willis Towers Watson, January 28, 2020. https:// www.willistowerswatson.com/en-US/Insights/2020/01/cyber-risk-poses-ongoing -challenge-for-first-party-property-damage-lines-of-business.

HM Government. "UK Cyber Security: The Role of Insurance in Managing and Mitigating the Risk." UK Cabinet Office, March 2015. https://www.gov.uk/gover nment/publications/uk-cyber-security-the-role-of-insurance.

Holiday Inns Inc. v. Aetna Insurance Co. 571 F. Supp. 1460. United States District Court for the Southern District of New York 1983.

Inc, IDG Network World. *Network World*. IDG Network World Inc, 2000.

Innovak International Inc. v. Hanover Insurance Co. 280 F. Supp. 3d 1340. United States District Court, Middle District of Florida, Tampa Division 2017.

Insurance Europe. "Template for Data Breach Notifications, Part I: Identification of Data Controller." March 19, 2018. https://www.insuranceeurope.eu/downloads /2289/Template+for+data+breach+notifications+-+Section+1.pdf.

Insurance Europe. "Template for Data Breach Notifications, Part II: Principal Information on Data Breach." March 19, 2018. https://www.insuranceeurope.eu /downloads/2290/Template+for+data+breach+notifications+-+Section+2.pdf.

Insurance Europe. "Template for Data Breach Notifications, Part III: Complementary Information." March 19, 2018. https://www.insuranceeurope.eu/downloads /2291/Template+for+data+breach+notifications+-+Section+3.pdf.

Insurance Europe. "Template for Data Breach Notifications: Press Release." March 19, 2018. https://www.insuranceeurope.eu/news/297/gdpr-data-breach-reporting -templates-developed-by-insurance-industry/.

"Insurance Industry Working Session Readout Report: Insurance for Cyber-Related Critical Infrastructure Loss: Key Issues." National Protection and Programs Directorate, Department of Homeland Security, July 2014. https://www.cisa.gov/sites /default/files/publications/July%202014%20Insurance%20Industry%20Working%20 Session_1.pdf.

Interactive Communications International Inc. v. Great American Insurance Co. 731 Fed. Appx. 929. United States Court of Appeals for the Eleventh Circuit 2018.

International Monetary Fund (IMF). *Brazil Financial Sector Assessment Program: Technical Note on Insurance Sector Regulation and Supervision*. Washington, DC: International Monetary Fund, November 2018.

Ives v. South Buffalo Railway Co. 201 N.Y. 271, 94 N.E. 431. Court of Appeals of the State of New York 1911.

Jaeger, Jaclyn. "More Companies Turning to Data Breach Insurance." *Compliance Week*, August 1, 2011. https://www.complianceweek.com/more-companies -turning-to-data-breach-insurance/4512.article.

Jones, Sam. "Finger Points at Russian State over Petya Hack Attack." *Financial Times*, June 30, 2017.

Keat, Heng Swee. "Speech by Minister for Finance Heng Swee Keat at the 15th Singapore International Reinsurance Conference." October 29, 2018. https://www .mof.gov.sg/news-publications/speeches/speech-by-minister-for-finance-heng-swee -keat-at-the-15th-singapore-international-reinsurance-conference.

Kim, Saskia. S.B. 1386 Senate Bill: Bill Analysis, Committee on Judiciary. 107th Cong. (2002). http://www.leginfo.ca.gov/pub/01-02/bill/sen/sb_1351-1400/sb_1386 _cfa_20020617_141710_asm_comm.html.

Knowles, Scott Gabriel, and Howard C. Kunreuther. "Troubled Waters: The National Flood Insurance Program in Historical Perspective." *Journal of Policy History* 26, no. 3 (2014): 327–353.

Kumar, Kavita. "Target Sues Insurer for up to $74 Million in 2013 Data Breach Costs." *Star Tribune*, November 19, 2019. https://www.startribune.com/target -sues-insurer-for-at-least-74-million-in-2013-data-breach-costs/565169292/.

Kumar, Ram Shankar Siva, and Frank Nagle. "The Case for AI Insurance." *Harvard Business Review*, April 29, 2020. https://hbr.org/2020/04/the-case-for-ai-insurance.

Laszka, Aron, and Jens Grossklags. "Should Cyber-Insurance Providers Invest in Software Security?" In *Proceedings, Part I, of the 20th European Symposium on Computer Security—ESORICS 2015—Volume 9326*, 483–502. Berlin: Springer Verlag, 2015. https://doi.org/10.1007/978-3-319-24174-6_25.

Lemos, Ronaldo, Natalia Langenegger, Juliana Pacetta Ruiz, Sofia Lima Franco, Andréa Guimarães Gobbato, Daniel Douek, Ramon Alberto dos Santos, and Rafael A. Ferreira Zanatta, trans. "Brazilian Data Protection Law (LGPD, English Translation)." October 28, 2020. https://iapp.org/media/pdf/resource_center/Brazilian _General_Data_Protection_Law.pdf.

Li, Tracy. "Cyber Insurance Market Set to Grow Significantly: Zurich." Shine, January 2, 2019. https://www.shine.cn/biz/company/1901027546/.

Lloyd's and AIR Worldwide. "Cloud Down: Impacts on the US Economy." 2018. https://www.lloyds.com/~/media/files/news-and-insight/risk-insight/2018/cloud -down/aircyberlloydspublic2018final.pdf.

Lloyd's Underwriters' Non-Marine Association Ltd. "Electronic Data Endorsement B." January 25, 2001. https://www.commund.com/Forms/cargo_rater/NMA 2915.pdf.

Lubin, Asaf. "Public Policy and the Insurability of Cyber Risk." *Journal of Law and Technology at Texas* (forthcoming 2021).

Macht, Joshua. "Safe Haase." Inc., September 15, 1997. https://www.inc.com /magazine/19970915/1427.html.

Margherio, Lynn, Dave Henry, Sandra Cooke, and Sabrina Montes. *The Emerging Digital Economy*. Washington, DC: US Department of Commerce, April 1998. https:// www.commerce.gov/sites/default/files/migrated/reports/emergingdig_0.pdf

Matthews, Denise. "Report on the Cybersecurity Insurance and Identity Theft Coverage Supplement." National Association of Insurance Commissioners and Center for Insurance Policy Research joint report, September 12, 2019. https:// content.naic.org/sites/default/files/inline-files/Cyber_Supplement_2019_Report _Final%20%281%29.pdf.

Mazzei, Patricia. "Another Hacked Florida City Pays a Ransom, This Time for $460,000." *New York Times*, June 27, 2019. https://www.nytimes.com/2019/06 /27/us/lake-city-florida-ransom-cyberattack.html.

Mazzei, Patricia. "Hit by Ransomware Attack, Florida City Agrees to Pay Hackers $600,000." *New York Times*, June 19, 2019, https://www.nytimes.com/2019/06 /19/us/florida-riviera-beach-hacking-ransom.html.

McCabe, Matthew. "NotPetya Was Not Cyber 'War.'" Marsh McLennan, August 2018.

Medidata Solutions Inc. v. Federal Insurance Co. 268 F. Supp. 3d 471. United States District Court for the Southern District of New York 2017.

Medidata Solutions Inc. v. Federal Insurance Co. 729 Fed. Appx. 117. United States Court of Appeals for the Second Circuit 2018.

Mehr, Robert I., and Emerson Cammack. *Principles of Insurance*. 3rd ed. Homewood, IL.: Richard D. Irwin, 1961.

Meier, Kenneth J. *The Political Economy of Regulation: The Case of Insurance*. Albany: State University of New York Press, 1988.

Methodist Health System Foundation v. Hartford Fire Insurance Co. 834 F. Supp. 2d 493. United States District Court for the Eastern District of Louisiana 2011.

Miller, Lauren. "Cyber Insurance: An Incentive Alignment Solution to Corporate Cyber-Insecurity." *Journal of Law and Cyber Warfare* 7, no. 2 (2019): 147–182.

Mondelez International Inc. v. Zurich American Insurance Co. No. 2018-L-011008. Circuit Court of Cook County, Illinois October 10, 2018.

Morgus, Robert. "Cyber Insurance: A Market-Based Approach to Information Assurance." In *Cyber Insecurity: Navigating the Perils of the Next Information Age*, edited by Richard M. Harrison and Trey Here, 155–170. Lanham, MD: Rowman and Littlefield, 2016.

Mulford, Joshua P. "Non-State Actors in the Russo-Ukrainian War." *Connections: The Quarterly Journal* 15, no. 2 (2016): 89–107. http://dx.doi.org/10.11610/Connections.15.2.07.

National Bank of Blacksburg v. Everest National Insurance Co. No. 7:18-cv-310. United States District Court for the Western District of Virginia, Roanoke Division June 28, 2018.

National Cyber Security Centre. "Russian Military 'Almost Certainly' Responsible for Destructive 2017 Cyber Attack." February 14, 2018. https://www.ncsc.gov.uk/news/russian-military-almost-certainly-responsible-destructive-2017-cyber-attack.

National Protection and Programs Directorate (NPPD). *Cyber Risk Culture Roundtable Readout Report*. Washington, DC: US Department of Homeland Security, May 2013.

National Protection and Programs Directorate (NPPD). *Cybersecurity Insurance Workshop Readout Report*. Washington, DC: US Department of Homeland Security, November 2012.

National Protection and Programs Directorate (NPPD). *Insurance Industry Working Session Readout Report: Insurance for Cyber-Related Critical Infrastructure Loss: Key Issues*. Washington, DC: US Department of Homeland Security, July 2014.

New York Life Insurance Co. v. Bennion. 158 F.2d 260. United States Court of Appeals for the Tenth Circuit 1946.

Nicol, Chuck. S.B. 1386 Senate Bill: Bill Analysis, Committee on Appropriations. 107th Cong. (2002). http://www.leginfo.ca.gov/pub/01-02/bill/sen/sb_1351-1400 /sb_1386_cfa_20020813_145811_asm_comm.html.

Nordman, Eric. "The History of No-Fault Auto Insurance." *Journal of Insurance Regulation* 16, no. 4 (1998): 457–466.

Oliker, Olga. "Russian Influence and Unconventional Warfare Operations in the 'Grey Zone': Lessons from Ukraine." Statement before the Senate Armed Services Committee Subcommittee on Emerging Threats and Capabilities, March 29, 2017. https://www.armed-services.senate.gov/imo/media/doc/Oliker_03-29-17.pdf.

Orland, Kyle. "Sony to Pay up to $17.75 Million in 2011 PSN Hacking Settlement." Ars Technica, July 24, 2014. https://arstechnica.com/gaming/2014/07 /sony-to-pay-up-to-17-75-million-in-2011-psn-hacking-settlement/.

Overend, William. "Cyber Crime Fighters Escape Funding Cut." *Los Angeles Times*, November 10, 2002. https://www.latimes.com/archives/la-xpm-2002-nov-10-me -cyber10-story.html.

Pan American World Airways Inc. v. Aetna Casualty & Surety Co. 368 F. Supp. 1098. United States District Court for the Southern District of New York 1973.

Pan American World Airways Inc. v. Aetna Casualty & Surety Co. 505 F.2d 989. United States Court of Appeals for the Second Circuit 1974.

Paul v. Virginia. 75 U.S. 7 Wall. 168. United States Supreme Court 1869.

Pearce, Andrew. "Brokers Told to Wake up to Cyber Liability." *Insurance Age*, September 10, 2012.

Perlroth, Nicole, and Elizabeth A. Harris. "Cyberattack Insurance a Challenge for Business." *New York Times*, June 8, 2014, sec. Business. https://www.nytimes.com /2014/06/09/business/cyberattack-insurance-a-challenge-for-business.html.

Personal Data Protection Act of 2019. Bill No. 373 (2019) [India].

Pestmaster Services v. Travelers Casualty and Surety Company of America. No. 2:13-cv-5039-JFW, 2014 U.S. Dist. LEXIS 108416. United States District Court for the Central District of California July 17, 2014.

Pestmaster Services v. Travelers Casualty and Surety Company of America. 656 Fed. Appx. 332, 2016 WL 4056068. United States Court of Appeals for the Ninth Circuit 2016.

Pinchuk, Denis. "Russia Denies British Allegations That Moscow Was behind Cyber-Attack." Reuters, February 15, 2018. https://www.reuters.com/article/us-britain -russia-cyber-kremlin/russia-denies-british-allegations-that-moscow-was-behind -cyber-attack-idUSKCN1FZ102.

Port of Seattle v. Lexington Insurance Co. 48 P.3d 334. Court of Appeals of Washington, Division 1 2002.

PricewaterhouseCoopers. "Insurance 2020 & beyond: Reaping the Dividends of Cyber Resilience." 2015. https://www.pwc.com/gx/en/insurance/publications /assets/reaping-dividends-cyber-resilience.pdf.

Radcliff, Deb. "Got Cyber Insurance?" Computerworld, August 21, 2000. https:// www.computerworld.com/article/2596915/got-cyber-insurance-.html.

Ralph, Oliver. "Beazley and Munich Re Join up in Cyber Insurance Push." *Financial Times*, April 10, 2016.

Raphael, Adam. *Ultimate Risk: The Inside Story of the Lloyd's Catastrophe*. New York: Four Walls Eight Windows, 1995.

Renn, Ortwin, Klaus Lucas, Armin Haas, and Carlo Jaeger. "Things Are Different Today: The Challenge of Global Systemic Risks." *Journal of Risk Research* 22, no. 4 (2017): 401–415. https://doi.org/10.1080/13669877.2017.1409252.

Report by the Committee to Study Compensation for Auto Accidents to the Columbia University Council for Research in the Social Sciences. Philadelphia, 1932.

Ricken, Keith. "The Missing Piece: Buyer Interest." *Risk & Insurance*, December 1, 2001.

Roberson, Jason. "Time to Sign up for Cyber Insurance?" *Orlando Business Journal* 17, no. 51 (2001).

Romanosky, Sasha, Lillian Ablon, Andreas Kuehn, and Therese Jones. "Content Analysis of Cyber Insurance Policies: How Do Carriers Price Cyber Risk?" *Journal of Cybersecurity* 5, no. 1 (2019). https://doi.org/10.1093/cybsec/tyz002.

Rosenau v. Idaho Mutual Benefit Association of Canada. 65 Idaho 408, 145 P.2d 227. Supreme Court of Idaho 1944.

Rosenfield, Harvey. "Auto Insurance: Crisis and Reform." *University of Memphis Law Review* 29, no. 1 (1998): 69–136.

Rossi, Michael. "The End of Computer Virus Coverage as We Know It?" International Risk Management Institute, May 2002. https://www.irmi.com/articles /expert-commentary/the-end-of-computer-virus-coverage-as-we-know-it.

Satariano, Adam, and Nicole Perlroth. "Big Companies Thought Insurance Covered a Cyberattack. They May Be Wrong." *New York Times*, April 15, 2019. https://www .nytimes.com/2019/04/15/technology/cyberinsurance-notpetya-attack.html.

Sawyer, E. W. *Comprehensive Liability Insurance*. New York: Underwriter, 1943.

Scheuermann, James E. "Cyber Risks, Systemic Risks, and Cyber Insurance Symposium." *Penn State Law Review* 122, no. 3 (2018): 613–644.

Schoenberger, Chana. "Payout: Times of Terror Are Good Times for Hacker Insurance." *Forbes*, December 24, 2001.

Shalal, Andrea. "Massive Cyber Attack Could Trigger NATO Response: Stoltenberg." Reuters, June 15, 2016. https://www.reuters.com/article/us-cyber-nato-idUS KCN0Z12NE.

Sheehan, Matt. "Pipeline Cyber Attack Not Surprising, Says Swiss Re's Mumenthaler." Reinsurance News, May 13, 2021. https://www.reinsurancene.ws/pipeline-cyber-attack-not-surprising-says-swiss-res-mumenthaler/.

Shen, Alice. "Asian Companies See Little Need for Insurance against Cyber Attack, with Less than 20pc Insured." South China Morning Post, April 22, 2018.

Shortland, Anja. Kidnap: Inside the Ransom Business. Oxford: Oxford University Press, 2019.

Stankus v. New York Life Insurance Co. 312 Mass. 366. Supreme Judicial Court of Massachusetts October 29, 1942.

Stilgherrian. "Blaming Russia for NotPetya Was Coordinated Diplomatic Action." ZDNet, April 11, 2018. https://www.zdnet.com/article/blaming-russia-for-notpetya-was-coordinated-diplomatic-action/.

St. Paul Fire & Marine Insurance Co. v. Rosen Millennium Inc. 337 F. Supp. 3d 1176. United States District Court for the Middle District of Florida, Orlando Division 2018.

St. Paul Fire & Marine Insurance Co. v. Rosen Millennium Inc. Complaint. No. 6:17-cv-540-ORL-41-GJK. United States District Court, Middle District of Florida, Orlando Division March 24, 2017.

Strom, Shelly. "Egghead Favors Security over Cyber Insurance." Portland Business Journal 18, no. 1 (2001). https://www.bizjournals.com/portland/stories/2001/03/05/focus2.html.

Sturgeon, Jeff. "National Bank of Blacksburg Settles with Insurer over Losses from Suspected Russian Hacking." Roanoke Times, January 29, 2019. https://roanoke.com/business/national-bank-of-blacksburg-settles-with-insurer-over-losses-from-suspected-russian-hacking/article_acc2cff5-9ad1-57aa-bb20-d4c1f6d524b6.html.

Subcommittee on Oversight and Investigation. Failed Promises: Insurance Company Insolvencies. Washington, DC: US House of Representatives Committee on Energy and Commerce, February 1990.

Sullivan, Bob. "ID Theft Rampant; Options Limited." MSNBC, May 29, 2002.

Sullivan, Sean. "Obama: North Korea Hack 'Cyber-Vandalism,' Not 'Act of War.'" Washington Post, December 21, 2014.

Talesh, Shauhin A. "Data Breach, Privacy, and Cyber Insurance: How Insurance Companies Act as 'Compliance Managers' for Businesses." Law and Social Inquiry 43, no. 2 (2018): 417–440. https://doi.org/10.1111/lsi.12303.

Terrorism Risk Insurance Act of 2002. Pub. L. No. 107–297, 116 Stat. 2322 (2002).

Travelers Indemnity Company. "Travelers CyberRisk Policy Template (CYB-3001)." July 2010. https://www.travelers.com/iw-documents/apps-forms/cyberrisk/cyb-3001.pdf.

Unified National Program for Managing Flood Losses, A: A Report by the Task Force on Federal Flood Control Policy. H.R. Report No. 89–465 (August 1966).

United States Cyberspace Solarium Commission (CSC). "Final Report." March 2020. https://www.solarium.gov/report.

United States Cyberspace Solarium Commission (CSC). "Legislative Proposals." July 2020. https://www.solarium.gov/report.

United States Department of Homeland Security. "Enhancing Resilience through Cyber Incident Data Sharing and Analysis: Establishing Community-Relevant Data Categories in Support of a Cyber Incident Data Repository." Cyber Incident Data and Analysis Working Group (CIDAWG) White Paper, September 2015. https://www.hsdl.org/?view&did=788825.

United States Department of Homeland Security. "Enhancing Resilience through Cyber Incident Data Sharing and Analysis: The Value Proposition for a Cyber Incident Data Repository." Cyber Incident Data and Analysis Working Group (CIDAWG) White Paper, June 2015. https://www.hsdl.org/?view&did=767778.

United States Department of Homeland Security. *The National Strategy to Secure Cyberspace.* (Washington, DC: White House, February 2003). https://us-cert.cisa.gov/sites/default/files/publications/cyberspace_strategy.pdf.

United States Department of the Treasury. "Guidance Concerning Stand-Alone Cyber Liability Insurance Policies Under the Terrorism Risk Insurance Program." *Federal Register* 81, no. 248 (2016). https://www.federalregister.gov/documents /2016/12/27/2016-31244/guidance-concerning-stand-alone-cyber-liability -insurance-policies-under-the-terrorism-risk.

United States General Accounting Office. *Auto Insurance: State Regulation Affects Cost and Availability.* Washington, DC: United States General Accounting Office, August 1986.

United States, Office of the Press Secretary. "Statement from the Press Secretary," February 15, 2018. https://trumpwhitehouse.archives.gov/briefings-statements /statement-press-secretary-25/.

United States Securities and Exchange Commission (SEC). "CF Disclosure Guidance: Topic No. 2." Division of Corporation Finance, October 13, 2011. https:// www.sec.gov/divisions/corpfin/guidance/cfguidance-topic2.htm.

United States Securities and Exchange Commission (SEC). "Form 10-K: Yahoo! Inc.: Annual Report Pursuant to Section 13 or 15(d) of the Securities Exchange Act of 1934 for the Fiscal Year Ended December 31, 2011." February 29, 2012. http://edgar.secdatabase.com/1700/119312512086972/filing-main.htm.

United States v. South-Eastern Underwriters Association et al. 322 U.S. 533. United States Supreme Court 1944.

Universal Cable Products LLC v. Atlantic Specialty Insurance Co. 929 F.3d 1143. United States Court of Appeals for the Ninth Circuit 2019.

Vance, William Reynolds. *Handbook of the Law of Insurance.* St. Paul, MN: West, 1904.

Vanderbilt v. Travelers' Insurance Company, 112 Misc. 248, 184 N.Y.S. 54. Supreme Court of New York 1920.

Vijayan, Jaikumar. "Recent Breaches Raise Specter of Liability Risks." Computerworld, June 3, 2002. https://www.computerworld.com/article/2576023/recent-breaches-raise--specter-of-liability-risks.html.

Voreacos, David, Katherine Chiglinsky, and Riley Griffin. "Merck Cyberattack's $1.3 Billion Question: Was It an Act of War?" Bloomberg, December 3, 2019. https://www.bloomberg.com/news/features/2019-12-03/merck-cyberattack-s-1-3-billion-question-was-it-an-act-of-war.

Wang, Frank. "Cyber Insurance Ready for Take-Off in China." Gen Re, November 2017. https://media.genre.com/documents/cmchina1710-en.pdf.

Webel, Baird, and Carolyn Cobb. "Insurance Regulation: History, Background, and Recent Congressional Oversight." Congressional Research Service, February 11, 2005. https://www.everycrsreport.com/files/20050211_RL31982_1d5eff403f858929157d365c96ccc029206575a7.pdf.

Weiss, N. Eric, and Rena S. Miller. "The Target and Other Financial Data Breaches: Frequently Asked Questions." Congressional Research Service, February 4, 2015. https://fas.org/sgp/crs/misc/R43496.pdf.

"Why Brazil's Data Law Will Boost Cybersecurity Insurance." BNamericas, October 24, 2019. https://www.bnamericas.com/en/features/why-brazils-data-law-will-boost-cybersecurity-insurance.

Winston & Strawn LLP. "2017 Insurance Review." February 2018. https://www.winston.com/images/content/1/3/v2/135129/2017-China-Insurance-Review-MAR2018.pdf.

Winston & Strawn LLP. "2018 China Insurance Review." April 8, 2019. https://www.winston.com/images/content/2/2/v2/227694/Corp-2018-Insurance-Review-A4-Brochure-APR2019.pdf.

Wojcik, Joanne. "Y2K Bug Is Still Biting." Business Insurance, July 16, 2000. https://www.businessinsurance.com/article/20000716/STORY/10002453#.

Wolff, Josephine. "As Ransomware Demands Boom, Insurance Companies Keep Paying Out." *Wired,* June 12, 2021. https://www.wired.com/story/ransomware-insurance-payments/.

Wolff, Josephine. "Cyberinsurance Tries to Tackle the Unpredictable World of Hacks." *Wired,* April 6, 2018. https://www.wired.com/story/cyberinsurance-tackles-the-wildly-unpredictable-world-of-hacks/.

Wolff, Josephine. "Perverse Effects in Defense of Computer Systems: When More Is Less." *Journal of Management Information Systems* 33, no. 2 (2016): 597–620. https://doi.org/10.1080/07421222.2016.1205934.

Wolff, Josephine. *You'll See This Message When It Is Too Late: The Legal and Economic Aftermath of Cybersecurity Breaches*. Cambridge, MA: MIT Press, 2018.

Wolff, Josephine, and William Lehr. "Degrees of Ignorance about the Costs of Data Breaches: What Policymakers Can and Can't Do about the Lack of Good Empirical Data." Paper presented at the 45th Research Conference on Communications, Information and Internet Policy (TPRC), Washington, DC, September 9, 2017.

Wolff, Josephine, and William Lehr. "Roles for Policy-Makers in Emerging Cyber Insurance Industry Partnerships." In *TPRC 46: The 46th Research Conference on Communication, Information and Internet Policy 2018*. Washington, DC: Social Science Research Network, 2018. https://papers.ssrn.com/abstract=3141409.

Woods, Daniel W., Tyler Moore, and Andrew C. Simpson. "The County Fair Cyber Loss Distribution: Drawing Inferences from Insurance Prices." Paper presented at Workshop on the Economics of Information Security (WEIS). Harvard University, Cambridge, MA, June 3–4, 2019. https://informationsecurity.uibk.ac.at/pdfs/DW2019_CountyFair_WEIS.pdf.

Woods, Daniel W., Ioannis Agrafiotis, Jason R. C. Nurse, and Sadie Creese. "Mapping the Coverage of Security Controls in Cyber Insurance Proposal Forms." *Journal of Internet Services and Applications* 8, no. 8 (2017).

Woods, Daniel W., and Rainer Böhme. "How Cyber Insurance Shapes Incident Response." Paper presented at Workshop on the Economics of Information Security (WEIS). Online conference, June 28–29, 2021.

Woods, Daniel W., and Andrew C. Simpson. "Policy Measures and Cyber Insurance: A Framework." *Journal of Cyber Policy* 2, no. 2 (2017): 209–226.

Woods, Daniel W., and Jessica Weinkle. "Insurance Definitions of Cyber War." *Geneva Papers on Risk and Insurance: Issues and Practice* 45, no. 4 (2020): 639–656.

Yang, Rui. "China Liability Insurance Market Trend Report." Swiss Re, May 2019. https://www.swissre.com/dam/jcr:64625acc-dd25-4719-bf2b-935b65727ed5/China%20Liability%20Insurance%20Market%20Trend%20Report%20-%20updated.pdf.

Zhu, Julie. "Greater China Cyber Insurance Demand to Soar after WannaCry Attack: AIG." Reuters, August 9, 2018. https://www.reuters.com/article/us-aig-china-cyber/greater-china-cyber-insurance-demand-to-soar-after-wannacry-attack-aig-idUSKBN1AP12E.

Zurich American Insurance Co. v. Sony Corporation of America. 2014 WL 8382554. Supreme Court of the State of New York February 21, 2014.

"Zurich Cyber Insurance Policy U-SPR-300-A CW." September 2018.

INDEX

INFORMATION POLICY SERIES

Edited by Sandra Braman